Readers share about Dr. Lesslie's previous book, the bestselling *Angels in the ER*

"I am a busy working mother but managed to read the entire book in less than three days. The way you described the people and the situations was brilliant... You see things in a very special way and have made me see...thank you."

Jamie

"I am currently applying to medical school, MD/PhD program...Thank you for providing such a bright and shining example of what medicine should be."

Svetlana

"I loved every bit of it. It touched me greatly and I have told my friends about it...It also gave me a much better understanding on what goes on in an ER. I sincerely believe it should be read in high schools, colleges, etc."

Mosheh

"Just read your book *Angels in the ER* and loved it. Couldn't put it down. Very well written. Excited to see another one is on the way! God bless you."

Bill

"Having spent ten years as a coordinator for our emergency department, I was very intrigued to read your stories...You have a very eloquent way of relating things that most people will never experience, but probably should...Your kindness, care, and compassion shine through."

Alicia

"I couldn't put the book down...but when I got to a certain chapter I broke into tears and couldn't read anymore...I would like to know if you are planning to come to Australia at anytime."

"Your stories touched me deeply…I am a retired RN…7 years in infant ICU. We got the worst of the worst. It was a hard job, but so worth it…On a brighter note, your book made me feel that I still might have a purpose…I keep praying for God's will to be done in my life."

Jackie

"Your book is full of life lessons as well as heart struggles…I have recommended this book to many of my friends. I find myself going back to read the stories over and over…Thank you for sharing yourself."

Valerie

"So nice to read about you finding good in such terrible situations. The way you wrote made the book very easy to read…I was able to pick it up and put it down without feeling lost when I got back to it. Thank you."

Jenika, RN

"It's *so* refreshing to hear a doctor comment on patient care in a positive way, despite the gravity of many situations…Thank you for writing such uplifting stories! May God continue to grant you success in your medical practice and writing."

Phyllis, RN

"I recently visited the USA from Finland…My husband and I have enjoyed these little stories…Great book and wish you would write more."

Inka

"The Bible verses, along with the stories, had me searching my heart for peace and grace (something I haven't felt in some time). Thank you for your dedicated care to all of the people whose lives you have touched, and thank you for reminding me that God really is with us all of the time."

Terri

More praise for *Angels in the ER*

"People caring for people. Compassion and lovingkindness in difficult circumstances. This is the medicine we need the most, and it is administered on every page of *Angels in the ER*, a chronicle of mankind at its best."

—Richard Thomas
Film, television, and stage actor
"John-Boy" on The Waltons and host of It's a Miracle

"I read it in one sitting…I couldn't lay it down."

—Debra Gaynor
ReviewYourBook.com

"If you enjoy watching medical dramas on television, then you will absolutely love *Angels in the ER*…Keeps you on edge wondering what the outcome of various patient situations is going to be."

—5MinutesforBooks.com

"Each situation shows the spiritual dimension of life and death in a way most of us will never experience on our own. I can only compare the demand for moment-to-moment decision-making with my time on the basketball court. I enjoyed every story."

—Bobby Jones
cofounder 2XSALT, four-time NBA All-Star,
and member of the 1983 World Champion Philadelphia 76ers

"In an age when patients are viewed as Social Security numbers, Dr. Lesslie recovers the fading image of a caring doctor for whom the patient is center stage…If I ever land in an emergency room, I hope Dr. Lesslie is there waiting for me."

—Randall Ruble
President, Erskine College and Seminary

"Dr. Lesslie...drew me into this book from the first story and held me captive until the last. He combines wit and drama to describe what really happens in the ER."

—BookBargainsAndPreviews.com

"We meet an amazing cast of characters who come through the doors of a South Carolina hospital emergency room...But Robert Lesslie is also there, a faithful, empathetic physician with a heart for compassion and a keen eye for the presence of God in the midst of human need."

—Thomas Long
Bandy Professor of Preaching,
Candler School of Theology, Emory University

ANGELS ON CALL

Robert D. Lesslie, M.D.

HARVEST HOUSE PUBLISHERS

EUGENE, OREGON

Cover by Left Coast Design, Portland, Oregon

Cover photos © ER Productions Ltd / Blend Images / Getty Images

Back-cover author photo © Penny Young

All the incidents described in this book are true. Where individuals may be identifiable, they have granted the author and the publisher the right to use their names, stories, and/or facts of their lives in all manners, including composite or altered representations. In all other cases, names, circumstances, descriptions, and details have been changed to render individuals unidentifiable.

ANGELS ON CALL
Copyright © 2010 by Robert D. Lesslie, MD
Published by Harvest House Publishers
Eugene, Oregon 97402
www.harvesthousepublishers.com

Library of Congress Cataloging-in-Publication Data
    Lesslie, Robert D., 1951-
    Angels on call / Robert D. Lesslie.
        p. cm.
    Includes bibliographical references and index.
    ISBN 978-0-7369-2740-6 (pbk. : alk. paper)
    1. Hospitals—Emergency services—Popular works. 2. Emergency medical personnel—Popular works. I. Title.
    RA975.5.E5L473 2010
    362.18—dc22

                                                    2009047433

Printed in the United States of America

            10 11 12 13 14 15 16 17 18 / VP-SK / 10 9 8 7 6 5 4 3

To Lori, Rob, Amy, Dave,
Robbie, Jeffrey, Katie—
the arrows in my quiver
(Psalm 127:5).

...And to the memory of Virginia Granger.

Contents

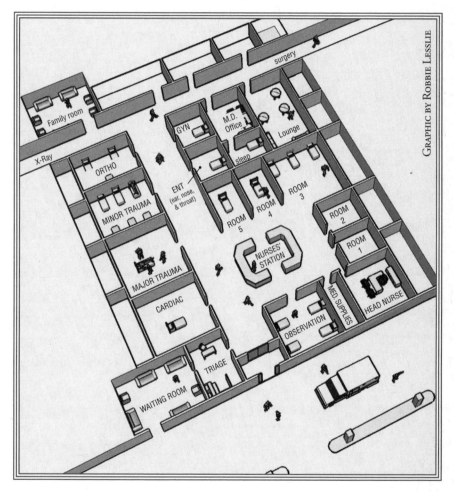

Layout of the Rock Hill ER

First Things

The ER has a lot to teach us about living and dying, about other people, and about ourselves. It's a classroom that never closes.

In these pages, I share some of my experiences from over two decades of working in the emergency department. Throughout all those years, I learned that one thing never changes: Every person who walks, or is wheeled, or is carried into the ER is unique and has a story to tell. Each has something to share. And most importantly, each has something to teach us, if we only take the time to listen.

One of those lessons is that we all need someone to lean on. At some point each one of us will ask, "Who can I turn to when I'm in trouble?" "Who can I count on when all hope seems gone?" "Who is on call for me?"

Maybe you know who those people are, or who that Person is, in your life.

And maybe you have come to understand that the more important question is, "Who am I on call for?"

1

Into the Deep End

Then you will understand what is right
and just and fair—every good path.
For wisdom will enter your heart,
And knowledge will be pleasant to your soul.

PROVERBS 2:9-10

Thursday 7:05 a.m. Jack was standing at the nurses' station rubbing his eyes, as if that would clear the cobwebs from his brain. He was not used to getting up this early. His "early" classes the past two semesters at Appalachian State had started at 10 a.m., and the alarm clock this morning had been an unpleasant intrusion.

This was the first morning he was going to spend in the emergency department with me this summer. He wanted to see how his father spent his time as an ER doc, and he wanted to get an idea if a career in medicine was something he wanted to pursue. He would be a senior next fall, and he was twenty-two years old. Hard to believe.

"Wake up, buddy!" Amy Connors chided him. "Things are gonna get hoppin' here in just a little while. EMS is already out on a couple of runs."

Amy was our unit secretary this morning. And she was the best I had ever worked with. She was in her late twenties and had been in the department for the past six years. Nothing seemed to bother her—no amount of stress or being yelled at by impatient physicians (of course, that wouldn't be any ER doc), or even an overwhelming workload. She just rolled with whatever came her way. What I really appreciated was her anticipation of what needed to be done, regardless of the situation. She always seemed to be one step ahead of me, which is what every emergency physician needs.

I was drinking my first cup of coffee, and I looked over at Jack as Amy needled him. He smiled at her and said, "I'm awake, Amy. Don't worry about me."

We had gotten to the ER a little before seven, relieving Tom Anders, the overnight doc. He had left me a clean board, and the department was empty.

Jack sat down beside me, behind the nurses' station.

"Dad…or Dr. Lesslie," he hesitated. "Which should I call you? I hadn't thought about that."

"Why don't you call him what we do?" Amy impishly suggested. "In fact, you could take your pick from a couple of names."

Without looking in her direction I said, "Amy, don't you have something to do?"

And then I said to Jack, "You know, we need to think about that. It might be best to call me Dr. Lesslie. That way, none of the patients would be confused or bothered."

Before Jack could respond, our attention was drawn to a commotion coming from the triage area. The voices of several men could be heard, and they sounded pretty excited and angry. Over this din, I could hear the voice of Jeff Ryan, our triage nurse. He was trying without success to calm down the boisterous group.

"Hold on just a minute!" I heard him shout.

"We ain't holdin' on!" someone responded angrily. "Johnny needs some help and he needs it right now!"

Then the door from triage burst open and a tangled mass of people spilled into the department. Amy and I just sat and watched, but Jack immediately stood up and stared in surprise. I noticed his mouth had dropped open.

The group stumbled over to the nurses' station, and it was then I noticed they were all dressed in bikers' garb—blue jeans, chaps, and leather jackets. A few still had their helmets on. In the middle of this group stood Jeff Ryan, still trying to regain some semblance of order.

"Alright, guys," he bellowed. "Just hold it right here, and we'll get Johnny taken care of!" His voice reached a new level of intensity, and even this cantankerous audience stopped where they were and listened.

"We're going to take him to the trauma room, and I want two of you—*just two*—to come with me. Everybody else needs to go back to the waiting room."

There was some murmuring and muttering from the group, but slowly they began to do as instructed. These were all big men, and pretty intimidating. Most had long, unkempt beards and seemingly perpetual scowls on their weathered faces.

But Jeff was not intimidated by them. He was thirty-six and had been working in the ER for over twelve years, starting just before our family had moved to Rock Hill. He was a big, seemingly gruff mountain of a man, intimidating in his own right in size and demeanor. His mere presence usually calmed the most belligerent and rambunctious of our patients. And if his presence didn't calm them, a firm hand on a shoulder would quickly bring them into line.

Jeff's reddening face was a sure indication that he meant business, and the bikers must have sensed this as well. They were finally beginning to follow his instructions. It was then I noticed the knot of men standing behind Jeff. Three of them were holding a companion in their arms, trying to be as gentle as possible. That must be Johnny, their injured friend.

As the other members of the group began to shuffle out of the way and back toward triage, Jeff turned around and said, "Alright, three of you then. You guys follow me down the hall." Then he turned and headed briskly toward the trauma room.

We got a glimpse of Johnny as they passed by the counter. He was moaning in pain and his face was a pasty white color. He was clutching his left hip, grimacing with each step taken by his carriers. I stood up and walked around the nurses' station, motioning Jack to follow me.

Jeff directed the group to the side of the trauma stretcher, which was positioned in the middle of the room.

"Here, put him down gently," he told them. They tried their best, but Johnny gave out a loud, anguished cry as they laid him on the thin mattress.

"Oww! My hip!"

His three buddies stepped back from the stretcher, and I tapped the one nearest to me on the shoulder. He turned around and I said, "Tell me what happened here."

"You the doc?" he asked.

"Yes, that's me," I answered him. "I'm Dr. Lesslie. What happened to your friend here?"

"Dr. Lesslie?" he remarked. "I think you're the one who sewed up my head last summer." As he said this, he took off his helmet and began parting his hair, searching for his scar.

"That's great," I said. "I probably did, but tell me about your friend. How did he get hurt?"

"Oh, yeah," he muttered, sheepishly putting his helmet back on. "Johnny busted his leg this morning in a swimming pool."

He paused, as if this were all the information I needed.

"A swimming pool?" I finally prodded him.

"Yeah. We were comin' in late from Atlanta and were staying at the Sleep EZ Inn. Johnny sees the swimming pool and says he's gonna jump it. Done it before—but not quite that big a pool, and it wasn't six in the morning, and the other pool had water in it."

"The pool was empty?"

"Yeah, they must have been cleaning it or painting it or something. Anyway, it was empty, and there was a fence around most of it, and we didn't think he could get up enough speed to clear it. Told him that, but it didn't make no difference. He was determined to try, and sure enough, he couldn't get up enough speed."

He started giggling, and turned a little more toward me, making sure Johnny couldn't see his face. "Actually, it was pretty funny...almost like slow motion. He backed up, gunned his hog, and hunkered down.

When he hit the edge of the pool, he tried to pull up the front of the bike, but it just kind of froze in space and headed straight down. I didn't see him hit the bottom—it was in the deep end—but boy did I hear it. That was awful. That bike is all busted up, probably done for. And Johnny was throwed off and into the far wall. Must have hit it with his left knee, 'cause that's what hurts. Should have hit it with his head, then he'd probably be alright now." He started giggling again and quickly glanced behind him.

"Was he knocked out?" I asked.

"No. In fact, he tried to stand up, but he couldn't. Said his leg was comin' off and started hollerin'. That's when we threw him on the back of one of the bikes and brought him here."

The thought of that ride made me flinch.

"Okay, why don't you and your two friends head out to the waiting room, and we'll take care of Johnny," I told him.

Reluctantly, he and his two fellow bikers left the room, and Jeff, Jack, and I were alone with Johnny.

He was a big man, and in a lot of pain. Jeff was trying to get him quieted down on the stretcher, but it was difficult for him to find any comfortable position.

"It's my hip, Doc!" he moaned. "It feels like it's comin' off!"

We got him undressed, and as Jeff was carefully removing his jeans and chaps, I could see the source of his problem. His left hip was swollen and already bruised, and its angle of attachment to the socket was clearly abnormal. It was either severely fractured or dislocated, or both.

I asked Jeff to start an IV and then pushed the intercom button for the nurses' station.

"We need some portable X-rays in trauma," I told Amy. "Hip and pelvis, and a chest."

"Got it," Amy replied.

Jack was standing against one of the counters, being careful to stay out of our way. I explained to him what I thought was going on and what we needed to do.

Once Jeff had the IV started, we gave Johnny some pain medication, and then something to help him relax. Because of his size, it took a couple of doses before he seemed a little calmer.

When the X-rays were developed and brought back to the trauma room, I put them up on the view box and stood back, studying them.

"What do you see, Doc?" Johnny asked from the stretcher. "Is it bad?"

It was in fact the best of several bad possibilities, and was what I had hoped for. The hip was dislocated, but there was no fracture. The upper leg and pelvis were fine. Just the dislocation was the problem. That would be better for him in the long run. When he fell into the pool, his left knee must have hit the side wall, driving his upper leg and hip back and out of its socket. It takes a lot of force to do that, especially with someone as big as Johnny. And it was going to take a lot of force to get it back into place.

I told Johnny what the X-rays showed, and that we would need to get it back in place as quickly as possible.

"Once we do that, your pain should be gone," I told him. "You're going to be pretty sore for a while, but this should heal quickly."

His chest X-ray was fine. There was no evidence of any other injury, other than some scattered scrapes and abrasions. He was one very lucky guy.

Jack tapped me on the shoulder and asked, "How are you going to get that hip back into place? Will you need to knock him out?"

"We'll sedate him as much as we can," I explained, "and then we'll have to put some traction on it in order to get it reduced. You'll see. But we need to get it back in place as fast as we can. The longer it's out, the greater the chances for complications and problems later on."

This was an unusual injury, and I had treated only a few myself. I had been able to get all of those reduced, but some had proved to be very difficult, especially the cases involving a big, muscular person like our biker patient.

Johnny was still pretty uncomfortable and not yet relaxed enough, so I asked Jeff to give him more sedating medication. Then I showed Jeff what I wanted him to do.

"Here, let's get Johnny flat on his back," I told him. "And then I want you to stand beside him and hold his pelvis flat on the bed. You're going to need to put all of your weight into it, understand? He's going to try to come off the stretcher."

Jeff positioned himself beside our patient and then placed his hands firmly on Johnny's pelvis, one big hand on each side.

"This what you want?" he asked me.

"Perfect," I said. "Just be sure to hold on."

Then I climbed up on the stretcher and stood over Johnny's legs. There wasn't much room up there and it felt pretty precarious, but there was no other way to do this. He was drowsy, but was still awake enough to mutter, "What the…" Then he closed his eyes and his head turned to one side. Good.

I glanced over at Jack. He was staring at me in disbelief but didn't say anything.

Carefully bending over, I grasped Johnny's injured leg at the knee, and slowly brought it up until it was perpendicular to the stretcher. His thigh was huge, and his calves were enormous. I nodded at Jeff and then bent down further, hugging our patient's calf tightly against my chest. Johnny moaned a little with this movement, but then grew quiet. That was when I noticed the multicolored tattoo on his left thigh, right in front of my face: "MOTHER." I looked up at Jeff and he just grinned and nodded his head.

"Alright, here we go," I told him.

Jeff straightened his arms and applied all of his strength, determined to keep Johnny's pelvis flat on the stretcher. I began to pull up on his leg, raising his knee at a 90-degree angle to his pelvis.

Johnny moaned and began to twist on the bed, but Jeff was able to keep him in place. And I kept pulling, but nothing was happening. His muscles were knotted, and they seemed determined to keep his hip out of its socket.

I started sweating. This was hard work, but I couldn't back off from the traction. I would need to cause his muscles to fatigue and then relax, allowing me to pull the ball of the hip joint over the edge of the socket and back into place. So far, his muscles were fatiguing *me*.

I glanced at Jeff. His face was red too, and beads of sweat were forming on his forehead.

Then I thought I felt a little give. It was subtle, but I was sure I'd felt it.

"Hold on tight, Jeff," I encouraged him. "I think we're—"

Before I could finish, the hip suddenly slipped back into place, and I almost fell off the stretcher. As it did so, we all heard a loud clunking noise, followed immediately by a relieved "ooooooh" from Johnny.

It was the clunk that did Jack in. I heard some metal pans rattle on the countertop, and I looked over just in time to see him reaching behind himself with both hands. He was trying desperately to find something to grab, something to keep him from sliding down to the floor. I watched as his face went from a peculiar greenish color to a pasty and almost ghostlike white. Then his knees buckled. Jeff had seen this too, and with one large arm he reached out, grabbed Jack around the waist, and helped him gently to the floor.

"Just sit here for a minute, boy," he told him. "Take a few deep breaths, and you'll be okay in just a minute."

I climbed down and moved to the head of the stretcher.

"Johnny, how do you feel?"

"Doc, I feel great," he slurred, still under the influence of our medication. "I can move my leg again, and it doesn't hurt."

He tried to pick his leg up from the bed but I quickly put my hand on his thigh and held it down.

"You'll need to be still for a while, Johnny," I spoke loudly. "We don't want that hip going out again."

"No...don't want that," he mumbled, shaking his head and again closing his eyes. This time he had a smile on his face.

Then I turned my attention to Jack. He was sitting on the floor with his head in his hands. His color was a lot better, but not quite back to normal.

He looked up and quietly said, "I...I don't know what happened. I was fine until you pulled on his leg and that...that sound. That was awful. And then the room starting spinning...I'm sorry, Dad, I don't know..."

"Don't worry, Jack," I told him, suppressing a smile. "This happens a lot, and with bigger men than you. You'd be surprised how often. Anyway, just sit there until you feel better. And when you're ready to get up, let Jeff or me know and we'll give you a hand. We don't need another dislocated hip."

From the still-somnolent biker on the stretcher, we heard, "That's for darn sure."

❧

11:45 a.m. Jack had made a full recovery, and Johnny had been discharged on crutches in the company of his friends. He was instructed to follow up in the morning with the orthopedist on call. He would do fine if he didn't push himself. And if he didn't try to jump any more empty swimming pools.

It had been about an hour since Johnny and his friends had left the ER. We were standing at the nurses' station with our backs to the ambulance entrance. I heard the doors open behind me, followed by the quiet clicking of the wheels of a stretcher as it was rolled into the department. Busy with the chart in front of me, I didn't turn around.

Then the clicking stopped and I felt a light tap on my back.

"Robert, I'm so glad you're here today."

The voice was of an elderly woman, and I recognized it.

Turning around, I looked down at the stretcher behind me and saw Myra Donalds.

She stretched out her slender hand to me and said again, "So glad you're on duty today."

Myra Donalds was easily in her nineties. When we had first moved to Rock Hill, she was active in teaching the children in the church we joined. In fact, she had taught all of our own kids in Sunday school, including Jack. Her husband had died four or five years ago, and Myra had moved into one of the retirement centers in town. She had trouble getting around, and I hadn't seen her in church in a long time.

"Myra Donalds," I said, taking her hand in mine. It was tiny, and weak. She had aged since I had last seen her, and she had lost weight. Myra had always been slender, always prim and proper. But she knew how to handle the young people in our church, especially the more difficult ones in the middle-school years. It wasn't her size, or commanding voice, or gruff demeanor. She had none of those. It was because they knew she cared about them, and they cared about her. She was a favorite of all of our children, especially Jack.

It was unusual, really. Jack had been having a typical rebellious phase in the sixth and seventh grades, about the time he started attending Mrs. Donalds's Sunday-school class. Other teachers had tried various ways of dealing with him, but like his father before him, he had spent a good bit of time in trouble. Or at least until he sat down in Myra's classroom. It all changed then. Something clicked between the two of them, and his demeanor and behavior completely changed. And so did his life.

"What brings you to the ER today?" I asked her. "I hope it's just a social visit."

I knew better, having glanced down at her right hip and seeing its awkward angle and the way she was trying to hold it still.

"I wish it were, Robert," she said, smiling. "But I'm afraid it's this hip of mine," she explained, gently patting it. "I tripped over a rug in my apartment this afternoon and fell. I landed right on it. I'm afraid it's broken."

Denton Roberts, the paramedic who had responded to the call, was standing at the head of the stretcher. I looked over at him and he silently nodded his head.

Denton was one of our best paramedics. He was in his mid-forties and had been with the EMS for the past fifteen years. Tall, slender, and always smiling, I trusted his judgment in the field and frequently leaned on his experience. He had seen a lot.

He reached down and patted Myra on her shoulder. "This is one tough customer, Dr. Lesslie," he said respectfully. "Obvious hip fracture, but she didn't want anything for pain. Just wanted to be brought to the hospital. And she apologized for not having tea and something to eat for us."

"Well, young man," she said, straining to look back at his face. "If I could have gotten off the floor, I would have."

I laughed at this, knowing she meant it. Then I said, "Myra, we need to get you back to one of the exam rooms and get you taken care of." Then suddenly remembering Jack, I said, "And look who's here with me today."

Jack had been standing near Denton, and Myra had not yet seen him. He moved around the other side of the stretcher until he stood beside her.

"Mrs. Donalds, it's Jack Lesslie," he said, laying his hand on her elbow. "It's been a long time."

There was a mixture of emotions on his face. He was genuinely glad to see her, but at the same time he was surprised at how much she had changed. She seemed much older than when he had last sat in her classroom. Once he had started high school and now college, he had lost contact. Seeing her like this must have been a shock.

"Jack? Is that you?" Myra asked, her face brightening.

"Yes, Mrs. Donalds. It's me," he answered, now smiling himself, and more relaxed.

Myra let go of my hand and reached up and patted Jack on his cheek.

"My, my! You have grown up, young man," she said with obvious pride. "You're not a young boy anymore."

"No ma'am, I'm not," he said. "I'm in college now, and spending some time with Dad in the ER this summer."

"Well, I bet you didn't count on seeing an old lady like me, did you?" she kidded him.

"I...well..." he stuttered, taken off guard.

"Myra, let's get you on back to a bed and get you more comfortable," I said, coming to his rescue. "Denton, I think the first bed in ortho is open. How about taking her back there?"

Myra Donalds did have a fractured right hip, and it would need to be operated on, probably this evening. For a woman over ninety, she was in remarkable health. And perhaps even more remarkable, she was not taking any regular medications. This should be a routine admission and surgery, and then a routine discharge back to her retirement center. But I knew better.

After the orthopedist had examined Myra and written orders for her admission, Jack went back to talk with her before she went upstairs. After about twenty minutes, he came walking up the hall and stopped beside me at the nurses' station. I had just picked up the chart of my next patient, and I turned to him and asked, "Did you have a good chat with Mrs. Donalds?"

"I did, Dad," he answered, looking at the countertop and nodding his head. "It's been a long time since I've seen her, but she really hasn't changed at all. Not really. She's still as funny and sharp as ever. And somehow she knows just the right questions to ask you. She doesn't beat around the bush, does she?"

"No," I answered. "*That* she doesn't do. And she never has. Maybe that's why the two of you have always gotten along so well. She came into your life when you needed someone to shoot straight with you, someone outside of our family."

"Hmm," he mused. "You know, I think you're probably right. I didn't realize back then how much I really…liked her, I guess."

I studied his face for a moment, "Did you tell her that this afternoon?"

"It's funny, but I did." He looked up at me. "It was just so easy to talk with her, and she asked about everything I was doing, and what was going on in my life. It just came so naturally, and I wanted her to know how I felt about her."

He paused and looked down again.

"I'm just glad it's only her hip that she's injured," he told me, breaking this brief silence.

"What do you mean?"

"Well, it's just her hip," he began to explain. "Like that other guy this morning, the biker. He really hurt his hip bad but then he was able to go home on crutches. Like you said, he's going to be okay."

He waited for my response, and I said, "Uh-huh," wanting him to go on.

"I mean, she's going to be alright after this, isn't she?" he asked. My hesitancy seemed to concern him.

I put the chart in my hand down on the counter and looked into the eyes of my son.

"Jack, I know it seems like sort of the same thing, these two hip injuries," I began. "Johnny the biker goes home and should completely recover. But Myra, well, *this* hip injury is a completely different story. If Johnny had broken his hip instead of dislocating it, he still would have been okay. He would have been admitted to the hospital and had it operated on. And then he would have gone home and done fine. But when someone Myra's age breaks a hip…well, it can be the beginning of the end."

"The what?" he exclaimed. "She seems fine now, and it's only a hip… and…"

"I know that's what it seems," I explained. "But Myra is ninety-two years old, and even though she lives in a retirement center, she's still very lonely. She and Bill had been married for over sixty years, and when you lose a spouse after that long…well, it's really a hard thing to get over. And it was especially hard for Myra because she and Bill were so close."

I stopped and let Jack think about this for a moment.

"You mean Mrs. Donalds is going to give up?" he asked me.

"I don't know that it's *giving up* exactly," I answered, searching for the right words. "I think it might be coming to an understanding that you've reached a place in your life…a place where things really get difficult and you just wonder why you're fighting so hard. And then you come to a peaceful place, and you're ready to accept what comes next. Unfortunately, not everyone finds that peace. And don't misunderstand me—Myra might go back to the retirement center and do just fine. It's just that the odds are against her, and I sense…well, I sense that's where she is."

Jack just looked at me. And then he said, "Dad, now I understand what she was saying."

He stopped. I just waited.

"When I was back in the room talking with her, she said, 'Jack, it's important to live well, and it's important to leave well.' I didn't understand her, and I think she knew that because she said it again. She wanted to be sure I heard her, and that I remembered. Now I know what she meant."

Myra Donalds. Always teaching, always supporting, always thinking of someone else. She continued to be an amazing woman.

Over Jack's shoulder I could see her being wheeled out of the ortho room and around the corner toward the OR. I didn't say anything.

"And she said something else," Jack added. "She reminded me of a verse from the book of John. She had us memorize it when we were kids, but after all these years, I can't remember it. I'll have to look it up when we get home."

I picked the chart up from the countertop again and started down the hallway.

"When you look it up tonight, son, let me know."

Now before the feast of the Passover,
when Jesus knew that his hour had come
to depart out of this world to his Father,
having loved his own who were in the world,
he loved them to the end.

JOHN 13:1 RSV

2

Choose Life

Light is sweet,
and it pleases the eyes to see the sun.
However many years a man may live,
let him enjoy them all.
But let him remember the days of darkness,
for they will be many.

ECCLESIASTES 11:7-8

6:58 a.m. I walked through the ambulance entrance just as Sally Carlton was being brought in from triage in a wheelchair. Jeff Ryan was our triage nurse this morning, and he was pushing her down the hallway to room 4.

"Sally's here for another transfusion," he told me as they passed the nurses' station.

"Hey, Dr. Lesslie," she said, looking up. "Sorry, but it's me again."

"Sally," I said, smiling. "You know we're always glad to see you. Let Jeff get you settled and I'll be back with you in just a minute."

Jeff and Sally continued down the hallway, and I looked for Tom Anders, the nighttime doc I was relieving.

He stepped through the curtained entrance of room 2 and walked over to the nurses' station. Shaking his head in disbelief, he tossed the patient's chart onto the countertop.

"Twenty-one-year-old college student," he told me. "Too much beer and too much sun yesterday. You ought to see this guy's burns. Woke up a little while ago, or more correctly *sobered* up, and realized how much pain he was in."

Tom made some notes on the chart, wrote a prescription for pain medicine, and tossed the clipboard into the discharge basket.

"He's going to have a tough couple of days," he said. "Maybe he'll learn a lesson here."

"Doubt it," Amy Connors muttered, not looking up from the patient ledger she was studying.

"Yeah, you're probably right," Tom agreed. "Anyway, that's all I have, Robert," he said, turning to me. "Everything's taken care of."

"Thanks," I told him. "Now go get some rest."

He turned and headed toward the ER entrance. "See you tonight," he called over his shoulder.

Lori Davidson was walking up the hall with Katie Matthews. They were intently studying a notepad, and I could hear Lori explaining to Katie the importance of making sure each room was restocked at the beginning of a shift.

They were an interesting contrast. Lori had been working in the ER for almost ten years and had become one of our steadiest and most dependable nurses. She was a little more than thirty, yet had the judgment and patience of someone much older. Her presence in the department was calming, a rare quality in such a chaotic and stressful environment. Perhaps her greatest strength, though, was that she genuinely cared for her patients, and they quickly sensed that.

Katie, on the other hand, was twenty-two years old and had just completed her nursing degree, graduating with honors from the program at Clemson. She had grown up in Fort Mill, a small town just a few miles from Rock Hill, and had spent some of her college summers in the ER as a tech. She was enthusiastic but inexperienced. Lori would be a good teacher for her and a good role model.

"So, you think you've got that, Katie?" Lori was asking her. "This is our check-list, and when you're finished, just be sure to initial what you've done."

"I understand," Katie answered. "That way, if something's not right, you'll know who's responsible."

She was quick, and for the few weeks she had spent in the ER as a full-time nurse, she was catching on quickly.

Jeff walked back to the nurses' station and handed me Sally Carlton's clipboard. He had taken her to room 4 and was helping her get settled on the stretcher.

"Here's Sally's chart," he told me. "I'll get things ready."

As he turned and walked to the medication room, it occurred to me that this might be a good opportunity for Katie to meet Sally.

She was standing on the other side of the counter, still talking with Lori, and I interrupted them. "Katie, if you've got a minute…"

They both looked over at me. "Sure, Dr. Lesslie," Katie said. "What is it?"

"There's somebody I want you to meet," I told her. "She's in room 4, Sally Carlton. But I want to tell you about her before we go in there."

Lori nodded as I said this. "That's a good idea, Katie," she told her. "You'll like her." She walked around the counter. "I'll be out in triage."

I motioned for Katie to follow me into the empty observation room. In a quiet voice, I began to tell her about Sally.

Sally Carlton was twenty-five years old. Three years earlier, when she was a senior at the University of South Carolina, she had come home on Christmas break and complained of fatigue. Sally had always been healthy, and her parents were concerned enough to take her to their family doctor. He told them it was probably the stress of a heavy schedule and advised her to get some rest over the break. A week later she came to the ER feeling worse, and running a low-grade fever.

I had been on duty that day, and remembered that first meeting. She was a pretty girl, of medium height and slight build. She had long, dark hair and a spontaneous and infectious smile. But it was her eyes that grabbed your attention. They were alive, and there was a sparkle behind them. Here was a spitfire—and someone who didn't like the idea of being sick.

But it was also those eyes that bothered me. Below each of them were dark circles, almost bruises. And as we talked, I became more concerned about her and about her fatigue.

This had started a few weeks earlier and had begun to affect her ability to get around the sprawling USC campus.

"I can't go up and down stairs now," she told me. "I just seem to give out."

Her parents had been in the room with her, her father standing with his chin cupped in his hand, her mother nervously patting her on the shoulder.

She had no history of any medical problems and was on no medication. Her father described her as "the picture of health."

"We don't think this has anything to do with the pressures of being in school or stress or anything like that," he told me. "I don't think Dr. Jones has any idea what's going on, and he's wrong about that."

"Hmm," I mused. "What about any bruising, Sally? Anything unusual like that?"

She had looked up at her mother and then back at me. "You mean like this?" she answered, pulling up the right sleeve of her blouse and revealing several large, purplish areas. They were irregular in shape, and the multiple shades of blue and purple indicated they were of different ages. This had been going on for a while.

"When did you notice this?" I asked. Her parents leaned closer, staring at her arm. This was something new for them, as she had apparently tried to keep it hidden.

"I guess it started about two weeks ago," she answered sheepishly. "I thought I must have bumped into something and that it would go away."

"But it didn't, did it?" I remarked gently.

"No, and then these…" She pulled up the left leg of her loose-fitting slacks, revealing more extensive bruising about the outside of her thigh. Her mother had gasped, putting her hand to her mouth. And her father had just stood up straight, staring at his daughter's leg.

A CBC had given us the answer nobody wanted. Sally had leukemia, and was in trouble. That evening she was at Duke, under the care of a blood-and-cancer specialist. Within a few weeks, she would have a bone-marrow transplant.

And for a while, she had done well. The medication was working and her blood counts had returned to normal. Most importantly to Sally, her energy level had returned and she was able to go back to school and her classes. She wanted to finish her degree and pursue a career in nursing.

But that had lasted only a few weeks. Her white-blood-cell count started to rise again, indicating more problems. Then the fatigue returned, and her fevers. The specialists at Duke tried everything, and she would sometimes seem to be improving, to almost *will* this disease into remission. Then the blood work would be bad again. First it was her white count, exposing her to what could be a catastrophic infection. And then her hemoglobin began to fall, with the resulting anemia causing a fatigue that never seemed to leave her.

It was the anemia that had been bringing her to the ER. She would come in for a transfusion of a few units of blood and would then feel better for a few weeks. But it was always there, this thing that had destroyed her bone marrow, and her visits to the ER had become more frequent. It was all that could be done at this point. And there was no way of knowing how many more times we could do this, and how much more time she had. It probably wouldn't be very long.

"So there's really nothing anybody can do?" Katie asked. "I mean, how about another transplant?"

"No, I'm afraid she's run out of options," I told her. "But you wouldn't know that by talking to her. You'll see."

We walked around the nurses' station to room 4. Sally was lying on the stretcher, her blanket drawn up to her waist. She had folded her arms across her chest but now raised her right hand and waved as we entered.

She smiled and said, "I'm glad you're on duty today, Dr. Lesslie. And who is this with you?" she asked, looking at Katie.

"This is Katie Matthews," I said. "She just recently finished her nursing school and has started working here in the ER with us."

Sally held out her hand. "It's good to meet you, Katie," she said as they shook hands. "I'm sure Dr. Lesslie has a few things to show you. And I'm sure he has plenty of stories to tell you," she adding, winking at me. "You know, I'm going into nursing myself."

Out of the corner of my eye I thought I saw Katie tense just a little. But Sally's words were spoken with conviction, and her smile and expression did not change at all. She meant what she was saying. And yet she knew the reality of her condition.

"Where did you go to school?" she asked Katie.

"Well, that will give you two something to talk about," I told them. "Sally, we'll get your blood going as soon as it comes over from the lab."

Jeff had come back into the room and was preparing to start an IV.

"Want to give me a hand?" he asked Katie.

"Sure," she answered. "I'll be happy to."

Sally would be in good hands, and I stepped to the doorway. "I'll check on you in a while," I told her. "Keep these guys straight."

"Don't worry about them," she answered. "I'll make sure they behave."

As I stepped out of the room, I saw Virginia Granger standing in the doorway of the head nurse's office. She motioned for me to join her.

Virginia had been our head nurse for a lot of years, longer than I had been in Rock Hill. No one knew her real age (no one was brave enough to ask), but she must have been in her mid-sixties. The early part of her nursing career had been spent in the military, and her bearing continued to be rigid, overtly professional, and quite intimidating. She always wore a dazzling white, freshly starched uniform, and white scuffless shoes. And this morning, as always, her pointed nursing cap was bobby-pinned to her dyed-jet-black hair.

She commanded respect from her staff and demanded that we all take our jobs seriously and focus on the needs of our patients. That's what she did, and we were to do nothing less. Yet behind this rigid exterior, behind this intimidating façade, lived a woman with a big and warm heart. She didn't show that side to a lot of people, and I'm not sure why. But I knew it was there. I had seen it.

"Dr. Lesslie," she said to me. "Close the door, would you? And have a seat."

She pointed to the chair in front of her desk, and I sat down. "Tell me about Sally."

I knew Virginia didn't want to know temperatures or blood pressures or blood counts. She wanted to know how Sally was handling things, how she was *really* doing.

We talked for a few minutes and I told her I would get back with her before Sally left the department.

"That one's a fighter," Virginia said, slowly nodding her head.

Two hours later, Sally had finished receiving her blood transfusion. Jeff was wheeling her toward the exit. She was laughing at something he had said, and I noticed that her color was decidedly better. This time she was able to go home, but the time was soon coming when that would no longer be an option.

Her father had gone out to bring the car around to the ambulance entrance, and they were waiting for him to come back into the department.

Katie had walked up with them. They all stopped beside me at the nurses' station.

"Sally, are you feeling better?" I asked. "You certainly look like you do."

"I feel like a million dollars," she said, smiling at me. "I've had expert care this morning. What else would you expect?"

The ambulance doors opened, and her father stood beside the passenger door of their car. Jeff began pushing the wheelchair once again, with Katie walking close behind them.

Sally twisted around in her chair and waved at me. "I guess I'll see you next time." Then she turned and said something to her father as they disappeared through the closing doors.

A moment later, Katie walked back into the department and over to where I stood.

"You know, Dr. Lesslie, you're right. She really is a special person. Do you think she understands how sick she is?" she asked.

"Of course she does. It's just that she's not willing to give in to it. She wants to live. You can see it in her eyes. The day that's gone, the day that fire's not in her eyes, that's when I'm going to worry."

She stood there for a moment. "How much longer do you think she has?"

"There's no way of knowing for sure. But it's going to be measured in days and weeks, not months."

That seemed to bother her, but it was the truth.

"But you know, Katie, whatever time she has left, she'll make the most of it. She has a spirit I wish we all had. She appreciates every moment she has."

Katie was about to say something but was interrupted by the crackle of the EMS radio.

"Rock Hill ER, this is Medic 1. Is the doctor nearby?"

That's when it started.

Amy Connors picked up the receiver and handed it to me.

"Medic 1, this is Dr. Lesslie," I answered.

"Doc, this is Denton Roberts. We're at the scene with a twenty-six-year-old woman, complainin' of not feelin' right. She seems a little bit confused, but all her vital signs are good and she seems stable. Normally we wouldn't bring her in, but somethin' doesn't quite seem right. Any problems if I go ahead and transport?"

This was an odd request, but Denton had been doing this for a long time and I knew better than to second-guess him.

"Sure, Denton, go ahead and bring her in. What's your ETA?"

"About 5. I'll probably start a line, just to be safe."

"Fine," I told him. Lori had walked up beside me and heard this conversation. She got my attention and held up three fingers.

"And room 3 when you get here, Denton," I added.

A few minutes later, the ambulance doors opened and Denton Roberts and his partner brought their stretcher into the ER with the young woman.

"Room 3?" he confirmed with Lori as they reached the nurses' station.

"Right," she answered, making some notes on the chart in front of her. "I'll be just a second."

As they passed, the young woman looked up at me. She seemed alert enough, but there was something dull and remote about her gaze. I could see what had troubled Denton. Then from behind her there was a small commotion as another young woman tried to squeeze through the closing mechanical doors. She was able to pry them open enough to barely make it through.

Lori looked up from her charting and said, "Can I help you, miss?"

The woman standing just inside the ambulance entrance was probably in her mid-twenties, dressed in blue jeans and a loose-fitting T-shirt and wearing flip-flops. Her hair was a dirty blonde and probably hadn't met a comb in a few days.

"I'm with her," she answered, pointing to the stretcher disappearing into room 3.

Lori stepped over to the woman and motioned to the triage entrance. "You'll need to have a seat in the waiting room," she gently directed her. "We'll let you know something as soon as we can."

"But, she—"

"Come on, I'll show you." Lori cut off her protestations and led her out to waiting.

Wanda Bennett was the name of the young woman who had just been taken to room 3. I motioned for Katie to follow me. We stepped into the cubicle, pulling the curtain closed behind us. Denton and his partner had transferred Wanda to our bed and were preparing to push their stretcher out of the room.

"Everything's still stable," Denton told me. "Blood pressure is 115 over 70 and her pulse is 72 and regular. Pulse ox is 97 percent." He shrugged and shook his head. "If anything, she may be a little more confused, or something."

"Thanks, Denton," I told him, stepping back out of his way. "I'll let you know what turns up."

He left the room, and Lori continued to work with our new patient.

She attached the leads for the cardiac monitor and hung her IV fluid bag on the stand by the head of the bed.

"Oxygen?" she asked me.

The oxygen saturation of her blood was normal. She certainly wasn't in any distress. "No, we'll hold off on that," I told her, stepping closer to the stretcher.

I glanced down at the clipboard Lori had set on the counter, noting her name.

"Wanda?" I said, touching her lightly on her shoulder. "I'm Dr. Lesslie. What can we do for you today?"

She had absently been watching Lori and now turned to face me. Wanda was of a heavy build, used a little too much makeup, and had black hair of medium length.

"Who?" she asked, the word drawn out more than it should have been.

"I'm Dr. Lesslie," I repeated, a little louder this time. "What's the problem today?"

"Oh, Dr. Wesley, I…I…who brought me here?"

She seemed confused now and began to look around the room. Lori immediately stepped close and took her hand. "It's okay, Wanda. You're in the hospital. We're here to help you."

This seemed to confuse her even more, and she became a little agitated. She looked at Lori and asked, "The hospital? What's the matter?"

I tried to get some coherent information from her, but without success. She repeated my questions, but never answered them. Leaning closer, I tried to detect the odor of alcohol on her breath. Nothing there. A brief exam did not turn up anything unusual, and I was in a quandary as to what might be causing her decreased level of consciousness. She certainly wasn't helping, so we would need to use a broad, shotgun approach.

Katie and I walked back to the nurses' station, and she asked, "What do you think her problem is? She seems pretty out of it right now, doesn't she?"

She did seem out of it, and the problem was that it had appeared to be getting worse while we were in the room with her.

"I'm not sure at this point, Katie. We'll need to look at a bunch of things and see if something turns up. We'll need some blood work and probably a scan of her head." I paused and thought for a moment. "She told Lori she didn't take any medication, and Denton didn't report seeing any in her apartment. But you can't trust what she's telling us."

"What about her friend?" she asked. "What about that other woman who came in with her?"

Now there was a good thought. "Great idea, Katie. I'll ask Lori to bring her back and see if she can shed any light on this."

A few minutes later, Lori walked up to the nurses' station with the woman we assumed was Wanda Bennett's friend.

"Dr. Lesslie, this is Amanda Davis," Lori introduced her. "She's Wanda's roommate."

Amanda was nervously looking around the department, trying to locate her friend.

"Miss Davis," I said to her. "I need some information about Wanda."

"Okay, I'll be glad to help," she answered. But her eyes never met mine.

"When did she start getting like this? This confusion?" I asked her.

"She, uh, she was fine last night. I guess it started just a little while ago, right before I called 9-1-1."

"Was she complaining about anything when you called, any pain or headache? Anything unusual?"

"No, nothin' like that. She just wasn't acting right. Started talking funny, I guess. And didn't make much sense." She was becoming a little nervous for some reason. "Is she alright?"

"She's okay right now," I tried to assure her. "We're trying to figure out why she's acting this way. Is she taking any medication or using any drugs?"

I watched closely for any telltale change in her body language, any hint that what she might tell me was not the truth.

At this point she looked in my eyes and slowly shook her head.

"Nope. She doesn't take any medicine and doesn't use any drugs or stuff like that. She doesn't even drink."

I continued to study her face, and asked again, "Are you sure? No prescription meds or anything? Sleeping pills? Something for her nerves?"

"No, she doesn't take anything." She looked away after saying this, and asked, "Can I see her now?"

"Dr. Lesslie, can you come over here?"

It was Lori, standing in the doorway of room 3 and motioning for me to hurry over.

Amy Connors had been listening to this exchange and had heard Lori. She stepped around the nurses' counter and took Amanda by the elbow.

"Miss Davis, if you'll follow me, I'll take you back to the waiting room," she instructed her. Amy was polite, but left no room for questioning.

"But…" Amanda murmured, yet followed Amy obediently toward the triage entrance.

When I went into the room, one of our lab techs was drawing blood, adjusting the tourniquet on Wanda's right arm. Lori was standing at the head of the stretcher and pointed to the cardiac monitor as I pulled the curtain closed.

"Maybe she seems a little more confused, Dr. Lesslie," she explained. "But this is what has me worried."

My eyes followed hers to the monitor screen. There was a steady beep-beep-beep, nice and regular, but now the rate had fallen to 58.

"Her blood pressure is okay," she told me, anticipating my next question. "But her rate is slowing, and every once in a while she has what looks like a PVC. Look—right there," she said, pointing again to the monitor.

I had seen it as well. It looked like a PVC, an extra heartbeat, sometimes normal, but also at times associated with some underlying heart problem or irritability. There had only been one, and then it was gone.

"Let's get an EKG and see what it looks like," I instructed Lori. "And could we get those labs back as quickly as possible?" I asked the tech. She had finished drawing blood and was pressing a Band-aid over the puncture site.

"Should only be a few minutes." She hurried out of the room.

Wanda Bennett's EKG was troubling. I was sitting at the nurses' station, studying the tracing and trying to unravel this mystery. Somewhere in this multitude of undulating ink lines might be the answer, waiting to be discovered.

She continued to have a slow yet nearly normal pattern. But every few beats there was a slight lengthening of the whole electrical complex, and then it would tighten up again. That was strange and didn't make much sense. I wasn't sure I had seen it before.

Katie was standing behind me, looking over my shoulder. I pointed out the unusual finding on Wanda's EKG.

"What could cause something like that?" she asked. "She's too young for a heart attack, isn't she?"

She actually wasn't, but these findings didn't go along with a heart attack. Something else was happening here.

"I don't know, Katie," I answered honestly. "Maybe some toxin, or something like that. Something that's affecting her heart's electrical conducting system. Sometimes carbon monoxide poisoning can cause strange heart problems, but it's summer, and people probably aren't using space heaters now."

"Dr. Lesslie." It was Lori again. This time she stood in the doorway of room 3 and once she caught my eye, she stepped back into the room without another word.

We walked quickly around the counter and into the cubicle.

Wanda was relaxed on the stretcher, seemingly asleep. Her left arm hung limply over the side of the stretcher, and her mouth was open. She was quietly snoring.

"She won't respond now," Lori told me. "BP is about 60, and her heart rate is 40 to 50."

I looked at the monitor and immediately pressed the button that allowed a rhythm strip to print continuously. Her rate was 48, and now every complex was widened—and seemed to be getting wider as we watched.

I rubbed Wanda's sternum and loudly called her name in her ear. No response. Then I turned to Lori and asked her to give several medications in an attempt to speed up her heart and reverse this downward spiral.

"I'm going to find Amanda Davis and have another talk with her," I said, turning toward the door. "And I'll send Jeff in to help."

Amy Connors led Amanda into the department once more and toward the nurses' station. Room 5 was empty, and I motioned for her to follow me there. Once Amanda was in the room, I pulled the curtain closed behind us and asked her to have a seat.

"Miss Davis, this is very important. Your friend, Wanda, is not doing well. She's unresponsive. I can't wake her up now. And something's going on with her heart." I paused, letting these words sink in. "Is there anything you can tell me about her, about what she's been doing over the past few days? Is she taking any medication? Any recreational drugs?"

She looked down at the floor when I said this.

"Amanda, listen, I'm not the police. And nothing you say to me will be reported to the police. I'm trying to help Wanda. And if you know anything, anything that could be of use…" I pleaded. And then more sternly, "I need your help."

She turned her face up to me and was about to say something. There was a conflicted look in her eyes, but they hardened again and she looked down at the floor.

"No, I don't know of anything," she persisted.

She knew something, or I thought she did. And I was starting to get angry.

"Let me say this once more, Amanda," I said to her, my voice firm yet as measured as I could make it. "Wanda is in trouble. Real trouble. She may die. Do you hear me? If we don't determine what's causing this, she may very well—"

"Code blue, room 3!"

Jeff Ryan's voice spoke urgently over the department intercom.

"Code blue, room 3!" he repeated.

Wanda Bennett had crashed, and I sprang for the door, but not before nailing Amanda with a look of anger and disgust and accusation.

I threw the curtain aside and saw several people heading to room 3. Then from behind me I heard, "Dr. Lesslie! Please, Dr. Lesslie!"

It was Amanda Davis, and she was following me as fast as she could. I stopped and turned, facing her.

"What do you want?" I asked her, knowing I needed to get to Wanda Bennett, but also wondering if Amanda had something of value to tell me.

She was crying now and wringing her hands. Then she blurted out, "Dr. Lesslie, she made me promise not to tell. She made me promise! That's why I didn't…before…I couldn't—"

"What is it, Amanda?" I demanded.

"She took her daddy's pills. A bunch of them. Last night and again this morning. Said she was tired of livin' and puttin' up with everything. I didn't think she was really serious, 'cause that's all she took. She's talked about this before, but—"

"Amanda!" I snapped, getting her attention. "What did she take?"

"That's just it, nothin' serious. That's why I thought…She just took some of her daddy's blood-pressure medicine, that's all. That shouldn't really hurt her, should it?" she asked innocently.

My mind was sorting through the various classes of blood-pressure medications, searching for the answer that would fit this woman's problems. It was forming in my mind, but it was not quite there yet.

"What was the name of it? What was on the bottle?"

A puzzled look came over her face, and I gave up, turning toward room 3.

"Dalozam, or diltozam. Something like that," she mumbled.

The answer flashed like lightning across my brain. She had taken a huge overdose of a calcium-channel blocker, a commonly used blood-pressure medication. It blocked the movements of certain chemicals in various parts of the heart, slowing the heart rate and easing the force of contractions. It was obvious what too much of that drug could do.

I turned to Amy and said, "Take her to the waiting room." And then I hurried into room 3.

There was a flurry of activity around the stretcher, controlled chaos. Lori had set out the emergency airway tray and in less than a minute we had secured Wanda's breathing.

"She just stopped breathing and then went flatline," Lori told me, a little out of breath. Jeff was doing chest compressions. Just then the lab tech came into the room and handed me Wanda's lab reports. Everything was completely normal. I searched for the calcium level and it was normal too. But then it should be. She had plenty of calcium on board—it just wasn't able to do its job because of the medication. The only thing to do was give her *more* calcium, in the hopes of overcoming the blockade.

"Give her two amps of calcium," I told Lori.

"Two amps?" Jeff questioned. "Do you want to try some epi first?" He was only trying to help, following what should be standard protocol.

"No, Jeff. We're going to give her calcium, and a lot of it. We're going to need more amps from the main crash cart," I told one of the techs. Then I explained to Jeff and Lori what I had learned.

It all made sense now. The sleepiness, then the worsening confusion. And then the widening of her electrical complexes. It was all logical and explainable. And if I had known from the beginning, or had just had a clue…Why hadn't she told me? And why hadn't Amanda Davis seen the danger to her friend and told me from the outset?

"Nothing here," Lori told me, feeling for a carotid pulse. And there was no electrical activity on the monitor.

We continued our efforts for another 45 minutes, pumping Wanda full of calcium and other emergency medications. She didn't respond to anything.

Finally, I knew we had to stop. She was dead. We weren't going to change that.

Lori noted the time of death on her chart while everyone else filed out of the room. Everyone except Katie. I had forgotten she had been standing behind me the whole time, never uttering a word. There was a troubled look on her face as she stared down at the lifeless body of Wanda Bennett.

"Come on, Katie," I said to her, putting my hand lightly on her shoulder. "Let's go outside for a minute."

We stood together under the portico of the ambulance entrance, shielded from the afternoon sun.

"That was—really tough, Katie." I spoke, then became silent, wanting her to express her thoughts.

"I don't understand, Dr. Lesslie," she shook her head. "I don't understand a couple of things. I didn't know something simple like blood-pressure medicine could do something like that to you. And I wonder if she knew it." She thought for a moment. Then, "Do you think she had any idea this might happen? And I wonder if she really wanted to kill herself? What if—"

"That's something we'll never know, Katie. There's no way you can know the mind of another person, much less their heart. I don't have any idea what she was thinking, or what she was trying to do. It doesn't matter now," I told her. "I only wish…"

We were silent for a moment, and then Katie continued my thought. "Do you think it would have made any difference if you had known right away what she had taken? Do you think it could have been reversed or something?"

I had been struggling with the same question. My head told me that she must have taken a massive overdose of this medicine, and that by the time she'd come to the ER, there was nothing anyone could do to reverse its actions. It had all happened so quickly.

But my heart told me something different. I wasn't used to being in this position, and feeling helpless. And I found I was angry with Wanda. But I wasn't going to voice that to this young nurse. I wasn't the one lying on the stretcher in room 3, a sheet drawn over my face.

"No, Katie. I think she sealed her fate when she took all those pills. There was no going back."

"It just seems like such a waste. What makes someone want to die like this? What would make her want to kill herself?" she asked, not expecting an answer. Maybe not wanting one. "She's only a few years older than me, you know."

We didn't talk any further. And I thought of Sally Carlton.

Now choose life,
so that you and your children may live
and that you may love the Lord your God,
listen to his voice,
and hold fast to him.

DEUTERONOMY 30:19-20

3

All That Glitters...

Judgment comes from experience,
and great judgment comes from bad experience.

SAYING

Beware lest you lose the substance
by grasping at the shadow.

AESOP

Tuesday, 9:45 a.m. Amy Connors dropped the pen she was holding and stared in amazement over my left shoulder. "Good Lord," she murmured. "Would you look at that?"

I was standing at the nurses' station and turned around to see a young man behind me, not more than five feet away. He was staring straight at me, his arms hanging limply by his side, his knees slightly bent as if ready to pounce. The look on his face got my attention. There was a mixture of fear and pleading, and something else. His eyes were wild, and I began to wonder if he was dangerous.

He was barefoot, and his worn jeans were tattered at the edges. He wasn't wearing a shirt and I noticed the tattoo of a multicolored, robed wizard over his heart.

"Doc," he whispered in a shaky voice, "I need some help."

Lori Davidson, our triage nurse this morning, had walked up behind him.

"Sir," she said, reaching out and lightly tapping his shoulder.

Then his arms stiffened and his eyes widened in what looked like abject terror. His legs straightened and his arms went out zombie-like. His head twitched for just a second and he began to arch backward, first his head, and then his upper torso. He did this very fluidly, as if having practiced it over and over. His long hair dangled behind him, and when he finally stopped, he was almost nose to nose with Lori. Her eyes widened in surprise, and she seemed frozen on the spot. As for this young man, he looked like a pretzel. I was impressed with his flexibility.

Suddenly he let out a terrible and unnerving scream. "Aghh!" And that did it. The chart in Lori's hand flew ten feet into the air and we all jumped, seeking a safe distance from him. I reached for the countertop, trying to find something solid to hold on to. And then without warning he snapped back to his original position, arms hanging by his side, knees slightly bent. His eyes were once again fixed on mine.

"Doc, I need some help. I can't stop doing this. Do something," he pleaded.

"What in the world…" Amy muttered behind me.

Jeff Ryan was on duty today and was walking up the hall. He stopped beside me, intently studying our young patient.

"What's going on?" he whispered to me.

"I don't know," I answered him honestly. "This guy just walked in, and—"

Suddenly it started again. This young man's arms stiffened, his legs straightened, he began arching backward, and Lori moved further away. When his torso was parallel with the floor, he let out another scream and his body whipped forward, hair flying in all directions. This time I was prepared and didn't react with the same surprise. Jeff watched these startling contortions but seemed unfazed. After a brief assessment, he suspected mischief.

"This guy's wacko, Doc," he said. "I'm gonna take him to room 5 and get him to calm down. Look," he added, gesturing down the hallway at several patients and visitors who were peeking out from behind their curtains and watching this spectacle.

"Good idea, Jeff," I agreed. "But I'm not sure about this guy. This is pretty strange."

Jeff nodded his head. Then he addressed our new patient. "Why don't you come with me...uh...what's your name?"

"Jimmy Blake," the man answered, happy that someone was finally going to help him.

Jeff headed to room 5, with Jimmy obediently following behind him. Suddenly he stopped, still in the hallway, and the gyration began again. He immediately stiffened and then began slowly arching backward. Jeff didn't know his patient had stopped, and he continued on to room 5, talking. When there was no answer, he turned around just as Jimmy was snapping his body forward and screaming.

This time even Jeff jumped. "Come on in here," he told him, shaking his head and holding the curtain open. "Have a seat on the stretcher."

When Jeff had gotten Jimmy undressed and in a gown, he walked out of room 5 and over to where I stood. He handed me his chart, and said, "He's all yours. He did that goofy thing twice more while I was trying to get his vital signs. The blood pressure is probably pretty close, but I don't know. Anyway, it's the best I can do."

He walked toward the medicine room to wash his hands.

I looked over Jimmy Blake's chart. Twenty-three years old. Vital signs were normal. No medications and no allergies. "Denies alcohol or illicit drugs," Jeff had written. Not much to go on here.

Virginia Granger had walked up behind me and was glancing at the record.

"Better take a close look at this one," she said to me, slowly nodding her head. Then she turned and walked down the hall.

Jimmy was standing in the middle of the room as I entered. "Have a seat, Mr. Blake," I told him, pointing to the stretcher. "I'm Dr. Lesslie, and I'm here to help you."

I was hoping that having him off his feet and on the stretcher would distract him from his contortions. If he was malingering, maybe that would take his mind off it long enough to confirm to me that this was a voluntary thing. But if he *was* malingering, pretending to have these wild movements, what was in it for him? What did he stand to gain? This was really bizarre.

Jimmy followed my instructions and hopped up on the stretcher. But just as he settled onto the thin mattress, he jumped back down on the floor and began his strange dance. Once again it ended with a loud scream and his hair flying in my face.

"I'm sorry, Doc, I can't help it. Please help me stop!" he pleaded. Without being asked, he got back up on the stretcher.

While I was examining Jimmy, I asked him about any trauma, any medical problems, and especially about any medication.

"No, I don't take any medicine," he insisted.

"And what about any other types of drugs? Something without a prescription?" I questioned him, pressing a little.

"No nothing like that," he answered, shaking his head but shrugging his right shoulder at the same time. He was sending a mixed signal, and might not be telling the whole truth.

"Jimmy, this is important for me to know, if you want me to help you," I pushed.

"Well…I'll smoke a joint every once in a while, Doc," he finally admitted. "And maybe drink a couple of beers. But nothing hard, you know. No crack or anything like that."

Then he jumped down, and it started all over again. After the final jerking of his head, he looked up at me with frustration and a growing fatigue in his eyes. "Doc, please, do something!"

The consistency of each episode was worrisome. If he was faking this, it would be difficult for him to duplicate each "dance," but that was what was happening. It was the same every time. No—there was something else here.

"Alright, Jimmy," I continued, a little more sternly this time. "I have to know if you've taken anything unusual today, smoked anything, popped any pills, anything like that."

He looked me squarely in the face and began to shake his head. "No, nothing." But as he said this, some new realization seemed to dawn on him, and his eyes widened.

"Wait a minute, Doc," he said with a little excitement. "There *was* something I took last night. Yeah, maybe that's it! My girlfriend gave me one of her brother's pills—Haldol, I think it was. Yeah, it was a Haldol tablet. A little white pill. He's pretty messed up and I shouldn't have been takin' his medicine. I guess I should have known better. Made me feel pretty strange, and I thought I slept it off. Actually, Doc…it was three of them," he added sheepishly. "Could that be—"

"Are you sure it was Haldol?" I interrupted. "This is important, Jimmy."

"Yeah, I'm sure, Doc. I read it on the bottle. Do you think—"

I stepped to the curtain and pulled it aside. "Jeff, we need to start a line here, normal saline. And we need some IV Benadryl."

From across the nurses' station, Jeff acknowledged my request with a wave of his hand.

Turning to Jimmy, I began to explain the cause of his strange gyrations and how we were going to stop them.

The Haldol he had taken was a strong antipsychotic medication. It acts on several important areas of the brain, and even at normal doses it can cause involuntary muscle movements and cramps. Some of these can be really painful and very disturbing. At high doses, which was apparently where we were with Jimmy, all of these symptoms can be amplified.

Fortunately, the side effects of Haldol can be easily and quickly reversed with Benadryl, a simple and commonly used antihistamine medication.

"You're going to be okay, Jimmy," I assured him.

He hadn't been malingering after all. If we had followed our initial assumptions, things could have turned out much worse. There was a lesson here for Jimmy, and maybe for me. And once again, I was reminded to pay attention to Virginia.

I signed Mr. Blake's chart and tossed it into the discharge rack. Just as I did this, the curtain of room 1 opened. Blair Higgins stepped out. He pulled the curtain closed behind him and walked over in our direction, stopping right beside me.

Blair was a thirty-two-year-old internal-medicine specialist. He had only recently finished his training, having completed a fellowship in some specialty I couldn't remember at the moment. He was a very bright guy, and personable enough. But he exemplified the term "flea" as it was frequently applied to specialists in the field of internal medicine.

Years ago I had mentioned "flea" in Lori Davidson's presence, and she had asked me what it meant.

"Well, you see Lori," I began to explain. "The field of internal medicine requires a certain mind-set if you're going to be good at it. It's all about attention to detail, and following every possible lead until you run a problem to ground. When every other physician has scratched their heads about a patient and finally walked away, the internal medicine doc is the last to leave. Just like a flea is the last to leave a dying dog. Hence the term 'flea.'"

"Is that a good thing or a bad thing?" she had asked me.

"Well, if you're sick, really sick, I'd think you'd want a 'flea' taking care of you, wouldn't you?"

She thought for a moment, "Yeah, I think I would."

The problem with Blair Higgins was that he had not yet had enough practical experience to temper his extensive medical knowledge.

As we stood at the nurses' station, he began to write on the chart of the patient in room 1.

"What was all that commotion out here?" he asked me, not looking up from his writing. "What's with all that screaming? I could barely hear myself think."

"Just another interesting case," I answered, winking at Amy. "Everything's under control."

"Well, that's good," he said. And then, "Speaking of interesting, here—take a look at this, Robert, and tell me what you think."

He slid the chart of room 1 across the counter, right in front of me. He stood up straight and looked at me over the top of his glasses, adjusting them with the long finger of his right hand. For a split second I was transported back to my intern days, making rounds with one of the staff physicians and being quizzed on every minor detail of a patient. It didn't matter how much you knew about your patient or about his or her condition. The "attending" would continue questioning until you were finally stumped on some trivial finding, no matter how obscure. The goal seemed to be to remind you of your place in the pecking order of things, and how little you actually knew. I didn't like the feeling.

"Okay, let's see here, Blair," I responded, willing to play his game and focusing on the medical record before me.

The patient was a twenty-three-year-old male, presenting with complaints of nausea, vomiting, and diarrhea. It had started yesterday, and the triage nurse had noted that he "was unable to keep anything down."

His vital signs were stable, with only a slightly elevated pulse of 102. His temp was 99.8. Not really elevated. He was on no medications and listed no history of asthma, diabetes, or heart disease. He didn't smoke.

"His exam?" I turned to Blair and asked.

"Completely benign," he declared. "Maybe a little dryness of mouth, nothing more."

I glanced down again at the chart, looking for some hidden clue or some subtle piece of information. It seemed pretty straightforward to me.

"Well, it looks to me—" I began, but was interrupted.

"Take a look at this," he said knowingly. "Maybe this will give you a clue."

He placed a lab slip on top of the chart, patting it for effect.

It was the CBC report of this young man. I picked up the piece of paper and glanced through the multiple numbers on it.

His white count was elevated, a little over 18,000, and consistent with an infection of some kind. His hemoglobin was fine, no evidence of anemia. And his platelet count was normal, no obvious evidence of any bone-marrow problem.

"Okay, is this all you have? Any other lab studies?" I asked him, trying to figure where he was going with this.

"No, this is all. Just this CBC. That's all I need," he answered. Then he impatiently started drumming his fingers on the countertop. "Well, what do you think now?"

I looked at the chart again, and then at the lab slip. I must have been missing something here. It seemed pretty simple.

"Well?" he persisted. "What do you think?"

"Okay, I would say he has a mild to moderate case of gastroenteritis," I answered him. "Probably a viral infection. We've seen a bunch this week, and a few already today."

Out of the corner of my eye I could see Amy nodding in agreement.

"He might be getting dehydrated," I continued. "So I would consider giving him some IV fluids while he's here. Then I'd treat him symptomatically. That would be the extent of it," I said, sliding the chart back over to him.

"Hmm…well, that's not what I think." Blair placed his palm on the chart. "This young man has leukemia."

Amy looked up at this pronouncement and rolled her eyes.

"Leukemia?" I responded. "What makes you think that?"

At some point during this conversation, Jeff had walked over to the nurses' station. When he heard this proclamation, he had sidled a little closer, trying to get a peek at the chart. Something interesting was going on here.

Dr. Higgins sighed with obvious impatience. "Well, for one thing, this young man has some vague symptoms, some that are not easily explained. But the most important thing is his white count. It's entirely too elevated for a simple and benign process."

"Blair," I tried to reason with him, "I've seen white counts in the 20,000s with viral gastroenteritis. They come down in a couple of days and don't mean anything. I've pretty much stopped getting them in this scenario. It just confuses things."

Just like this time.

"Nope, I don't believe that's the case here," he said, obviously not listening to me. He began to stroke his chin thoughtfully and then said, "I'm going around to the lab and order some more tests. Maybe a bone-marrow analysis. This young man will need to be admitted to the hospital and worked up."

"But Blair—" I tried once more.

"Thanks anyway, Robert," he dismissed me. "I'll let you know what turns up."

He spun around and started down the hallway. Suddenly he stopped, then slowly turned and once more placed his hand to his chin, stroking it professorially.

"You know, Robert, the key here is observation," he spoke with great gravity. "That's right—observation. You...uh...*we* need to pay attention to every detail, look under every rock, *observe* every possible thing about our patient. That way, we won't be led astray."

Allowing no opportunity for a response, he turned and walked off, leaving me standing there with Jeff and Amy, all of us wondering what was to happen with the young man in room 1.

"Doc," Amy interrupted my thoughts, "that is a classic example of too much head sense and not enough common sense."

Then Jeff looked up at me and said, "Yeah, and that's a case of bein' a real jerk. Does he think he's some kind of a professor?"

That part of it didn't bother me. I had come to expect such remarks from Blair. But a few years earlier, fresh out of residency, I would probably have bowed my neck.

Then Jeff said, almost apologetically, "What if he's right? What if that guy has leukemia? What about the white count?"

"The white count doesn't bother me at all," I told him. "It's just a red herring."

"A what?" He looked confused.

"A red herring," I repeated, realizing I would need to explain the remark. "A red herring," I began, "is something that leads you away—away from the main point or object. It's a distraction. You know, something that takes you down the wrong path."

"You mean this guy's white count would be a distraction, and lead Dr. Higgins in the wrong direction?"

Jeff understood. "Yes, that's right. He's intent on chasing that lab value when it's really not the problem at all."

"Okay then, why do they call it a red herring?" he asked.

Another good question. Fortunately I was ready for this one. I made it a habit to look up the origin of obscure sayings and metaphors, especially the ones I used from time to time. "One fell swoop." "Wet your whistle." "Son of a gun" (now *there's* an interesting one).

"Well, that's a good story," I began to explain. "It seems that if you cook a herring by smoking it, the fish will turn a reddish color. Now apparently, several hundreds of years ago, there were animal lovers in England who didn't particularly like the idea and the cruelty of a fox-hunt. They would sabotage these hunts by tying a smoked herring to a string and then dragging it on the ground across the fox's trail. This confused the hounds and led them off in the wrong direction. Much as Dr. Higgins is being led in the wrong direction right now."

Amy Connors cleared her throat and skeptically asked, "Dr. Lesslie, is that true? Or have *you* been smokin' somethin' other than herring?"

"Of course it's true!" I insisted. "It makes sense, doesn't it?"

"Well, sort of…" Jeff said, feigning allegiance with Amy. "But then again, it does seem a little far-fetched."

"Okay then," I countered. "Just what is the origin of the term 'far-fetched'?"

"Oh Lord, here we go," Amy said, giving up. "This could go on all day."

Jeff chuckled, and I picked up the chart of the next patient to be seen.

She was a thirty-two-year-old woman, with a "laceration of left index finger." Apparently she had cut it on a broken glass in her kitchen sink.

"Well, that doesn't change the fact that Dr. Higgins is a jerk," Jeff stated again flatly.

I put the chart back down on the counter, a thought having come to my mind. "Well, you know, he *did* mention something about observation, didn't he?" I asked. Amy looked up from the ER registration ledger, nodding her head.

"Yeah, he did," Jeff answered. "But I didn't pay much attention."

"Well, let me tell you something that happened when I was in medical school."

Amy settled back in her chair, and Jeff turned to face me.

"There was a pathology professor, a Dr. Black," I began. "He was one of our favorites, a real character, and I'll never forget a lesson he taught us one morning. It had to do with developing this essential skill of observation."

We had been sitting in our main lecture hall, about a hundred and twenty of us. It was our first year of medical school—we were all pretty green. This was one of our first pathology classes, and the instructor, Dr. Black, was going to lecture on diabetes. I can still see him now, walking across the stage, his lab coat barely covering a pretty good-sized belly. And then he stopped right in front of us and held up a beaker of yellow liquid.

"Young men and ladies," he had addressed us. "Tell me how you would make a diagnosis of diabetes in a middle-aged man."

He waited for a response from some brave soul. There were in fact a few murmurs of "get a blood sugar" or "what are his symptoms?" but nothing very assertive. He feigned being hard of hearing, cupping his hand to his ear and leaning toward his audience.

"No thoughts, eh? Well, here we have the urine of a person with diabetes," he said, holding up the beaker of liquid. "And what can you tell me about this?"

There was a painful silence in the large auditorium as he scanned the group for some willing volunteer. That person not forthcoming, he pointed to an unfortunate student on the front row and motioned for him to come up on the stage.

As the student approached, Dr. Black continued. "You can tell a lot about a person's health from a thorough examination of his urine. Specific gravity, pH, chemistries. But what can you tell me by inspection of this specimen?" he asked the student, now standing by his side.

Dr. Black held the beaker in the young man's puzzled face and swirled it a little. "I, uh...it...it looks like urine to me," he stammered.

"That's very good," Dr. Black congratulated him, and we all nervously chuckled, glad we were still in our seats.

"You see," he went on, "with diabetes, your blood sugar is elevated, sometimes to very high levels, and the sugar spills into your urine. If you are at the bedside of a patient and don't have access to a laboratory, you can perform a simple test to check for the presence of sugar in a urine specimen, such as this."

With that, he held the beaker out in front of him, stuck his finger deep into the urine, swirled it around a little, and then put it into his mouth.

"Hmm...definitely sweet," he stated. "This man's blood sugar is probably two or three hundred. Maybe more."

He then held the beaker out in front of the student. "Tell me what you think," he instructed him. There was a collective moan from those of us sitting in the room, which Dr. Black quickly silenced with a stern glance.

The student's eyes widened, and like a deer frozen by the headlights of a car, he dutifully held out his hand, stuck a finger into the beaker, and then into his mouth.

"Ugh!" he couldn't help but uttering.

We all moaned again, and this time Dr. Black only chuckled and nodded at us. "Any comments, young man? he asked.

The student just grimaced, wiped his mouth with the back of his hand, and shook his head.

"And how about you?" he asked, turning to those of us in the auditorium. No one said a word.

"Hmm...we have some work to do here. Go have a seat, young man," he instructed his reluctant assistant.

Dr. Black walked over to the podium and placed the beaker on a small table standing beside it.

"This is an important lesson for you," he told us. "And I want you to remember it. *Observation.* That's one of the essential requirements of being a good physician. Listening, seeing, touching, smelling, maybe even tasting. But mainly close and focused observation. If this young man had been watching closely, if he had been paying close attention and *observing*, he would have noticed something very important."

At this juncture he held out his hands, an imaginary beaker in one, and the index finger of his other pointing straight at the ceiling.

"You see, when I tested the urine specimen, I dipped my index finger into the beaker," he said while elaborately demonstrating this maneuver, twirling his finger in mid-air. "And then I stuck my long finger into my mouth"—again showing us what had actually happened.

"I of course would never taste a person's urine specimen."

There was a moment of silence as this revelation had its effect on us. And then there was hesitant laughing and a nodding of heads. No one had caught this sleight of hand, certainly not his student assistant, who had now jumped up from his seat and was heading for a water fountain in the back of the room.

"Observation!" Dr. Black intoned. "Don't take anything for granted—and always, always pay attention to detail!"

Jeff chuckled. "That's great," he said. "I bet if Dr. Higgins had been there, he would have been the one up on that stage."

"Maybe so," I agreed. "I'm just glad it wasn't me." I knew I would have done the same thing.

The next morning, I asked Amy to call upstairs and check on the status of the young man who had been in room 1, Dr. Higgins's patient. He had been admitted to the fourth floor and placed in isolation.

"Yeah, that's him," she said into the telephone, nodding her head at me. Then after a moment she said, "Okay—thanks, Sally. Talk to you later."

She hung up the phone and then looked at me. "They gave him some fluids overnight and repeated his white count this morning. Completely normal. He's up and walking around, and being released as we speak. 'Viral gastroenteritis' is his discharge diagnosis."

It is not good to have zeal without knowledge,
nor to be hasty and miss the way.

PROVERBS 19:2

4

Dogged Perseverance

*It ain't what you don't know
that gets you into trouble.
It's what you know for sure
that just ain't so.*

Mark Twain

Ι t's remarkable how quickly a moment of relative calm in the ER can be shattered. And sometimes it happens in the strangest of ways...

❧

Sunday afternoon, 4:45. The department was under control, an unusual thing for this time on a Sunday. I was sitting behind the nurses' station, talking with Jeff about nothing in particular.

The doors of the ambulance entrance suddenly burst open, pushed aggressively inward by the backside of a tall, slender, middle-aged woman. She was dressed in a nurse's uniform and was pulling an antiquated stretcher behind her.

As soon as she had cleared the doorway, she yelled out, "Hey, ya'll! We need some help!"

The volume of her voice didn't match her slender frame, and it got our attention.

Jeff had jumped up from his chair and was already around the corner of the counter.

"What's going on?" he asked the woman.

When she turned to face him, I recognized her as one of the clinical staff at Peaceful Acres, a local retirement center. She frequently came to the ER with some of their clients, usually after a fall or some minor mishap. *Modine.* I seemed to remember that was her name.

She was flushed and out of breath, obviously upset by whatever circumstances had brought her to the ER. I walked up behind Jeff and noted her nametag. I was right. "Modine." Then I noticed the stretcher behind her. It had just now cleared the doors.

It required a moment to take in the full picture. There, on a rickety gurney that listed dangerously from side to side, was an elderly gentleman, easily upwards of eighty years old. He was on his back, arms strapped to the side of the stretcher. Straddled across his abdomen, barely supported by this conveyance, was a *healthy* young woman, actively performing chest compressions. She weighed at least three hundred pounds, and with each chest compression the stretcher lurched precariously, creaking loudly, as if calling out for help. Sweat was dripping down her forehead and onto the helpless old man beneath her.

"Liza Sue, keep up them compressions! And make sure his chest is goin' in enough!" Modine directed the young woman on the stretcher.

Jeff tapped Modine on the shoulder and repeated his question. "Modine, what's going on here? What happened to this man?"

Then he stepped around her to get to the side of the patient.

By this time, the entire group had made it through the entrance and had now stopped in front of the nurses' station. Amy was standing up behind the counter, her eyes wide as she studied the action before her.

I had stepped around to the other side of the stretcher and was trying to examine this unfortunate individual. It was difficult, with Liza Sue's elbows flying in my face after each compression and her sweat flinging itself in all directions. I took a chance, and after a particularly aggressive chest compression, I wedged myself against the stretcher and reached out to check for a pulse. The man's color was surprisingly good, and his skin was warm and dry—all good signs.

"He had a card-yac arrest," Modine explained to Jeff. "We found him flat out on the floor in the hallway, and he wasn't breathin' or nothin'. Liza's certified in BCL...or BCS...or...anyway, she knew what to do and what to check for. He was done gone, and she called for help."

She caught her breath and nodded in the direction of Liza Sue. "She was doin' CPR when I came runnin' up. And we've been doing it for the last twenty, maybe thirty minutes, switchin' off and takin' turns."

Jeff had positioned himself at the head of the stretcher and was shining a light into the man's pupils.

"They're still reactive," he told me. "But I can't tell if he's trying to breathe."

My fingers had found a strong, regular carotid pulse on the right side of his neck that seemed to be in rhythm with Liza Sue's compressions. I watched closely, but saw no respiratory effort.

"Like I said," Modine continued, "he was completely unresponsive, so after we started to get him stabilized, I called for a stretcher and told the staff to get our ambulance ready."

Peaceful Acres was the oldest retirement home in the county. As evidence of that fact, they still kept an ancient ambulance on the premises and used it from time to time. It might have seen its earlier years as a hearse. In my experience, they had used it only to transport minor problems, never anything as serious as a cardiac arrest. I was a little confused as to what made this case different, and why they hadn't called EMS.

"Modine, what—" I was about to ask her about this, but she silenced me with a wave of her hand, seeming to anticipate my question.

"We didn't have time to call for the EMS. Mr. Wood was in real trouble, and we just did what we thought was best. Somebody pushed the stretcher down the hall. Then Liza Sue threw him on it and kept on doin' CPR. Never missed a beat." She paused here and looked over at her assistant. "Liza, you're doin' good, honey! Real good!"

Liza Sue tried to blow some errant hair out of her face and only succeeded in blowing sweat in mine. "Sure thing," she answered.

"Do you need anything, Dr. Lesslie?" Amy called out from behind the nurses' station. "X-ray or lab? An EKG?"

We were going to need all of these, but first I needed to get a better handle on the patient's status.

"Yeah, Amy. Get them all coming, and we'll head to the cardiac room."

Jeff had grasped the end of the stretcher, gently moving Modine to one side. He began to carefully lead the group into cardiac. Liza Sue kept doing chest compressions, balancing as best she could on top of her patient.

"What did you say his name was, Modine?" I asked her. "Mr. Wood?"

"Yeah, Mr. Wood. Wesley Wood," she answered. "And he's a fine gentleman. One of our favorites. Never has a harsh word for anyone." She paused, shaking her head. "Hmm, hmm. This is a real shame."

Once we were in cardiac, I motioned for Jeff to help me move Mr. Wood to our bed. Jeff's eyes widened a little, and he glanced in the direction of Liza Sue. She wasn't about to stop what she was doing. I shared Jeff's concern, but it was time to get the woman off this poor man. Something didn't add up here.

I laid my hand on Liza Sue's shoulder and firmly said, "Hold on a minute here, Liza. Let's check Mr. Wood and see what we've got."

She stopped her chest compressions and sat up straight, blowing out a long breath of air. She had been working hard.

I leaned down, my face close to Wesley Wood's.

"Mr. Wood, can you hear me?" My fingers remained on his carotid artery, and I could still feel a strong, regular pulse, this time without Liza's chest compressions. But other than that, there was no response. Something was peculiar here, and I—

Liza Sue had been watching closely, and when she could see no apparent sign of life, she leaned forward, straightened her arms, and before I could stop her, she applied a vigorous compression to the middle of Wesley's chest.

Then she was at it again.

"One-one-thousand, two-one-thousand—"

"Hold it!" I demanded. "Just stop everything!"

Reluctantly, Liza Sue complied.

I searched Mr. Wood's face for any response and for any evidence of a respiratory effort. There was none. And then suddenly, his mouth seemed to move. He appeared to be trying to form some word, but I heard nothing. I leaned closer, my ear inches from his mouth.

There was a lot of noise in the room, and I raised my hand for quiet. And I listened.

Then, there it was.

"Get her off me."

It was only a whisper, and I wasn't exactly sure what he had said.

"What did you say, Mr. Wood?" I asked him. His words had been so quiet that no one else in the room could possibly have heard them.

And there it was again.

"Get…her…off…me."

It was no louder this time, but he was emphatic. And I understood him clearly.

I straightened and looked at Liza Sue. "Let's hold off on any chest compressions for a minute, Liza. We need to check him over."

She had a puzzled look on her face, but she understood, and once again sat up straight and placed her hands on her hips.

We all looked down into the face of Wesley Wood. For a split second there was nothing, and I wondered if I had imagined hearing his request.

Then his eyelids flickered—and suddenly he took a deep breath. He exhaled loudly and began looking around the room.

"Have mercy! Praise the Lord and thank you, Jesus!"

The exclamation came from right behind me and caused me to jump. It was Modine, and she began clapping her hands in my ear.

"Liza Sue, you done saved his life! Look, he's breathin'! You done it!"

Mr. Wood's eyes were now wide open. He continued to look around the room and tried to free his arms, which were still strapped down and pinned beneath Liza's knees.

She sat up even straighter, surprise and amazement clearly written on her face. She wasn't sure what to do or say. None of us were.

Modine kept clapping and shouting, "You done it! You saved his life, Liza!"

Wesley Wood looked up at me again. This time his eyebrows were furrowed in determination. "Get her off me!" he whispered with a newfound strength in his voice.

"Jeff," I said. "Let's help get Liza Sue down off the stretcher and then get Mr. Wood over to our bed. We need to check him out, make sure he's okay. And good work, Liza Sue," I added.

"You sure he's alright?" she asked me. "I don't want him to stop breathin' again…" She clasped her hands together as if to resume her CPR.

"No, no, he's fine," I assured her, waving her back.

"Here, be careful," Jeff said, helping her get off the stretcher. There was a precarious moment as she shifted her weight to one side. The rickety contraption almost went over, but then she was off and standing on the floor. Wesley Wood was lying flat on his back, somehow looking even smaller than when Liza was straddling him. But there was a look of relief on his face.

"Why don't you two go out to the nurses' station and fill out your report?" I motioned with my head to Jeff. He nodded and began to herd them toward the door.

"Way to go, Liza!" exclaimed Modine once more. They gave each other a high five as they left the cardiac room. Jeff closed the door behind them and walked over beside the bed. He began to check Mr. Wood's blood pressure and pulse, and then his oxygen saturation.

Wesley's shirt had been torn open during the episode, Liza Sue wanting to expose his chest for CPR. He was gently rubbing his sternal area, and I could see reddish-blue discoloration over most of his chest. He was going to have some bruises, at the very least.

"110 over 80," Jeff told me. "Pulse is 92 and regular, and his pulse ox is 98 percent."

"How do you feel, Mr. Wood?" I asked. His vital signs were fine.

He looked up at me and shook his head.

"How do you think I feel?" he answered, his voice stronger now, no longer a whisper. "Did you see the size of that woman? My chest is killing me. I think she busted my ribs."

"Here, let me take a look," I said, reaching out and gently beginning to examine his bruised thorax. "Do you remember what happened?"

"Remember? Doc, it was a nightmare. A complete nightmare." He glanced over his head toward the door. "They gone?" he asked.

Jeff nodded his head, and I said, "Yeah, they're out of the room, Wesley. It's just us."

"Okay—well, here's what happened."

We couldn't wait to hear this, and out of the corner of my eye I saw Jeff cock his head.

"It's Sunday, you know, and we always have a big dinner. Families come over, and there's a lot of visiting. I usually eat with one of my friends, Neal Wingate. He doesn't have any family either, so we are usually alone. And he needs some help now, 'cause he seems to be getting a little forgetful...and, well...none of us are getting any younger."

"I understand," I told him, and then waited for him to continue.

"Well, after that, we sat around in the sunroom for a while, and then I walked him down the hall to his room. He wanted to watch some baseball. Heck, it's not even baseball season. Anyway, I got him situated and then I headed for my room. Gonna do some reading. Well, I was walking down the hall, and I thought I was being careful. Always watch out for stuff on the floor, electrical cords and stuff like that. But I guess I didn't see the water. Somebody must have spilled some in the hallway. I stepped in it and—wham! There I was on the floor, flat on my back. It happened really fast, and I didn't have time to catch myself or anything. One minute I was standing up, walking, and the next minute I was flat on my back. I must have bumped the back of my head when I fell, 'cause I was seeing stars."

He paused here, and began rubbing his head. "You know, it's really true, Doc. You really *do* see stars when you bang your head."

"Do you think you were knocked out?" I asked him. "Do you remember everything?

"Oh, no. I wasn't knocked out. Just startled, I guess. I thought about that too, but I was clear as a bell. My butt hurt a little, and then the stars, but that passed pretty quickly. And then I remember thinking to myself, *Did I break anything?* So I started moving everything, my arms and legs, and I moved my head from side to side. Everything was working, and nothing really hurt. And I remember feeling relieved. Then I decided it would be best if I just rested on the floor for a few minutes, sorta collecting myself, you know? So I relaxed and closed my eyes. In a minute or two I was going to get up, and everything would be fine. And then it happened."

A troubled look came over his face, and he began rubbing his chest again. He tried to turn his head so he could see the door.

"They're still gone," Jeff told him. "It's just us."

He sat back and continued his story.

"Like I said, I was just lying there, collecting myself. First thing I know, I start to feel the floor shakin'. It got stronger and stronger. Then I heard this stomping sound and a blowin' and a pantin'… and I opened my eyes…and there she was—'Big Liza'—standing over me, blocking out the light, and then she started screaming and her arms were flailin' everywhere. And I remember thinkin', *Lord, take me quick!* Well, she gets right in my face and starts yelling my name. But I was so surprised I couldn't say nothin'. And then she jumped on top of me and started mashing on my chest. Hurt like the dickens, let me tell you! And I couldn't say a word. She was knocking the wind out of me. Tried to get her to stop, to tell her I was okay, but I couldn't make a sound."

Wesley shook his head and took a deep breath, wincing a little from the effort, but grateful to be able to do so.

"And then the other one comes along, and she starts in. 'Faster—faster, Liza Sue!' she yelled at the big one. Well, I didn't need to hear that, 'cause she was already beating on me pretty good. But she kept pressing on my chest faster and harder. I knew I was done for."

Jeff chuckled quietly at this. Wesley heard him and cut a sharp glance in his direction. Jeff cleared his throat and backed out of Mr. Wood's vision.

"Then, Doc, they somehow got me on the stretcher, and Liza Sue jumped on top. She's been pounding on my chest all the way to the hospital and up till just now. I want you to know, you saved my life. I mean it. I don't know how much longer I could have lasted."

Jeff had pursed his lips and was nodding his head. With great difficulty, I maintained a straight face.

"Well, Mr. Wood, I know they were doing what they thought was the right thing. They were only trying to help you," I told him.

"Help me? Heck, they almost killed me!" He folded his arms in anger across his chest, his chin set resolutely. "And keep them crazy women away from me! I ain't going back to that place. No sir."

"Let's see what's going on before we talk about that, Wesley. We'll need to get some X-rays to make sure you haven't cracked any ribs."

"*I* didn't crack my ribs!" he interrupted. "If they're busted it's 'cause of that big girl, Liza Sue."

"Okay, okay." I tried to calm him. "You've been through a lot, Mr. Wood. The main thing is to check out your ribs and make sure your heart is alright." The crunching I noted as I had examined his chest told me he would have a few broken ribs, maybe a bunch. And I needed to be sure his heart had not been bruised by Liza Sue's compressions.

"Okay, Doc, but I'm not going back to that place. Not ever."

"We're probably going to need to keep you overnight at least, Mr. Wood. And then we'll figure things out."

"I'm telling you, I'm not going back—"

"Jeff, let's get an EKG, and then we'll get him around to X-ray. And Mr. Wood," I said, patting him on his shoulder. "I just want you to relax now and let us take care of you."

"Fine, fine," he muttered. "But I ain't goin' back there."

I nodded at Jeff and headed toward the door. As it closed behind me, I glanced over to the nurses' station. Amy looked up from her desk, shook her head, and pointed in the direction of the ambulance entrance.

The doors were open, and Liza Sue and Modine were getting ready to walk through. Something made Liza turn and look in my direction. She took Modine by the arm and they walked toward me.

When they came up to where I stood, Liza Sue was the first to speak.

"Dr. Lesslie, I was just thinkin'….Maybe we should just check on Mr. Wood once more, make sure he's alright."

"Yeah," added Modine. "We at least got to tell him good night."

The imp on my shoulder said, *Go ahead, Robert…let them go back into cardiac and visit Wesley. And then just watch his reaction.* Hmm. Now that would be interesting.

But I knew better.

"Liza Sue, Modine—Mr. Wood needs some rest now. He'll never forget what you've done to, uh, for him today," I told them.

They stood there a moment and then nodded their heads.

"You're right," Modine said. "He needs to get some rest. I guess we'll be goin'. Come on, Liza Sue."

They turned and walked out of the department.

The difference between perseverance and obstinacy
is that one comes from a strong will
and the other from a strong won't.

HENRY WARD BEECHER (1813–1887)

The Face of Evil

*Be very careful, then…
because the days are evil.*

EPHESIANS 5:15

I t was the darkest night I can remember.

⚜

6:15 p.m. Sergeant Joe Walters stood beside me at the nurses' station. He was investigating a routine fender bender. The driver of one of the cars had been brought in by ambulance. He had only minor injuries and would be released in a few minutes.

"Always happens around this time of day, doesn't it, Doc?" he said to me. "Around dusk, the light gets bad, people get tired, and they don't pay attention. Good thing for this guy he was only going twenty miles an hour. Ran right up the back of a big pickup."

I was going to say something but was interrupted by Joe's radio. There were a couple of loud beeps and then some scratchy voice asking for his location. He put the receiver close to his ear, and I didn't hear anything else.

Amy Connors, sitting across from me at her secretary's station, slid a clipboard across the laminated countertop.

"Here's the chart of the belly pain in room 2," she informed me. "All his labs have been ordered."

As I reached for the chart, I heard Joe Walters utter, "A signal what?"

He dropped the paperwork in his hand and pressed the receiver closer to his ear. We couldn't hear anything, but the tone of Joe's voice and the sudden change in his demeanor told us something was going on.

"10-4," he hastily told the person on the other end. "Got it, and I'm about seven or eight minutes away."

He jammed the radio back into its holster and headed for the ambulance doors.

"Whatcha got?" Amy called out after him.

Joe was almost running, but he turned to her and said something I couldn't make out. A signal "something." And then he was gone through the doors.

Amy had heard him and had reached into one of her drawers for a laminated sheet of paper. It contained an extensive list of all of the official codes used by the police and fire departments. A "10-50" was an auto accident. But that was about all I knew.

"What did he say?" I asked. It was unusual for Joe Walters, a seasoned police officer, to act like this.

"I heard him, but I don't recognize the signal," she said, sliding her index finger carefully down the long list of numbers. "Here it is—10… Holy smoke!" she exclaimed.

"What is it?" I asked, now very curious.

"It's a…multiple homicide…"

Jeff Ryan listened closely to the police dispatcher. We were able to pick up police transmissions in the ER, and used them to prepare ourselves for what was happening out on the street. Sometimes we listened for entertainment, but not tonight.

For the previous thirty minutes, the airwaves had been alive with chatter. Several police units had been dispatched to the scene of an apparent double murder, and we were now hearing the voice of Joe Walters as he passed on information and asked for assistance. No one was alive at the scene. When an EMS unit arrived, they weren't needed and were turned away.

This kind of violence was unusual for Rock Hill, though we had our share of stabbings and shootings.

"I wonder what's goin' on," Amy stated. "Joe still sounds pretty upset on the radio."

I had noticed the edge in Joe's voice as well. Something was obviously getting to him.

It wasn't long before we found out what that something was.

Denton Roberts's EMS unit had responded to the initial call. They had only been told "multiple gunshots," nothing more. When Denton and his partner arrived at the scene, there were police cars everywhere.

"I've never seen anything like it," he told us. "Marked and unmarked cars all over the place. And there was yellow tape already going up around the whole house and yard. We could barely get down the drive, and then Joe Walters came out and told us what happened and that we wouldn't be needed." Denton stopped and shook his head. "It must have been awful."

It was indeed a murder scene, and in one of the nicer parts of Rock Hill. Denton told us what he knew.

Joe Walters said the perpetrator had smashed the glass beside the front door and then reached in and unlocked it. The noise he made must have alarmed the two owners, James and Joy Easterling. They were in their sixties, husband and wife. She had been the first the shooter had seen, and he had killed her instantly with the blast of a 12-gauge shotgun. When James had come down the hallway, the killer had turned the shotgun on him and fired twice. Neither of them had a chance.

"No apparent motive," Denton told us. "Maybe robbery, but it seems to be a random act. Just doesn't make sense. I knew the Easterlings, and they were good people."

"Any idea who did it?" Amy asked.

"Turns out a neighbor heard the shotgun blasts and got a look at the pickup truck in the front yard. Managed to get the license number too. Pretty quick thinking. Anyway, the police are on that now, and there's a county-wide search going on."

"Hope they catch that lowlife…" Amy muttered.

Just then, the police scanner got our attention. The dispatcher was notifying everyone in the vicinity of a little-traveled crossroads in the western part of the county to be on alert. The suspect's pickup truck had been spotted and was heading in that direction at a high speed.

"Maybe he'll run off the road and hit a tree and save everyone a lot of trouble," Amy remarked coolly.

"Humph," Jeff muttered, having just walked up to join us. "They'd better get him now before he gets loose on those back-country roads. It'll be the devil to find him then."

We didn't have to worry about the devil, at least not just yet. We listened as one of the county sheriff's units reported sighting the truck and forcing him off the road and into a hay field. The driver of the truck was quickly apprehended, uninjured. On the front seat of the pickup was a 12-gauge shotgun along with a half-empty box of shells.

After that, things in the ER returned to normal, and there was no more squawking of the police scanner. EMS was bringing in three individuals from a 10-50. A young man with a fishhook in his eyelid was being led to minor trauma. And the waiting room was filling up. Normal.

10:15 p.m. The nurses' station was a flurry of barely controlled activity, and I was finishing up the chart of the last of the auto-accident victims. It had been almost two hours since we had heard anything about the murders. That was when the ambulance doors burst open and it all changed.

Two police officers strode into the department, grim-faced and all business. I recognized them but couldn't recall their names. They were followed by a quickly moving group of more officers, one menacingly holding a police shotgun. In the middle of this cluster, only occasionally being glimpsed within this blue-clad moving mass, was a young man dressed in standard prisoner's garb. He had on a tan short-sleeved shirt and matching tan trousers. He wore brown flip-flops and shuffled awkwardly along, trying to keep up with the officers. It was then

I noticed the cuffs on his ankles and hands. And the bloody bandages on his wrists.

The group made its way to the nurses' station and stopped. Joe Walters appeared from behind and walked up to Jeff Ryan and me.

"Is minor trauma open?" he asked us.

I looked at Jeff, who quickly glanced at the patient ID board.

"Minor trauma C and D are open," he told Joe. "What you got here?"

"This guy," he said, pointing to the man in the midst of his officers. Then he walked up close to me and quietly said, "This is the guy who killed the Easterlings. We need to take care of him in a hurry and get him out of here. Don't want any one to know he's in the ER. There are a lot of really upset people in town right now."

"What happened to him, Joe?" I asked, trying to get a glimpse of the man.

Jeff grabbed the clipboards of minor trauma C and D and motioned to the officers to follow him down the hall with their prisoner.

"Doc, I don't know how he did it," Joe began to explain. "When we caught him out on 324, his truck was pretty busted up, but he didn't seem hurt. Actually, he was trying to run. We got him without any trouble, but he must have grabbed a piece of broken glass from the wreck and stuck it in his pants. Anyway, we took him straight downtown and booked him. Then we put him in a cell—and before I knew it, one of the guards was hollerin' that he had cut himself. He had managed to sneak that glass into his cell, and as soon as the guard's back was turned, he did a number on his wrists. I mean, we're talkin' about some deep cuts. It's a wonder he hasn't bled to death."

"It's a wonder he didn't use that glass on the guard."

"You're right about that, Doc," Joe agreed. "I thought of that myself. This is one bad actor. That's why we need to get him fixed up and out of here as quick as you can."

"What's his name?" I asked.

He looked around the room, as if to make sure we were alone, which of course we weren't. Then he leaned close and whispered, "Frankie

Sifford." Standing a little straighter and speaking a little louder, he added, "We don't want that to get out yet. Like I said, there are a lot of upset people out there. The Easterlings had a lot of friends and if they knew…Well, we just need to keep it under wraps for the time being. Anyway, if you could help us here, Doc, I'd really appreciate it."

"I'll do everything I can," I assured him. I understood his position. And considering the disruption that had already occurred in the department, I would also be happy to get this man out of the ER as quickly as possible.

Jeff had wisely pulled the curtains closed for both C and D. They could be arranged to form one large cubicle, and by pushing the stretcher in room D against the wall, he had created some needed floor space. It had quickly been filled by the dozen or so officers who accompanied Frankie Sifford.

"When beds A and B are discharged," he whispered to me, referring to the two other patients in the room, "I'll make sure nobody uses those beds until we're done."

"Good idea, Jeff. Thanks," I told him. "What does this look like?"

Jeff had on a bloody pair of examining gloves. He took them off and tossed them into a nearby trash can. "Pretty good lacerations," he told me. "You're going to be here a while. I can't imagine how, but I don't think he cut any tendons." He paused, then shook his head. "He was serious about this, though. This is the worst I've ever seen for self-inflicted cuts. It's almost as if he couldn't feel himself doing it. You'll see."

He stepped around to the supply cabinet and began taking down the material necessary to repair this man's wounds. And I stepped over to the stretcher of bed C and the young man lying on it.

The officers surrounding the bed parted a little as I approached, allowing me access to Frankie Sifford. My attention should have been drawn to the gaping wounds on both of his wrists. But instead, my gaze fastened on his eyes—and I couldn't look away.

These were terrible eyes, and they seemed to bore right through me. And yet there was nothing there. They were hollow, vacant, and completely without any feeling. There was no hatred, or anger, or fear.

Nothing. And as I stood staring at him, a smile slowly spread across his face. No, it was more of a leer, or something worse. He seemed to know me, to know something about me…but I had never seen him before.

"What's up, Doc?" he quipped in a flat voice. There was no emotion in his words, nothing, just like his eyes.

I tore myself away from his gaze and focused my attention on the task before me.

"Mr. Sifford," I addressed him. "Let's take a look at those wrists."

"Call me Frankie, Doc," he answered. "Just Frankie."

One of the police officers standing behind him looked down scowling and shook his head. There was a lot of bad tension in this room.

"Okay, Frankie, let me see what's going on here," I repeated.

He was handcuffed, and his leg cuffs were attached to the stretcher. He wasn't going anywhere. I turned to one of the officers and said, "We'll need to take his handcuffs off, or at least loosen them. I'll need to examine these wounds."

They apparently hadn't thought about this and were obviously reluctant to take him out of the cuffs. They whispered together for a moment, and then one of them took a key out of his shirt pocket and unlocked the cuff on Frankie's left wrist. I was standing by his left side and when the officer removed the cuff, he pulled it across Frankie's chest and then quickly snapped it around the rail on his right side. They weren't going to take any chances.

While they were doing this, I studied the man lying before me. He was in his early twenties, slight of build. His hair was light brown, uncombed, and hung to his shoulders. There was nothing really remarkable about him—other than his eyes, and the fact he had just murdered two people in cold blood.

Jeff positioned Frankie's left arm and wrist on a board that slid under the mattress of the stretcher. He had draped it in sterile cloth. I sat down on a rolling stool, slid it toward the stretcher, and began to examine Frankie's wrist.

It was a mess. He had three long, deep gashes running perpendicularly across his anterior wrist and lower forearm. They were gaping open, and I could easily see exposed tendons. There was not much bleeding, just a slow ooze, indicating that he had probably not severed any major blood vessels. But he had been serious about this. These were big cuts, and must have hurt.

Then I noticed something strange. There were no hesitation marks. Usually when a person is trying to harm themselves with a blade, or piece of glass, or some other sharp object, they will be unable to do so with one clean incision. It hurts, and there will be evidence of one or more initial efforts, usually just superficial scratches. Sometimes that's all we see, these hesitation marks. They ultimately couldn't go through with it.

But not this time. These were clean, deep, and almost surgical. He had never hesitated.

Something made me look up. Frankie was staring at me with the same leering smile on his face. He didn't say a word.

Usually at this point, I'm looking for an opportunity to ask the patient about why they tried to hurt themselves. I would be trying to assess the risk of another suicide attempt. I didn't have to worry about that this time. It didn't matter, since Frankie Sifford would be locked up in jail, probably for the rest of his life, however long that might be.

Then I began to wonder why he would do this. And I thought I might know the answer. Not infrequently, incarcerated individuals will feign an injury or illness in order to be taken out of the jail and to the hospital. It might be just to have a change of scenery, or it might be in the hope of escaping. It had happened before. Once, an inmate had faked having abdominal pain and was so convincing that two officers had to bring him to the ER. As soon as the police car had pulled up to the ambulance entrance and the door was opened, he bolted, straight for some nearby woods. He made it as far as the corner McDonald's before he was apprehended.

I was pretty certain that was the case here. Frankie Sifford was not trying to kill himself. Rather, he was looking for an opportunity to escape. And he knew his injury would need to be something serious.

As if reading my mind, he said, "Pretty bad, isn't it, Doc?"

I looked up at those dead eyes once again and answered, "Well, we've seen worse." Some primitive part of me wanted to be sure he didn't receive any satisfaction from this. "We're going to put these lacerations back together and send you back to the jail with these officers. It shouldn't take too long."

And there it was. Just the tiniest flinch of his eyelids. That had bothered him. He was hoping to be admitted to the hospital with these wounds, maybe even have surgery. That would give him time and opportunity to find a way to escape.

He didn't say a word, and his eyes returned to their vacant stare. And that crooked smile remained on his face.

When I took a closer look at his wounds, I hoped I hadn't misspoken. These were bad cuts. I knew it was going to take awhile to repair them. But there were no major structures injured, and it was only going to be a matter of carefully sewing them up.

I looked at his right wrist, moving his bandages around the handcuff. There were three lacerations there as well, almost identical to those on the left. Deep, long, and down to his tendons. And like the other wounds, there were no significant structures injured.

Curious. There was really no difference in the wounds.

"Are you right- or left-handed?" I asked him.

"Amphibious," he smirked.

I didn't look up, and certainly didn't smile.

The policeman standing at the head of the stretcher popped him on the shoulder with the back of his hand.

"Don't get smart," he said. "Answer the doctor."

"That's okay, officer," I told him. "It doesn't matter."

Jeff looked over at me, and I nodded. He began setting up a suture tray and getting some packs of suture material out of the cabinet. He had a half dozen of these in his hand and said to me, "I'll get some more when you need them."

This was going to take awhile.

Joe Walters walked up behind me as I began to work.

He leaned closed to me and asked, "Whatcha think, Doc? How long?"

Normally, this question would be a little aggravating. But this was a different circumstance.

"Probably about an hour on this side, and the same on the other," I estimated.

"Hmm. Okay," he muttered. "We're just gonna stay right here. Let me know if anyone gets in the way."

I was pretty accurate with my guess. Two hours and fifteen minutes later, Jeff was finishing up with the bandaging of Frankie Sifford's wrists. His cuffs were put back on, and he was ready to go.

"Thanks, Doc," Joe Walters said. "We'll be getting him out of here now."

A few minutes later, Frankie Sifford and his entourage were walking toward the ambulance entrance. He was looking down at his shackled feet. But when he reached the nurses' station, he looked up and directly into my eyes. Someone has said that the eyes are the portal to the soul. If that's true, then Frankie's soul was a dark and forbidding place.

Outside, the darkness was thick and somehow threatening, and a cold wind was beginning to blow. A gust found its way into the department, and Amy Connors shivered.

It took me a while to write up Frankie Sifford's chart. I described the wounds and the repair that was required. And then I slid the chart over to Amy.

"We can file that," I told her. "But you'd better make a few copies." We would probably all be testifying about this at some point in the near future.

I stood at the nurses' station, and suddenly realized how tired I was. Putting Frankie's wounds back together had not been physically taxing. It was the whole picture. Who he was, what he had just done. And while I was sewing him up, I couldn't help but think that those very hands, only a few hours before, had taken the lives of two innocent and unsuspecting people. And I thought about their family, and what must be going on with them at that very moment. Those are the things that wear you down.

Forty-five minutes later I stepped out of room 4 and walked across the hallway. Jeff was on the phone and motioned for me to come over.

"Thanks, officer," he was speaking into the receiver. "We'll be expecting you. And he'll be in the same room, just like before."

He hung up the phone and looked at me, shaking his head.

"What is it?" I was beginning to have a hunch, and it was troubling.

"Frankie Sifford," Jeff said. Amy turned in her chair to listen. "He's on his way back in," he continued. "Seems that when they got him back to the jail, they strip-searched him and found another piece of broken glass. Nothing else, so they locked him up. The officer on duty was supposed to be watching him closely, and perhaps he was. Anyway, Frankie apparently turned on his side away from the door and somehow started chewing on his bandages. He got them off, and then he started chewing on his sutures. Took every last one of them out. The officer said the place is a mess, and they're on the way over right now. I guess you heard me tell them to take him back to minor trauma."

I had heard that part and had glanced at the patient ID board. The room was still empty.

"That's fine, Jeff," I told him. "But what in the world…" I just stood there and didn't say anything else.

It was Amy Connors who spoke. "That's one crazy dude," she said with contempt. "They're gonna have to put him in a straitjacket."

That might not be a bad idea, if anyone still had one of those.

I sat down wearily behind the counter and waited.

The group that led Frankie into the department looked exactly as they had a few hours earlier. A mass of blue seemed to glide down the hallway and into the minor trauma room. Jeff and I followed close behind them.

They put him on the same stretcher, in the back right corner of the room, and again cuffed him to the rails.

Joe Walters was with him, and he stepped over to Jeff and me.

"Do what you need to do," he said, shaking his head. "And I can promise you this won't happen again."

From the steely determination in his voice, I knew it wouldn't, whatever that would take.

"Frankie, I'm going to need to take a look at those wrists again," I told him, stepping beside his stretcher. His face remained an impenetrable mask, but I thought I detected a hint of desperation in his eyes. He didn't say anything.

Jeff was removing his bandages, leaving the handcuffs in place. When I looked down at his wounds, I felt my face flush with anger. I had spent a couple of hours putting him back together, and he had undone that work in only a few minutes.

Every single one of the stitches was gone. I don't know how, but he had managed to rip them out with his teeth. There were tears along some of the edges of the lacerations where he had pulled the sutures through his skin. He had obviously been determined.

"Frankie," I said, unable to restrain myself. "Just why did you do this?"

He just stared at me, with that same smile on his face, and remained silent.

That was enough. I wasn't going to play any more of his games.

I turned to Joe. "There are a couple of ways to deal with this. These wounds need to be cleaned really well. And in some instances, I would probably suture them again. They'll heal more quickly and be easier to take of. However, that's not what we're going to do."

I stopped and looked down at Frankie. Then I turned again to Joe.

"He would probably find another way to screw things up, and I don't want to waste your time or mine. We're going to clean him up and bandage these again and let you go. The jail nurse can check on him tomorrow and redress him every day. It'll take longer to heal, and he'll have some bigger scars, but that will work."

"That sounds like a plan to me," Joe said. "I don't think he's gonna be worried about any scars. And like I said, this is the last time you're gonna see him for this."

The two officers closest to Frankie Sifford nodded their heads.

Jeff cleaned up the open wounds, scrubbing them with saline and Betadine. Frankie showed no emotion during this, and never flinched. He either had an unbelievable pain threshold or a stony determination to show no weakness in our presence. Whichever the reality was, it was all pretty spooky.

It didn't take long to have him redressed and on his way back to the jail. As he and his entourage slowly made their way down the hallway, Joe Walters told me more about the murder scene and about what had happened. It was a gruesome story, and was obviously the work of a sick and twisted individual.

"I would have thought there would be drugs or alcohol involved, Doc," Joe said to me. "But this guy is stone-cold sober. Nothing. He's just mean. No, he's more than that. I've never seen anyone quite like him."

As Joe was saying this, Frankie Sifford was passing by the nurses' station. He looked over in my direction and once again fixed his eyes on me. He wasn't a big man, and didn't have an impressive or threatening physical presence. In fact, he almost looked like a boy among those police officers. Yet there was something about him—something dark and ominous, something that disquieted my spirit. I was glad when he turned his head and looked away.

"Okay, Doc, I guess that's it for tonight," Joe said. "Thanks again for your help and—"

There was a sudden outburst of shouting at the ambulance entrance and the blue mass of police officers become a scrambled, moving mound of arms and legs. Several of them seemed to collapse on the floor and we heard, "Get that gun!" and "Quick! Put him down!"

Joe ran over to help his men.

As they had reached the automatic doors, Frankie had twisted his body to one side and had managed to grab the pistol from the holster of the officer walking nearest him. It had been careless on the part of the policeman, and Frankie had taken the opportunity. The only thing that saved us was that his wrists were cuffed together, and any coordinated movement was going to be awkward. Still, he managed to get the gun loose and jerked it up and away from the officer. As he did this, he struck the officer across his face, splitting open his left eyebrow.

Two other officers had immediately grabbed Frankie's arms and then thrown him to the floor, knocking the gun loose and away from him. Thankfully, no shot was fired, and no officer was seriously injured. Frankie Sifford left the department with a few more bruises than he had come in with.

The officer with the busted eyebrow stayed behind, and I closed it with about ten stitches. It would leave only a small scar. But it would forever remind him of what had happened here tonight.

When the excitement was over, Jeff and I sat at the nurses' station and were silent, each deep in our own thoughts. Then he said, "I've never seen anything quite like that. And I don't think I've ever seen anyone as…I guess, as just plain evil as that guy."

I didn't say anything, but was having the same thoughts.

"I guess he'll be meeting Ole Sparky in the not-too-distant future," he added.

Ole Sparky was the state's electric chair, located in Columbia. And it wasn't long before he and Frankie did meet.

But Frankie Sifford had sadly and permanently torn the fabric of our community, and more tragically, that of one of our families. The lives of a lot of people were forever changed that night.

In every man's heart there is a devil,
but we do not know the man as bad
until the devil is roused.

James Oliver Curwood,
"The Case of Beauvais"

6

Walking the Walk

Greater love has no one than this,
that he lay down his life
for his friends.

JOHN 15:13

Tuesday, 5:26 p.m. "Rock Hill ER, this is Medic 2, do you read me?"

Amy Connors rolled her chair toward the ambulance radio, getting to it just before Lori Davidson. She picked up the receiver, smiled at Lori, and said, "This is the ER, Medic 2. Go ahead."

Then she pushed the hands-free button and replaced the phone in its cradle.

"ER, this is paramedic Roberts," the familiar voice informed us. We could all hear now, and Lori had picked up a notepad, prepared to record Denton Roberts's information. I stood on the other side of the counter, listening.

"We're on the way in with a fifty-three-year-old man, complaining of shortness of breath and chest pain. Also with pain and swelling in his legs…" Denton's voice trailed off, and he added, "It's Jimmy Bostick."

"Oh my word," Amy muttered as she rolled her eyes, slamming her pen on the countertop and turning away.

A cloud seemed to pass over Lori's face for a moment, and then it was gone. She was all business. "Vital signs stable?" she asked.

"BP is 150 over 100, and his pulse is 92 and regular," Denton responded. "Looks okay."

"Room 3 on arrival," Lori told him. "And what's your ETA?"

"10 to 12. And roger, room 3 on arrival."

Lori pushed the bottom on the receiver, terminating the call.

"Jimmy Bostick," Amy said with obvious contempt. "I don't understand it sometimes how we see young people, good people, just all of
a sudden fall over dead, or get killed in an auto accident, or whatever.
And somebody like Jimmy Bostick just keeps hangin' in there. He
must be too mean, or too evil to die. It's a mystery, and just not right."

"Now Amy—" Lori began.

"Lori, now you hold on," Amy interrupted. "You feel the same way
about him, you know you do. You know what he did to his brother.
You were here the night Dan came in and coded. Don't tell me you've
forgotten that."

Lori didn't say anything, but just kept writing on the notepad. I
remembered.

November, five years earlier. The atmosphere in the cardiac room was
tense and electric, but controlled. A forty-eight-year-old man had stumbled into the ER, clutched his chest, and then promptly collapsed on
the floor in front of the nurses' station. He wasn't breathing when Jeff
got to him, and he didn't have a pulse.

One of his "friends" told us he had OD'd on cocaine. He had been
smoking it most of the day and then "just seemed to start comin' loose,
you know."

We had seen him in the ER on previous occasions, enough to know
he had a significant substance-abuse problem. Tonight might be the
end of that.

We worked with him for over an hour, getting a pulse back minutes
after his arrival, but unable to get much of a blood pressure.

And then he began to respond.

"Seems to be making some respiratory efforts on his own," Jeff told
me. He had been bagging him for most of this time, checking for voluntary breathing every few minutes.

"80 over 60," Katie told me. His blood pressure was starting to improve. We had been pumping him full of fluids and potent medications, hoping for such a response. But he had gone a long time without a decent blood pressure, and perfusion to his vital organs would be the big question. If he woke up and was clear, then his brain would probably be all right. His kidneys might be another matter. A prolonged time of diminished blood flow to the kidneys could do severe damage, sometimes irreversible. But you wouldn't know that right away. Sometimes it took hours or days for kidney failure to declare itself.

"100 over 72," Katie informed us, making a notation on the code record. "Getting better, and he's starting to move around some."

I had noticed the same thing. First his legs began to move, and then he began to reach up for the endotracheal tube taped to the corner of his mouth.

"Better restrain his arms," I told Katie. "I don't want him grabbing that tube."

Over the next twenty minutes, Jimmy Bostick continued to improve. His blood pressure stabilized and he became a little more responsive. He ultimately required sedation in order for us to keep him calm and quiet. When he was transferred to the ICU, his vital signs were stable, his pupils were reactive, and his breathing was controlled. All good things.

A few days later, we learned that he had left the hospital AMA (against medical advice). He had improved to the point where they were able to take him off the ventilator and move him out of the ICU to a step-down unit. He required close monitoring but was making steady progress. And then he decided it was time to leave.

When one of the nurses went in to his room, she found the IV line hanging from the pole beside his bed, the remaining fluids having run out over the floor. And his hospital gown was gone.

Jeff and I were talking with her as we all stood in the ER hallway.

"Probably got some attention when he walked into McDonald's wearing that thing," she had told us. "And he left the IV needle in his arm. Must have taped over it, knowing he could use it to shoot up with. You guys might be seeing him later on tonight."

Jeff shook his head and muttered, "Jimmy Bostick. Hmm, hmm. Doesn't surprise me that he jumped AMA. He's done that before."

"A couple of times," the nurse responded. "But don't worry, if you don't see him tonight, it won't be too long before he shows up again."

"What makes you say that?" I asked her. She seemed to know something more about Mr. Bostick.

"Well, Dr. Shaw's been following his labs, and this morning he was pretty worried. Jimmy might feel okay now, but his kidneys are dead."

Eight days later—1:30 a.m. Jimmy Bostick followed the triage nurse into the department. He was shuffling along, his hair unkempt, his color gray, and his face bloated. He looked like death. This was a big change from the last time I had seen him.

The nurse took him to room 4, then stepped out and pulled the curtain closed behind her. She walked over to where I stood.

"He's in pretty bad shape, Dr. Lesslie," she said, handing me his chart. "Fever, short of breath, you name it. And he looks terrible."

She headed back out to triage, and I studied the ER ledger in my hands.

"Was that Jimmy Bostick?" Amy asked me. "I just caught a glimpse as he walked by, but…if it is, somethin' bad's goin' on."

It *was* Jimmy Bostick, and something bad *was* going on. His workup told us he was in kidney failure. His blood pressure was sky-high, almost every one of his lab studies was abnormal, and his heart was enlarged. He was a train wreck. No slipping out AMA tonight.

I talked with the kidney specialist on call for the ER and we arranged for Jimmy to have emergency dialysis. He was again admitted to the ICU.

While he was still in the ER, his family members came to the hospital to check on him. His mother and father were there, as were his younger sister, Susan, and older brother, Dan. It was a little bit of a shock for us when they came back into the department. We had known Jimmy for years as a druggie—no job, always dirty, always abusive when he was high on something. But his family was just the opposite. His parents were quiet-spoken, well-dressed, and very courteous. His brother and sister were the same, though Susan, out of Jimmy's hearing, was outspoken about the grief he had caused all those who cared about him.

"He's going to be the death of Mother and Dad," she had told Lori. "I don't know how much more of this they can take."

Dan told us they had tried everything: counseling, rehab hospitals, even involuntary commitment. Nothing worked. It was always the same. He would straighten out just long enough to be released, then disappear again. And in a few weeks or months, he would surface in the ER, in trouble.

Tonight he was in big trouble, and I tried to explain his condition to them.

"Jimmy is in renal failure, complete shutdown. No kidney function at all, and he probably won't get any back. We think it started the last time he was in the hospital, after the cocaine overdose."

"That's when he left against medical advice," Susan said, looking over at her parents.

"That's right," I told them. "And I don't know if it would have made any difference in his condition, but we are where we are. Jimmy's going to have dialysis tonight, and we'll see how that goes. The problem is that when the kidneys go, everything else gets out of kilter, and things go downhill. Sometimes pretty quickly, like we're seeing with Jimmy."

"Is he going to die?" his father asked.

That was a real possibility, and they needed to know the truth.

"Your son is a very sick man, Mr. Bostick," I answered him. "And yes, he may die. If the dialysis helps, the kidney doctors may be able to turn things around for a while. But he'll need to be on regular dialysis, maybe three or four times a week. And then there's his heart, and his—"

"What about a kidney transplant?" his mother asked hopefully. "Wouldn't that help him? Wouldn't that fix things?"

"That's putting the cart before the horse," I gently told her. "We need to take one day at a time and try to get your son better. Then we can talk about what might come next."

"I'm sure the transplant waiting list for drug abusers is a short one," his sister said cynically.

"Now Susan, he's your brother," Mrs. Bostick chided. "And if it would save him…"

It turned out that a transplant was going to be the only thing that would save the life of Jimmy Bostick. Initially, dialysis had seemed to be helping. But then he developed an infection, and his labs started getting worse. He spent six weeks in the ICU and his doctors weren't holding out much hope. And they weren't being very optimistic about a kidney transplant. Susan was right about that waiting list.

That's when Dan Bostick walked up to one of Jimmy's doctors one day and asked about donating a kidney to his brother. There were discussions about studies for compatibility, inherent dangers to both parties, and then questions about Dan's overall health status.

It turned out that Dan had mild high blood pressure and had been on medication for over ten years. It was under good control now, but Jimmy's doctors were leery about pursuing this. They didn't want to take any chances with Dan's health, even though people live long and full lives with only one kidney.

And Dan's family was opposed to the idea. His mother didn't want to lose both of her sons, but it was Susan who was especially vocal.

"You're only putting yourself at risk," she told him. "And if Jimmy gets better, he's just going back to doing the things he's always done. And do you think for one minute that if things were reversed, he'd give you one of his kidneys?"

"I don't know the answer to that," Dan said. "But if I don't give Jimmy one of my kidneys, what chance does he have of living?" He had asked this of the doctors in the presence of Susan and his parents.

"Well, to be honest, none," one of them replied. "He has a month, maybe two."

"Then that's the answer," Dan had said resolutely. "When do we do it?"

And so Jimmy received one of Dan's kidneys. The operation went well, and Dan was out of the hospital in a few days, doing great. Jimmy's hospital course was miraculous. He seemed to turn on a dime, and within a few weeks, his blood pressure was good, his labs normal, and his heart was returning to normal size. He was released from the hospital and instructed to follow up with the kidney doctors in a few days. He was on some powerful antirejection medicines and would need to be closely monitored. A big concern was the risk of him getting a serious infection.

He didn't make it to that appointment, or the next. Jimmy Bostick just seemed to disappear—again.

Though he left the hospital feeling great, things didn't go so well for Dan Bostick. One month after the transplant, his doctor found some protein in his urine, and his blood pressure was beginning to creep up. Then he began to develop some swelling in his legs.

His cardiologist told him the difficult truth—his remaining kidney was being overworked. And while it was not in danger of failing, it was not able to keep up with the demands placed upon it. Apparently, his long-standing elevated blood pressure, though mild, had taken its toll. And in spite of aggressive medical management, Dan's overall health was being negatively impacted. His cholesterol began to rise, and he developed evidence of vascular disease.

Three years after the transplant, Dan Bostick had a heart attack. He didn't die, but he came very close. When he got to the ER, his blood pressure was dangerously low and his initial labs indicated extensive heart damage. He was improving with some pain medication and careful IV fluid replacement.

Then suddenly he coded. That was what Amy was reminding Lori of. One minute he was sitting up and talking with us, and the next he was unconscious, his heart fibrillating like a quivering mass of jelly. Lori was the first to see the monitor and had quickly charged up the paddles and shocked him. Fortunately, he had quickly returned to a regular and effective rhythm.

We had stabilized him in the cardiac room and were waiting to send him around to the cath lab when his family arrived. His mother and father were there, as was his wife and Susan, his sister. But not Jimmy. I didn't ask.

Dan was in the hospital for a week, and then in an aggressive rehab program. His doctors were able to keep his blood pressure under control, but his heart catheterization had revealed blockages in a lot of vessels, some of which couldn't be fixed. It would be a day-to-day thing for Dan, and hoping for the best.

❧

And so, here we were, waiting on Jimmy Bostick to arrive in the ER. I wondered what his story would be this time.

A few minutes later, the ambulance doors opened and the Medic 2 team came into the department with their patient. Denton rolled the stretcher into room 3, and Lori headed in that direction. I had looked down at Jimmy as he rolled by, and he managed to give me a slight nod. Once again, he looked awful.

I gave Lori a few minutes to get him settled. Then I walked around the counter toward his room. Denton was backing his stretcher into the hallway, and he pulled me aside.

"Dr. Lesslie, he looks terrible this time," he told me. "Worse than I can remember."

"Where did you pick him up?" I asked. "I didn't know he was back in town."

"Over on Wisteria Drive. You know, down by the old bus station."

That was one of the worst parts of town, a place that generated a lot of business for the ER. That would usually be gunshots, and stabbings, and overdoses. It was a tough street.

"I recognized a few of the guys he was staying with," he continued.

"Some of the usual characters, or maybe usual suspects. The place was filthy."

"Did he say when he got back in town? I wonder if his folks know he's here."

"Says he's been in Atlanta for the past few years," Denton told me. "And just came in yesterday on the bus. Hooked up with some of his old buddies, and they called us when he kept complaining of feeling bad. You heard my report, I guess. Shortness of breath, swollen legs. Looks like he might be in heart failure. And he's got these nasty-looking places on his neck and elbows. All red and draining. Like I said, Doc, he's a mess."

"Hmm. I wonder if he's started using drugs again," I mused.

"Come on, Doc, what do you think?" Denton shook his head. "Needle tracks up and down his arms. Even on his ankles. And he's staying with Bubba Burns, the biggest dealer in the county."

"Oh man," I sighed. "After all he's been through. And after all he's put his family through."

"Some folks just don't learn," Denton said. "And Jimmy Bostick is one of them."

He was right.

Jimmy later told me he had been living in Atlanta ever since the kidney transplant. He had done well for a while and felt good. And then he had stopped taking all of his medicines. Too expensive, and he didn't want to go to the trouble of registering with one of the free clinics down there.

His family had tried to find him, but he didn't want anything to do with them. Dan had somehow figured out where he was staying and had showed up one morning. Jimmy threw him out, threatening to hurt him if he ever came back. And that was the last contact he'd had with any of them.

"I guess you know about Dan," I said to him.

"Dan? No, is something the matter? He looked fine when I saw him in Atlanta."

I thought it best to wait for a while before I told him about his brother and his health problems. But then, he might not even care. So I changed the subject and asked him about any recent substance abuse.

He did admit to falling back into his old drug habits. He could hardly tell me otherwise, with the evidence screaming from the ruined veins of his arms.

And that's when he told me about his HIV. He and his friends shared needles—and girlfriends. When he learned that one of his buddies had advanced AIDS, he decided it was time to be tested, to make sure he was clean.

The day he was tested he was put in the hospital. His white count was dangerously low, and he had pneumonia. On top of that, Dan's kidney was failing. Without the antirejection medication, Jimmy's body was destroying the very organ that stood between him and his own death. It was a perfect storm. His defense systems were compromised, he had multi-organ system problems, and the AIDS virus was rapidly replicating. There were not many options open to him or his doctors.

He had refused dialysis in Atlanta, and after several courses of high-powered medicines, he had once again left the hospital AMA.

"I just decided to see what was gonna happen," he told me. "One day at a time, just see where all this takes me."

And the bus had brought him back to Rock Hill. I found that part interesting. He could have stayed in Atlanta with his "friends," but he'd chosen to come home. But what was there here for him? He had driven away his family by turning his back on his parents and threatening Dan.

I asked him about that, and why he had come to Rock Hill.

"Look at me, Doc," he said holding his hands out as if showcasing his decimated body. "I don't have much time, do I? You know that."

He was right. His blood work indicated he had little if any kidney function, and a chest X-ray showed his heart was once again enlarged. Worst of all, he had a bad-looking pneumonia. That's what usually kills people in this situation. And usually pretty fast.

"You're right, Jimmy," I agreed. "You've got some serious problems. Do you want me to get in touch with your family? I'll be glad to call—"

"No! I don't want them to know I'm here," he said emphatically. "Just do what you need to do, and don't bother them. I've been enough of a burden…about fifty years of heartache, I'd say. They can find out when this…when it's over."

His eyes were vacant as he said this. I was looking at the shell of a man, and it was impossible for me to know what he was thinking. But I knew I needed to honor his request. I didn't want to think how his mother and father might react if they saw their son like this.

"Okay, Jimmy. But if you change your mind, just let me know."

"Thanks," he said heavily, and I walked out of the room.

Standing at the nursing station, talking with Lori Davidson, was Dan Bostick. How did he know his brother was here?

Lori looked over at me and raised her eyebrows. Dan followed her glance, turned, and walked toward me.

"Dr. Lesslie, how's Jimmy?" he asked, grabbing my hand and shaking it. But his grip had no strength, and his skin was cool and damp. "One of my friends with EMS called and told me he had been brought in. Can I see him?"

I immediately thought of Jimmy threatening to physically hurt him in Atlanta, and of his request that his family not be notified of his presence here. While Jimmy was not in any condition to do much resisting, this could turn into a pretty ugly scene. And yet, he was dying, and here was his brother.

"He's over in room 3," I told him, pointing to the cubicle. "And he's pretty sick."

Then I quickly added, "Actually, Dan, he's very sick. He's not going to make it this time. I don't know how long he has, but—"

"I understand, Doctor," he interrupted. "I knew this was coming. I'm just glad he's home, and that he's here."

Dan walked over to room 3, pulled the curtain open, and stepped inside. I looked at Lori and she just shook her head.

We didn't know what to expect. I waited about fifteen minutes and then went to check on the two brothers. As I approached, I didn't hear any voices from within and felt a little nervous. I pulled the curtain back and was about to step into the room. But I stopped abruptly in the doorway.

The head of the stretcher had been raised to a sitting position, and Jimmy was leaning back against it. His head was resting comfortably and his eyes were closed. His breathing was regular and unlabored. Dan was sitting on the edge of the bed with his arm around his brother's shoulders. His head hung down on his chest.

Neither of them looked up at me, and I left them alone.

7

Just Plain Stubborn

An obstinate man does not hold opinions,
but they hold him.

Samuel Butler (1835–1902)

I don't know what I said or what I did, but when Amy Connors remarked, "Dr. Lesslie, you're starting to act like Dr. Candler," I stopped what I was doing and stared at her.

"What do you mean by that?" I asked, bothered by the comparison.

"You know what I mean," she said. "You're being stubborn here."

Jeff Ryan was standing nearby and he chuckled.

"Might be starting to look like him too," he quipped.

I glared at him and then turned again to Amy. "Wait just a minute, Ms. Connors. You need to explain yourself."

"Now don't get all riled up." She smiled. "I'm just kiddin'…though you *were* pretty rough on that lab tech."

"Rough?" I exclaimed, trying to think of what I might have said that could have triggered this. "I was only telling her how to run the tests on the knee fluid from the guy back in ortho. She wanted to do it her way, and—"

"See, there you go. And you wanted to do it *your* way. She was just doin' it the way her supervisor told her to. You almost had her in tears."

I hadn't noticed that, and I looked around to see if she was still in the department.

"Don't worry about it, Doc," Amy said. "She'll be okay. And you're not quite as bad as Dr. Candler...not yet, anyway."

"Yeah," Jeff added. "We still have our phone."

He was referring to an episode that had occurred in the ER a few months ago. It was late at night, and Dr. Ray Candler had been called in to see a trauma patient. Ray was a neurosurgeon, well-trained and very capable. But he had a short fuse, and we had learned to stay clear of him when certain warning signals were present. The most obvious was a flushed face—and then, when he rolled up his shirtsleeves, we knew someone was in for it. That someone turned out to be the nursing supervisor on that particular evening.

The patient he had been called in to examine would need to be taken to the operating room for a head injury. Amy Connors had called the nursing supervisor to get the OR crew organized. Apparently, the response and the time frame she was given didn't satisfy Dr. Candler.

"Here, give me that phone," he brusquely ordered Amy after she had told him it would be at least forty-five minutes before things would be ready.

"Who is this?" he demanded of the person on the other end of the line. There was a pause and then some expletives, and then his face went from bright red to scarlet and finally to a dangerous maroon.

And then the phone came off the wall. Actually, it flew off the wall as he hurled it down the hallway. Wires went everywhere and plaster showered onto the counter at the nurses' station as he stomped down the hall. If you look closely, you can still see the repair job where the new phone has been attached.

"Well, maybe I need to go around to the lab and apologize," I suggested, not knowing what to do. I didn't want to hurt the tech's feelings. But I knew how I wanted things done.

"No, she'll be fine," Amy answered. "It wasn't a big deal."

I needed to think about this one. There was a fine line sometimes between insisting on what was right and insisting on having your way. Or maybe it wasn't so fine.

"Do you remember the night you called Dr. Candler about the young Webb boy?" Amy said, interrupting my thoughts. "Jason Webb, remember?"

"Yeah," I said, chuckling, happy for the release from my thoughts. "Now that was something."

∽∾∾

Wednesday, 3:00 a.m. This was not a call I had wanted to make, but it had to be done.

"Dr. Lesslie," Amy said, shaking her head, "it's Dr. Candler."

She handed the receiver across the countertop to me, but at the last minute covered the mouthpiece with her hand and whispered, "Doesn't sound like he's in a very good mood."

I didn't expect him to be. After all, it was the middle of the night, and it was Dr. Ray Candler, not the happiest of guys even in the middle of the day.

Amy took her hand from the receiver and I grabbed it, placing it to my ear.

"Ray, this is Robert."

"Hmm" was the response from the other end.

"Sorry to bother you this time of the morning," I apologized. "But I've got a twenty-year-old here with a neck injury. Moped accident, out on a dirt road. Apparently he ran off the trail and hit a tree. No helmet on, but no obvious injuries except for some neck pain. He's completely awake and alert, and complaining of numbness and weakness in his right arm and leg."

I paused, wanting to be sure my colleague was still awake and listening. There was no response.

"Ray?" I said, checking.

"What!" The response was not really a question, but more of a statement. He obviously was not very interested in what I was telling him.

"Anyway, he does have some weakness on that right side, and his cervical X-rays look like a fracture and maybe a jumped facet." This was a potentially unstable injury, and one that would need surgery. Especially the "jumped facet" part. That meant the spine was no longer normally fitting together, but was out of place. Making matters worse was the fact that the hospital's one CT scanner was down for repairs. We would have to make do with these plain X-rays.

I waited for his response, and after what seemed like a long time, he mumbled, "Are you sure about that?"

"Sure about what?" I asked him, getting a little aggravated now.

"About the X-rays," he said. "Are you sure they're abnormal?"

I took a deep breath before I answered. "Ray, I'm not a radiologist, but I can tell if a neck is broken or not. And this one is broken."

Amy looked up at this, her eyes wide with surprise. And she just shook her head again.

Then he said something I will never forget. In fact, it was so bizarre I had to ask him to repeat his request.

"Robert, go get those films and hold them up to the phone," he told me.

What? He sounded like he was awake, but—

"You want me to do what?" I asked incredulously.

This got Amy's attention. She looked at me questioningly. I leaned across the counter and cocked the phone away from my face, allowing her to hear Dr. Candler.

"Go get those X-rays and hold them up to the phone," he repeated. "I want to take a look for myself."

Amy almost burst out laughing, and had to cover her mouth with both hands. She rolled away from the counter, putting distance between herself and the phone. She was snorting loudly.

"Ray, do you really want me to do that?" I asked him patiently, hoping he was only partially awake. I couldn't look at Amy or I would start laughing myself. "Do you really want me to hold the X-rays up to the phone? Don't you think you need to come in and see the kid and look at the X-rays yourself?"

"I…uh…what?" he muttered, apparently trying to collect himself.

"Of course, I'll…I'll come over. Be there in a minute. But it sounds like a waste of time."

There was a loud click as he slammed his phone down.

Amy laughed out loud as we both remembered this episode. "I would never believe that if I hadn't heard it myself!" she declared. "Not in a hundred years! He must have been out cold—sleepwalkin' or sleep-talkin' or something!" She kept laughing and shaking her head. "Sometimes that man can be just plain…well, just plain stubborn as a mule. I guess that best describes it. And even when he knows he's wrong. I don't know what makes a person do that, but boy, he can really dig in his heels. As if he has something to prove."

She paused, suddenly thinking of something. "About the only person I've ever known to be more pigheaded was Maggie Reynolds. Remember that woman?" she asked me, a mischievous look on her face.

"Maggie Reynolds," I repeated thoughtfully. And then it came to me. "Yeah, I remember Maggie! And I bet I remember the night you're talking about. It happened right over there," I said pointing to room 3.

"Yep, you're absolutely right," Amy confirmed. "It was right over there."

❧

Maggie Reynolds was a fifty-year-old nurse, sent to the emergency department from a temp agency. Why in the world the hospital administration would send us someone with little or no ER experience was beyond us, but there she was. Lori Davidson had been the charge nurse that day, and she decided to give Maggie a limited assignment. She would be covering only rooms 3 and 4, and hopefully wouldn't get into too much trouble.

From the moment she arrived in the ER, Maggie began asserting herself.

"Why do you people put this paperwork over here?" she had asked

Amy. The questions went on. Why don't you do this? Why don't you do that?

Amy Connors would have committed manslaughter had we not been so busy that morning. And that was a good thing for Maggie Reynolds.

Lori had instructed our triage nurse to send the serious patients to beds other than rooms 3 and 4, and to use those only if absolutely neces-sary. Throughout the morning, she had been able to give Maggie simple sore throats and a few coughs. Nothing serious or complicated.

And then Michael Beck came into the department.

To be fair to our triage nurse, Michael had been less than forthcom-ing about his reason for being in the ER. He told her he wanted to be checked by the doctor, but reported nothing specific. His vital signs were completely stable, and he looked fine. She brought him on back without any real concerns.

Michael was a veteran of the Vietnam War. He had been moving around a lot, working various jobs and trying to find his space. He had settled down in Rock Hill for the past few years and had been work-ing as a technician with a local telecommunications company. He had been in Special Forces and was still in great physical condition.

I looked up as he came by the nurses' station with the triage nurse. He was neatly dressed and his hair was close-cropped, betraying his military background. His eyes held mine with an intensity that was anything but threatening. He was obviously intelligent, and there was a gentle spirit behind that rough and tough façade. He was an inter-esting man. I noted he was being taken into room 3.

Maggie noticed this as well and quickly headed into the cubicle.

I was writing up the record of a patient in the cardiac room and was standing within earshot of room 3. I heard the entire exchange between Maggie and Mr. Beck.

"Mr. Beck," Maggie began. "I will be your nurse today, and I'm here to help you. And my name is Maggie Reynolds. Do you under-stand me?"

With a half-perplexed, half-humorous look on his face, Michael replied, "Yes, Ms. Reynolds. I understand you."

"Good. Now, what is the problem this morning?" she asked him, busying herself around the room, straightening the countertop, and rearranging our supplies.

"I've been stabbed," he said matter-of-factly.

Maggie stopped what she was doing and turned to stare at him. I thought I had heard the word "stabbed" as well. I looked over in his direction. Everything seemed calm, and he still looked fine. Then Amy Connors handed me the phone and said, "Here's Dr. Shaw. He's on for cardiology and he's returning your call about the heart attack in cardiac."

"You what?" Maggie asked Mr. Beck, now beginning to lose her patience.

"I've been stabbed," he repeated calmly.

"What in the—" she mumbled. "Now see here, Mr. Beck. We've no time to spend with any tomfoolery. If you think I'm going to—"

"Ms. Reynolds, I'm telling you, I've been stabbed in the back with a pair of scissors," Michael explained, still surprisingly calm. "I was in the elevator of our building, and these two guys tried to mug me. One grabbed my arms and I felt the other one punch me in the back. Then I saw he had a pair of scissors in his hand, and I knew I was in trouble. That's when I knew he had stabbed me."

"What…you say he…" she muttered incoherently, totally taken off guard by what he had just said.

"I've handled much worse, and I left the two of them on their butts in the elevator—you'll probably be seeing them soon enough—and then I went back upstairs to our lounge. I remember seeing some Saran wrap in one of the cabinets, and I found it and wrapped it around myself and came straight over here."

Maggie Reynolds was trying desperately to collect herself and regain control of this situation.

"Are you telling me you've been stabbed in the back?" she asked.

Michael shook his head, showing the first sign of frustration. "That's what I've been telling you, Maggie."

"It's Mrs. Reynolds, young man," she asserted herself. "Now, about this stabbing—"

"Here, take a look," Michael said, taking off his shirt.

He was not wearing an undershirt, and his chest was completely encircled with several layers of Saran wrap. It extended from just below his armpits to his mid-abdomen.

He twisted around on the stretcher and tried to point to his right mid-back. "Here, this is where I think he got me."

Maggie glanced at his back and saw the pooled blood beneath the Saran wrap. Her eyes widened as she began to realize Michael might be telling her the truth.

His training in the Special Forces had prepared him for the possibility of such an injury. He knew that a stab wound of the chest was serious business and could rapidly prove fatal. If the stab penetrated the chest cavity and lung, you could develop a tension pneumothorax— where the cavity quickly fills with air from the outside, creating a pressure that forces the collapsed lung against the heart. Finally, the blood flow from your heart is compromised and you no longer are able to move air in and out of your chest. And then you die. Something adherent and waterproof like Saran wrap will close off the stab hole and prevent air from entering your chest. It will buy time until you can get help. Michael had saved his own life.

What happened next was a blur. I was trying to tell Dr. Shaw about the patient in the cardiac room, and at the same time it was beginning to dawn on me that I had a real problem in room 3. And Maggie was at the center of it.

"Let me take a look at that," Maggie said, stepping over to the stretcher.

"Just be sure not to remove that dressing," Michael warned her. "If you—"

"Now don't tell me my business," she clucked. "I know what I'm doing."

"Just be sure you don't—"

I heard the concern in our patient's voice and looked over at room 3 again. Maggie had not yet pulled the curtain closed, and I could easily see what was happening.

Michael was sitting sideways on the stretcher, his legs dangling over one edge. Maggie had walked around behind him, where he couldn't see what she was doing. It was a strange sight, this gentleman sitting on our bed with Saran wrap tightly encircling his chest. And then it happened. Before I could call out and stop her, Maggie took a pair of scissors out of her pocket and deftly and completely cut through the plastic wrap on Michael's back. It fell away as if it were the peel from an onion.

"No!" he yelled, turning and facing her. But it was too late. He tried to hold his breath, knowing it could prove fatal. But he couldn't, and with a sudden gasp, there was a terrible sucking sound, and the wound in his back began to bubble. Without saying another word into the phone, I dropped the receiver on the counter and slid it across to Amy. Then I raced toward room 3.

I reached the room and pushed Maggie out of the way, just as Michael Beck collapsed, almost falling off the stretcher. His color was a dusky blue, and he wasn't breathing.

"Get me an 18-gauge angiocath on a 50cc syringe!" I called behind me to Jeff. "And then I'll need a chest tube tray."

"What do you want me to do?" Maggie asked, still very assured and apparently unaware of what she had just done.

"I want you to step out into the hall," I told her, not looking up. "And stay there."

There was a rush of air when I punctured Michael's chest with the needle, buying us the time we needed to insert a larger tube between his ribs. Its purpose was to keep draining the leaking air from the wound in his lung until it had time to seal off and heal.

Half an hour later, he was stabilized, breathing, and talking. As I explained to him that he was to be admitted to the ICU for a few days, he kept looking over my shoulder and around me, searching for something—or someone.

I smiled briefly. "Don't worry, Michael. She's not here. And she won't be back."

"Now that was one pigheaded woman," Amy said. "And you know, the more I think about it, you can be pretty pigheaded too, Dr. Lesslie," Amy added with conviction.

I sighed, shook my head, and waited.

"Jeff," she said, glancing in his direction. He was sitting behind the nurses' station, drinking a cup of coffee. "Do you remember Kevin Mayer?" she asked him, but she was looking at me with eyebrows raised.

"Boy, do I," Jeff answered, smiling. He knew where this was going.

"Wait a minute!" I interjected. "That's not fair. I was only trying to give the guy a chance."

"Sure you were," Amy said. "And the rest of us were trying to tell you the guy needed to go. We were the ones having to work with him, not you. And we were the ones seeing what was going on."

"I know, I know," I muttered. "But he never hurt anybody, or at least no one you guys ever told me about."

"No, it was just that…well…he was just a screwball," Jeff tried to explain. "Something just didn't add up with him. In fact, some of us even wondered if he was really a doctor."

Kevin Mayer was in fact a doctor, having trained in several well-respected medical centers. He came to our ER with little experience, but an excellent resumé and references. We scheduled him for the weekday daytime shifts, since they were the quietest and most normal shifts we had. As if anything in the ER was normal.

From the outset, the nursing staff and Amy Connors were concerned about his performance. There was nothing concrete, as Jeff had said—just some vague misgivings about his medical judgment and experience.

"Give the guy a chance," I had vigorously responded on many occasions. "If you have something specific, let me know, and I'll address it. But remember—we all had to start somewhere."

I should have been suspicious when our most objective and reasonable nurses complained, especially Lori Davidson. She hadn't wanted to raise the issue, but she was concerned as well. Yet, there was nothing specific, nothing I could concretely address. Not until Madeline Waters came into the ER in congestive heart failure.

Madeline was in trouble. Her blood pressure was low. Her lungs were backing up with fluid from her failure. She had been in for this before, and we all knew her. But this was the worst Lori could remember seeing her.

Kevin Mayer was on duty, and with Lori's help, he made the right diagnosis. Then he slipped out of the department and hurriedly went around to our office. Unbeknownst to the staff or to me, when he came across something he didn't recognize or wasn't sure of, he would quietly retire to our office and consult our medical texts. That was fine, and I encouraged such activity. The problem this morning was that Kevin was looking at an internal-medicine book circa 1945. We had kept it in the office as a kind of interesting artifact. It provided some fascinating reading during slow times. Of course, there was no mention of pharmaceutical interventions or advanced monitoring techniques. Instead, the recommended treatment for congestive heart failure, referred to in this text as "dropsy," was rather primitive and of questionable effectiveness.

Kevin came back to the department armed with this newfound information and his treatment plan.

"We need to get some rotating tourniquets going," he ordered with authority. This was an interesting concept, incorporating the placement of tourniquets on both arms and both legs. The idea was that if you inflated one or two of the tourniquets, you would remove a significant portion of the blood volume from circulation, allowing the failing heart to beat more effectively. After a few minutes, you would let down the pressure in that tourniquet and inflate another one—hence the term "rotating." (I did say "primitive," didn't I? There hadn't been this kind of equipment in the hospital for twenty years.)

But it got worse.

"And…we need to draw off about a liter or two of blood." It was the old "cupping" idea. If you removed blood from the circulation, you would ease the work of the heart. It made sense, in a peculiar way. But we didn't have a "cupping" device in the department. And we probably didn't have any leeches, either.

"And we need to do it in a hurry!" he added.

Lori Davidson had stood in front of him and stared, her mouth open and eyes wide.

"Let's get going!" he ordered.

"But, Dr. Mayer——" Lori objected.

"I've got an idea how to do this," he mused, not paying her any attention. "Quick, get a big IV going, and we'll connect it to wall suction. That's it! And turn the suction on wide open. That should get it done. We'll take out about two liters of blood."

He was confident now, having determined his plan and now setting it in motion.

Or so he thought. When Lori realized he was dead-set on this, she slipped away to the nurses' station and called my home number.

I had worked the night before and was sound asleep. It took a moment for me to clear my head and for this strange tale to sink in.

"I'll be right there," I told her.

"Yep, he was stubborn and crazy—*and* a screwball!" Amy declared with a twinkle in her eye. "I'll never forget how you looked when you came through those doors. Hadn't even tucked in your shirttail or combed your hair. But you were bug-eyed and wide awake. And the next thing we know, there goes Dr. Mayer out the ambulance doors. Never did see him again either."

I was silent, letting Amy enjoy this moment of satisfaction.

She just sat there and smiled up at me. Then I turned and headed down the hallway.

"And where are *you* going?" she called after me.

"Where do you think I'm going?" I answered her over my shoulder.

When I reached the end of the hall, I turned and headed toward the lab. There was a certain tech who deserved an apology.

There are few, very few,
that will own themselves in a mistake.

JONATHAN SWIFT (1667–1745)

8

Foolish Pride

*Human pride is not worthwhile;
there is always something
lying in wait
to take the wind out of it.*

MARK TWAIN

When you think you're pretty good at what you do, when you think you can handle anything that comes through those ER doors, there it is, lying in wait. And that *something* is waiting to knock the wind right out of you.

❧

Friday, 9:15 p.m. Bill Thatcher was forty-eight years old. At least that was what his chart said. To me he looked a good bit older, maybe in his sixties. He had walked into the ER complaining of mid-to-upper back pain. "Nagging" was how the triage nurse had described it on his record.

He was at least fifty pounds overweight. I surmised that his two-pack-a-day cigarette habit was probably the cause of his premature aging. His skin had the sallow look of a veteran smoker, and he had a slight but audible wheeze as he walked down the hallway.

Once he had been settled into room 4, I picked up his clipboard and headed in his direction.

"Mr. Thatcher," I said to him. "I'm Dr. Lesslie. What can we do for you tonight?"

He had been struggling with his hospital gown and looked up as I spoke.

"First of all, Doc, have I got this thing on right?" he replied, gesturing to the light-blue gown.

I glanced at the garment, noted that he was wearing it correctly, and that he had already tied the strings in a series of knots that could only be undone with scissors. Then I noticed the hospital emblem on the front of the gown. It was from a facility a hundred miles distant, and fleetingly I wondered about the journeys of this particular cotton robe.

"You're fine," I assured him. "Just right."

Over the next few minutes, I asked him about his complaints of back pain—when it started, how bad it was, what made it better or worse. It seemed like a straightforward muscular complaint, maybe just a simple strain. It had started yesterday and had gotten worse over the past few hours.

His vital signs looked okay, other than a heart rate of 96. That wasn't dangerous, but it was a little bit of a red flag. It should have been around 70, but everyone is a little different. His pain might be causing it to go up. He described it as "maybe 5 on a scale of 10." Or it could be due to the recent strenuous activity of tying all those knots.

Still, something had brought him to the ER, something that had him worried. We needed to check this out and make sure nothing bad was going on.

His exam was unremarkable, eliciting no worrisome physical findings. His lungs sounded fine, his heart regular and strong, and his abdomen was completely soft. I considered the possibility of early shingles, but his back was clear of any skin lesions, and there was no pain when I palpated the area where he was hurting.

"Let's check a few things," I told him, picking up his chart from the counter beside his stretcher. "We'll start with a urine specimen and check that for blood or any sign of infection. Do you need anything for pain right now?" I asked.

"No, I'm okay," he answered. "Well, maybe a couple of Tylenols, if you've got some. That might be good."

"Sure, we can do that," I said, heading out of the room. "One of the nurses will be right back with that, and we'll get that urine."

At the nurses' station, I asked Lori to give Mr. Thatcher his Tylenol tablets, and I wrote some orders on his record. "Urinalysis." I was about to hand the chart to the unit secretary when I stopped and put it back down. Maybe we needed a CBC, just to check his white count and hemoglobin. His symptoms were vague. This might either help confirm that nothing bothersome was going on, or lead me in another direction. I would probably bet on the former—but I had thought about it, so I needed to do it. That was a lesson that had been drilled into my head by my earliest instructors. "If you *think* about doing something, you'd better do it." I had never had reason to doubt that wisdom.

I wrote "CBC" on his chart, slid it across the counter to the secretary, and picked up the record of the next patient to be seen.

Twenty minutes later, the urinalysis report was attached to Mr. Thatcher's chart, but the blood-work report was not yet back.

He had a small amount of blood in his urine, but nothing else. No abnormal chemicals or protein, no sugar, and no evidence of infection. The blood could go along with a kidney stone, but he didn't seem to be in that kind of pain. Usually people with stones would declare themselves by their inability to sit still. They would be pacing the floor, constantly moving around, unable to find any relief by lying or sitting. Bill Thatcher was doing none of that. Curious.

I stepped back into his room to see how he was feeling, and was struck by the change that had taken place over the past few minutes. He was sitting upright on his stretcher, staring straight in front of him, and actively inhaling-exhaling like a woman in labor. His color was good, but there was sweat on his forehead.

"How are you feeling?" I asked him, moving quickly to his side and checking his pulse. It was still regular, but now easily more than 100. "What's the problem?"

He looked up at me with a strained smile, not altering his forced breathing pattern. "I don't know," he stammered between breaths. "The pain is gone, but I just got a little short of breath."

I listened again to his heart and lungs. Nothing unusual there. No wheezes or abnormal sounds that would indicate asthma or pneumonia or heart failure. His skin was damp but warm, and while I was listening, his breathing seemed to return to normal.

He sighed loudly and sat back against the head of the raised stretcher, visibly relaxing.

"Boy, that was scary," he said, looking up at me. "Better now, though."

It *was* scary, and I wasn't exactly sure what to make of this. The thought of a pulmonary embolus crossed my mind—blood clots that would have originated in his legs, broken free, and traveled to his lungs. But he didn't have any risk factors for this, and he hadn't complained of any leg pain or previous shortness of breath. I examined his calves again, just to be sure there was no tenderness or swelling. Normal.

"What are you thinkin', Doc?" he asked.

There were several things flying through my brain, none of which were yet concrete.

"I don't know, Mr. Thatcher. You've got me a little worried here. I'm going to check on your blood work. But we'll need to do some more testing. I don't like your having trouble breathing, and I need to find out why that happened," I told him. "Any pain now, anything new?"

"No, no pain. I actually feel a little better, just weak, I guess," he answered.

"Okay, just let me know if something changes. I'm going to get some things going."

Lori was standing at the nurses' station, and I asked her to put Mr. Thatcher on a cardiac monitor.

"He'll need an IV going too, normal saline, just 100 cc's an hour right now. And we'll need to keep a close watch on him."

She nodded her understanding and headed to room 4.

"Amy," I addressed our unit secretary that day, Amy Connors. "We'll need an EKG, portable chest ray, and some blood work on Mr. Thatcher in 4. And a blood gas." I needed to check the oxygen content of his blood. A low level might indicate the presence of a blood clot. That might explain his unusual findings.

She had already begun filling out the necessary order slips, and she picked up the phone before I finishing speaking.

"Anything else?" she asked, looking up at me.

I thought for a moment. "Not yet. Let's see what turns up."

One of our lab techs had walked up the hall carrying her metal mesh basket. It contained an assortment of multicolored stoppered vials, syringes, needles, alcohol swabs, and Band-aids. When she reached the nurses' station, Amy slid an order form across the counter to her and said, "Room 4, Suzie."

Suzie had Mr. Thatcher's CBC report in one hand and exchanged it for Amy's order slip. "Thanks," she said, picking up the lab orders and noting what needed to be done. She turned and stepped toward Mr. Thatcher's room.

I picked up the CBC report and quickly scanned the automated results. His hemoglobin was normal, no obvious evidence of any excessive bleeding. And his platelet count was a little low, just borderline. But what was troubling was his white count…18,000. That was high, and indicated some infectious or stressful process going on. It still didn't make much sense, and I was having a hard time putting things together. I hoped that his X-ray was going to give me some clue, or maybe his EKG.

It was then that Richard Sanders walked out of the cardiac room and over to where I stood. Richard was one of the cardiologists on staff and had come in to see one of our patients. I had asked him to examine the elderly woman in the cardiac room. She was in congestive heart failure and would need to be admitted to the hospital.

"You're right about Mrs. Chambers," he said to me, gesturing with a nod of his head to the cardiac room. "She's in failure and will have to come in. Any family members with her?"

I told him her husband was in the waiting room and that a daughter was on her way in.

"Good," he responded. "I'll need to speak to them as soon as they're all here." He walked around the counter and sat down, beginning to write on Mrs. Chambers's chart.

"Richard, if you've got a minute, let me tell you about the guy I have in room 4."

I proceeded to run the strange case of Mr. Thatcher by him, hoping he might be able to shed some light on this enigma. As I was finishing, Lori walked out of room 4 with his EKG, followed by Suzie, the lab tech. She had collected several tubes of blood and was on her way back to the lab.

Lori handed me the EKG, and said, "You might want to check on him in a few minutes. He seems stable, just maybe a little confused. He's starting to repeat things."

I studied the heart tracing, relieved that it was completely normal, other than an elevated rate of 110. There was no evidence of a heart attack, and no evidence of any unusual strain. I slid it across the counter to Richard Sanders.

"Looks normal to me, Robert," he confirmed. "Puzzling, isn't it? And what's this about confusion? You think he might have early meningitis, with his elevated white count and all?"

That was a reasonable thought, but he had no fever and his neck had been completely supple. But things can change quickly, and I needed to re-examine him.

As I was about to enter room 4, the department's portable X-ray machine was being pushed out of the cubicle by the radiology tech.

"I'll be back in just a minute with the film, Dr. Lesslie," she told me.

"Fine, Carol. Just make sure I see it as soon as you come back."

Stepping into the room again, I immediately noticed a subtle change in Mr. Thatcher's behavior. His color was still good, and his breathing was normal, not labored. But he was nervously glancing around the room, seemingly unable to focus on any one object. He looked up at me as I walked toward him, and then he looked away.

"Bill, how are you feeling now?" I asked him, placing my hand on his shoulder.

He seemed to calm a bit, and said, "Doc, I…I…somethin's just not right. I…don't know what, but…somethin'…"

He stopped talking and just stared up into my face, slowly shaking his head.

I felt the side of his neck with the back of my hand. There was no obvious fever, but I would need to have his temperature rechecked. And then I grasped his head in my hands, moving it up and down, and then side to side. His neck was completely supple; no evidence of meningitis.

"Are you hurting anywhere, Bill?" I asked him.

"No, I'm not havin' any pain," he answered, again shaking his head. "Somethin's just not right."

"Dr. Lesslie." The voice came from behind me. It was Carol, having just returned from the radiology department. "Your X-ray is hanging on the view box."

"Thanks, Carol," I told her. And then turning again to Mr. Thatcher I said, "Bill, I'm going to look at your chest X-ray and then I'll be right back."

"Somethin's just not right," he repeated, once again glancing around the cubicle.

I stepped out of the room and over to the view box. Richard Sanders was already there, intently studying the chest X-ray.

"This is interesting," he mused, stroking his chin while he looked at the film.

I walked up behind him and looked closely at the size and shape of Bill Thatcher's heart, and then I examined his lung fields.

"Interesting?" I asked him. "This looks completely normal to me."

"That's what I mean, Robert," he said, nodding his head. "It *is* completely normal. That's what makes it interesting. There's no help for you here."

He turned and walked back to the nurses' station.

Richard was right. There was no help for me here. I continued to stare at the X-ray, hoping that something would appear, hoping that some answer to this man's problem would be forthcoming. But there was nothing.

"His labs are back," Amy called out, sliding several slips of paper toward me on the countertop. Lori was standing there, making some notes on Bill Thatcher's chart.

"Lori, would you repeat his temp and check his blood pressure again?" I asked her.

"Sure," she answered, and immediately turned toward his room.

I thumbed through the multiple lab studies that had just been returned. Glucose, electrolytes, liver studies, cardiac enzymes, blood gases—all normal. Nothing in all of his studies was out of line. I shook my head and attached the slips to his chart.

Richard Sanders looked up at me and was about to say something, when Lori suddenly called out from the doorway of room 4. "Dr. Lesslie, come quick!"

I immediately stepped across the corridor and into the room. Richard was right behind me.

Lori was now beside the stretcher, lowering its head and placing Mr. Thatcher flat on his back. He was staring blankly at the ceiling—and was barely breathing.

"I took his temperature—99," she told me over her shoulder. "And then while I was starting to take his blood pressure, he just mumbled something and stopped breathing."

Richard was feeling for a pulse and I moved to the head of the stretcher.

"Were you able to get a blood pressure?" I asked her.

"Just barely. I think I heard something at 60. Not any higher than that."

That was a dangerously low reading, indicating that something bad was happening. He was crashing right before our eyes.

"I've barely got a pulse here," Richard called out. "What do you want me to do?"

"Just hang in here a second, Richard," I told him, glad he was in the room. "Lori, get me the airway tray, and call respiratory therapy when you get a chance."

She had already anticipated this and was opening the tray behind me, spreading out the contents on a movable metal stand.

"Mr. Thatcher!" I spoke loudly in his ear. "Can you hear me?"

There was no response, and now he wasn't making any respiratory effort. He was turning a dusky blue.

"Richard, can you bag him for a minute while I get ready to intubate him?" I handed my colleague the ambu bag and face mask, not waiting for a response.

"Sure," he said, stepping around me and positioning himself by Bill Thatcher's head.

Within less than a minute, I had his airway secured with a tube in his windpipe. Richard was rhythmically inflating the ambu bag, watching the patient's chest rise and fall with his efforts. Bill was getting good air exchange, but his color was not improving.

"Any pulse?" I asked Lori while I instinctively felt for the carotid artery with my fingertips. Maybe there was a weak one, but I couldn't be sure.

"No pulse here," Lori said, her hand on his femoral artery.

Richard and I both glanced at the cardiac monitor. It showed a slow but regular cardiac rhythm, around 70 beats a minute. And it was a good, tight complex. But it wasn't doing anything. There was little if any blood moving.

The door to the room opened and two respiratory therapists walked in.

"Anything we can do?" one asked us. He was tall and muscular, and Richard and I spoke almost at the same time. "Yeah, we need to start chest compressions here."

The therapist quickly stepped over to the side of the stretcher, methodically noted the appropriate landmarks on Bill's breastbone, placed his palms in the correct position, and started depressing his chest. Richard timed his ventilations with the compressions. It was all textbook, perfectly orchestrated and carried off without a hitch. We began giving all the appropriate emergency medications through his IV line, following all the standard protocols. But nothing was working.

"Still no pulse," Lori told us. "Maybe a faint one with the compressions."

The respiratory therapist may have taken this as a challenge, and seemed to intensify his downward thrusts.

Yet there was no improvement in Mr. Thatcher's color. I glanced again at the cardiac monitor. It still showed a regular, tight complex, but now it was slowing—55 to 60 beats a minute.

"Any thoughts?" I asked Richard.

"I don't know, Robert," he answered, looking down at Mr. Thatcher's unresponsive face. "I guess he could have had a huge pulmonary embolus, or a stroke, or a tear in his aorta. But you checked all that out…and anyway, you're not going to save him if something like that's going on."

Save him? In the suddenness of Bill's collapse, my attention had been focused on the immediate things that needed to be done. Your training takes over—airway, breathing, circulation. And then you try to stabilize things as quickly as possible. Now, having done those things, and with the initial adrenaline rush beginning to fade, I had a moment to reflect. But "save him"? I hadn't had time to really consider that. He had been talking to me only moments ago. And though I knew he was in trouble, it had never occurred to me that I might *lose* him.

I immediately rattled off more orders, repeating doses of medications that might, just *might,* help him. And I again ran through a list of possible diagnoses that would fit this circumstance. Nothing new came to mind.

We continued working the code for another twenty minutes. His cardiac monitor showed a slowing electrical activity, and then a widening and more bizarre complex. His heart was dying. There was no response to anything we were doing. And when Richard stopped bagging him, there was no respiratory effort. He was dead.

I didn't want to stop. I didn't want to give up trying to save this man.

"Robert." It was Richard who finally spoke. "We need to stop. He's gone."

Lori Davidson had stepped behind me and lightly put a hand on my shoulder.

"10:58," she spoke quietly, noting the time on her wristwatch, noting the official time of Bill Thatcher's death.

And with that, all activity ceased, and people began to file out of the room.

"I'll see if there are any family members in the waiting room," Lori said, heading for the nurses' station, leaving Richard Sanders and me alone, standing by the stretcher and the lifeless body of Bill Thatcher.

We were quiet for a moment, and then he spoke. "I know how you feel, Robert. It's tough…when you do everything you know to do and it just doesn't work. But it happens. We can't save everyone, and some people are beyond saving. Whatever was going on with this man was going to take his life, no matter what you or any of us did."

I understood what he was saying. But it didn't make this moment any easier.

"I hear you, Richard. But I don't even know what killed him. I still don't have a clue."

I stared down at the body before me and shook my head. "I'm supposed to figure these things out. That's what I do, or—"

"Wait a minute, Robert," Richard interrupted. "Did you hear what I just said? Sometimes, hopefully not very often, we're all going to lose people, no matter what we do. Our patients are going to die. But we're not failing them when we do everything that can be done."

He paused for a moment, thinking. Then he nodded his head and quietly said, "Maybe that's it. Maybe it's all wrapped up in our not being able to handle failure, or what we *think* is failure. We fear it because it threatens our sense of invulnerability, our being able to handle every patient and every circumstance that comes our way. We think we're somehow invincible and all-knowing. But that's a dangerous place to be. That's when we find ourselves in trouble. We even think that life and death is in our hands. It's really not, is it?"

He paused, as if waiting for my response. Then he said, "I'm glad it's that way."

I listened to what he was saying, and I knew he was speaking the truth. Yet, I was having a hard time letting this thing go. Maybe it *was* my pride, but there was a heavy weight on my shoulders, and I couldn't shake it loose.

"Richard," I said, looking him squarely in the eyes and placing my hand on Bill Thatcher's motionless chest. "This man is dead. He walked into my ER, looked me in the face, talked with me—and now he's dead. Why is that not my failure?"

Nothing he could say at this point was going to change my mind. It was a hollow, painful feeling, and it struck to the core of who I thought I was as a doctor. There was no safe place to hide from this.

"You can call it what you want," Richard said. "But to my mind, this isn't your failure. It's tough, it's something terrible—but in the end, it was out of your hands."

He shifted his weight, placing both hands on the rails of the stretcher.

"Let me tell you something that one of my residency attendings told me years ago. He was a thoracic surgeon and did a lot of teaching with the cardiology residents. I'll never forget what he said and when he said it. Another resident and I were riding in an elevator with him, and he started talking about fear and about failure. Apparently one of his thoracic residents had freaked out during a chest case that had gone bad. I think a thoracic aneurysm had burst and the poor guy didn't know what to do. Anyway, the attending started telling us about this, and about how fear and the fear of failure can paralyze you. It can stop you in your tracks, and then you're no use to anyone. 'If you're afraid to fail,' he told us, 'You'd better find another profession.'"

Richard paused. "He was right, you know, Robert. That's especially true for you here in the ER. This is a tough place to work, and if you're going to be good at this, if you're going to help the people who need you, you can't be afraid. But you're not. I've never seen you paralyzed, never even close. You need to think through this, and you'll work it out."

He stepped to the door and turned around. "I'm going to check on our lady in the cardiac room. We *can* do something to help her tonight."

And then he was gone, leaving me alone with Bill Thatcher, and with my thoughts.

A week later I got a copy of the autopsy report. After reading it, I walked to the pathology department, confused by the findings. I wanted to talk with John Dial, the pathologist who had performed the autopsy.

"Yeah, Robert, this was a strange one," he said, scratching his head. "Absolutely nothing. No stroke, heart attack, blot clot, nothing. Your IV lines and endotracheal tube were all in the right places. There was just no obvious cause of death, nothing I could find to explain this. Happens sometimes. Sometimes we just don't know. I guess it was just his time."

I stood there for a moment thinking, trying to put all of this together.

This knowledge was of little consolation. It didn't change anything for me. And it didn't change anything for Bill Thatcher.

I thanked John, and headed back to the ER.

Perhaps God brings us to the end of our resources
so we can discover the vastness of His.

Dr. Neil T. Anderson

9

Idle Hands

Idleness is the devil's workshop.

GERMAN SAYING

Wednesday, 2:35 p.m. "You can tell the guy in 3 he's ready to go," I told Lori, tossing his chart into the discharge basket. He was the only patient in the ER, which was very unusual for this time of day.

Amy Connors, our unit secretary this afternoon, was sitting at the nurses' station, going through the daily log. She was doing some statistical work for Virginia Granger.

I looked across the counter at her, and I guess that's when it happened. It was the evil imp on my shoulder. And I couldn't muster the will to resist him.

For the past month, one of the area grocery-store chains had been advertising a promotional campaign. They were randomly drawing names each week and giving away hundred-dollar certificates for free groceries. Since they were the most frequently shopped grocery stores in town, almost everyone had filled out a form for the drawing. One of Amy's friends, an OR tech, had won two weeks ago, and I knew that Amy herself had filled out more than a dozen of the forms and kept her fingers crossed.

I walked down the hallway to our office as nonchalantly as possible. Alone in the room, I picked up the phone, got an outside line, and called the ER. This was in the days prior to caller ID, so I was anonymous.

The phone rang twice, and then, "This is the Rock Hill ER, Amy Connors speaking. How can I help you?"

I lowered my voice and affected an exaggerated Southern accent.

"Ms. Connors?" I paused and waited for a response.

"Yes, this is the ER. Can I help you? Is this an emergency?"

I searched her voice for some evidence of recognition, but detected none. So far, so good.

"No, no emergency," I told her. "My name is Rob Alexander and I've got some good news for you."

I waited for her response, and again for any sign that she might know it was me.

"Who did you say you were?" she asked, her tone completely unsuspecting.

"I'm Rob Alexander," I repeated, this time with more excitement in my voice. "The manager of the Giant Apple grocery store on Cherry Road. And like I said, I've got some good news for you."

"Uh…what is it, Mr. Alexander?" she asked. From the tone of her voice, I knew she was hooked and on the line. Now I was going to reel her in.

"Well, Ms. Connors, you registered for our grocery giveaway, I believe."

"I sure did, Mr. …What was your name again?" she asked, speaking a little faster now.

"Mr. Alexander. Rob Alexander. And I'm happy to tell you that you've won the one-hundred-dollar giveaway this week."

I waited again. I heard her say something, but it was muffled. She had apparently covered the phone with her hand and was speaking to someone at the nurses' station.

Then—"You say I won?" Still no hint of doubt in her voice, only a growing excitement.

"You most certainly have, Ms. Connors. And congratulations!"

"I—" she began, but I quickly interrupted. It was time to close the deal.

"Now, you understand you have to come by the store within the next thirty minutes in order to claim your prize?" I said.

"What…thirty minutes?" she seemed puzzled.

"Yes, that's the rule, you know. So we'll see you at the Cherry Road store. Just ask for Rob Alexander. And again, congratulations!"

I hung up the phone, not wanting to risk betraying my identity.

A sudden wave of guilt washed over me. Surely she was not taken in. But what if she was? What if she took off for the store? What if she got there and asked for Mr. Alexander and they said, "Who?" But that would be too good. Anyway, Amy was smart, and she wouldn't fall for something like this. Or would she?

The wave of guilt quickly passed.

I walked out of the office and up the hallway. And at once I knew I was in trouble.

Standing behind the nurses' station, hands on her hips, staring at me over the top of her horn-rimmed glasses, was Virginia Granger. I thought for a moment I saw smoke rising from the top of her nurse's cap.

And then I noticed that Amy Connors' chair was empty.

Lori Davidson glanced at me, shook her head, and gave me the palm of her hand in farewell. Then she walked quickly into the medicine room. She knew when to head for cover.

"Dr. Lesslie," Virginia said, her voice threatening. "I need to have a word with you."

How could she know?

"In my office," she added emphatically. Then she turned and walked around the nurses' station.

I followed her like an obedient puppy, my tail between my legs. But how did she know?

"Close the door," she told me, sitting down behind her desk.

I obeyed her without question and stood before her, not being brave or presumptive enough to sit down.

"Now," she began. "Tell me about Amy Connors and her winning the grocery giveaway," she asked.

How…?

"Well, I…she…did she win something?" I responded, not very convincingly.

"Dr. Lesslie, she's on her way there now. I couldn't stop her. She said she had to be there within thirty minutes." She was studying me intently as she said this.

I felt my face flush and knew I was cooked.

"Well...I...that's great! I'm glad she won," I stammered.

"Dr. Lesslie," she intoned, and then just waited.

I studied the tops of my shoes, and then the clock on the wall. Finally I looked at her. My shoulders slumped and my chin fell to my chest.

"Virginia, I...well..." And then I heaved a great sigh.

"She's going to want to kill you when she gets back," she said matter-of-factly. "And I think I just might let her."

I stood there, my hand in the cookie jar. I didn't know what to say. Then I mustered the strength to whimper, "I'll have to tell her I'm sorry, and that I won't do it again."

"Well, that might work, if you get down on your knees and plead for forgiveness. But she's going to be very hot."

"Maybe you could sort of cool her off," I suggested. "You know, maybe..."

"I'll do what I can," she answered, shuffling some papers on her desk. "But you know, Dr. Lesslie, this is not the first time you've done something like this."

She looked at me knowingly, and I knew what she was talking about.

A night in mid-February, 1:15 a.m. Dr. Johnny Gee. Now there was a piece of work. Johnny was an ER doc who lived in Charleston, about a three-hour drive from Rock Hill. He had worked with us for more than ten years and was a favorite of the nursing staff. More importantly, he was a good doctor and took care of his patients. And he was an animal when it came to picking up uncovered shifts. He would frequently make the trip to Rock Hill on a moment's notice, never seemed to need much sleep, and was always pleasant and cheerful. He was genuinely fun to have around.

This particular night, he had worked the 3 p.m. to 11 p.m. shift. He had left a couple of hours ago, heading across town to the Sleep EZ Inn. He was scheduled to relieve me at 7 a.m., and was going to get some rest.

"Now Robert, call me if you need me," he had told me as he was leaving. "You know I usually don't sleep much when I'm up here."

"We'll be fine," I told him. "Go and get some sleep, and I'll see you in the morning."

Jeff walked out of triage and over to the nurses' station. "We've cleared out the waiting room," he announced. "It's completely empty out there."

He walked around the counter and sat down heavily as I handed Lori Davidson the chart of our last patient.

"Here's his prescription," I told her. "And he needs to follow up with the orthopedist sometime next week."

She took the clipboard and headed to room 3 and the waiting patient.

I walked around the counter and sat down beside Jeff.

Amy Connors looked up and said, "Pretty quiet for a Friday night. Maybe it'll stay this way."

For the next hour, it did. Nobody checked in at the reception desk. Nobody called 9-1-1 for EMS transport. It was unusual, but we appreciated the calm.

"Do you think Johnny Gee really caught that marlin he was telling us about?" Jeff asked. He was referring to a fishing tale told earlier in the evening, one that sounded pretty tall to most of us.

"Maybe, but I doubt it," I answered.

"You know good and well he didn't catch any such fish," Amy flatly stated. "He wouldn't know a blue marlin if it bit him on the…well… you know."

"Might have, though," Jeff mused, nodding his head. "You never know with the G-man."

I guess that's when the idea began to form somewhere in the deep recesses of my mind. Maybe in a place that should be kept locked.

"Slide that phone over to me," I asked Amy. "I've got an idea."

As she did so, she saw the glint in my eye and pulled the phone back toward her. "And just what are you up to?"

"You'll see," I answered. "Just give me that phone and listen. Oh, and would you hand me the phone book?"

I looked up the number of the Sleep EZ Inn and called the front desk. The young girl who answered seemed a little skeptical, but when I told her who I was and that it was important that I get in touch with Dr. Gee, she gave me his room number and the number to dial to get his phone. I thanked her and hung up.

"You're not going to—" Amy began.

"Shhh!" Jeff hushed her. "Just listen."

Jeff knew me pretty well, and he had a mischievous streak that might have exceeded my own.

I dialed the number the clerk had given me, leaned back in my chair, and smiled at Amy. Jeff leaned close, trying to get his ear near the receiver. Amy couldn't help herself and did the same.

The phone rang once, twice, three times, and then, "Heeelooo." It was Johnny, and he sounded asleep.

"Is this Mr. Gee?" I asked, trying to disguise my voice. I doubted that in his sleep-drugged state he would be able to recognize me.

"Yes…this is Mr…. Dr. Gee. Who is this?" he asked, still sounding asleep.

"This is Sergeant Pepper with the Rock Hill Police Department," I told him in an official tone. Amy put her hand over her mouth, trying to suppress a chuckle.

"Sergeant Pepp…Who did you say you were?" He was beginning to wake up a little.

"Sergeant Pepper. And I want you to listen to me. First of all, do not leave your room. Do you hear me? Do *not* leave your room, under any circumstance."

There was silence on the other end, and then Johnny muttered, "Don't leave my…What's going on, officer? Is there a problem?"

"As I said, Mr. Gee, do not leave your room. Do you understand?" I repeated.

"Yes, yes…I mean no, I won't leave my room. What's the—"

"There's been a drug bust in the parking lot of the Sleep EZ Inn, right outside your door, room 112." I paused here for effect, letting this sink in.

"A what?" he asked.

"A drug bust. And the suspects stashed some bags of cocaine in a dark blue Volvo station wagon. Has a dented back fender."

"That's my car!" he exclaimed, and Jeff slapped his hands on the counter and squinted his eyes in devilish glee.

"I've got to go out there! There's been some kind of mistake. I don't know any—"

"I told you to stay where you are," I warned him again. "Don't go out in the parking lot. It's dangerous. Just let us handle this. I just wanted to let you know what was going on, in case you heard something. And if you hear gunshots—"

"What! Gunshots! Listen, officer—" he began, now obviously wide awake.

"Stay put!" I ordered him once more and hung up the receiver.

Amy let out a loud whoop and clapped her hands together.

Lori Davidson had been standing on the other side of the counter and just shook her head. "I'm not having any part of this." She walked off down the hallway.

"Now what?" Jeff asked. "What's next?"

I really hadn't thought about that. But it immediately came to my mind what the next call was going to be.

"We'll wait a few minutes," I told them. "And then we'll see."

"Do you think he's out in the parking lot?" Amy asked. "I bet he is. I bet he couldn't help himself and went outside to see what's going on."

"Well, we're just going to have to find out," I told her, and smiled. "You're going to make the next call, and here's what you need to say."

I told her what she should do, and after she stopped laughing, I dialed Johnny Gee's number again. Then I handed the phone to Amy, and Jeff and I leaned close.

This time, the phone only rang once.

"Hello?" There was no sleepiness in his voice now.

"Mr. Gee," Amy said, drawing out his name for effect.

"Yes, who is this?"

"This is…Nancy at the front desk." Amy had struggled for a split second to come up with a bogus name, and I hoped Johnny hadn't picked up on that.

"Nancy? What's the problem?"

He didn't seem to have a clue as to her true identity.

"Well, we've had a complaint. And it's about you," she told him, covering her mouth and squinting hard.

"A complaint? What kind of complaint?" he asked her, incredulous. "What's the problem?"

Amy quickly composed herself and went on, "Mr. Gee, someone called this desk and complained you were out in the parking lot in your underwear, walking around your car."

This was the gamble. We were taking the chance that he had not obeyed Sergeant Pepper and that his curiosity had overcome his good sense. It might be dangerous in the parking lot, but yet…

We were also gambling that he hadn't taken the time to get dressed but had bolted out of bed and out the door. The three of us leaned forward in our chairs, tense and hopeful.

"Well…" he stammered.

It was the pause that told us. He *had* been in the parking lot *and* in his underwear. That was all Amy needed.

"Mr. Gee, I don't know what you were up to or what's going on in your room, but it has to come to a stop. Do you hear me?" she reprimanded him.

"But…you see, there was a drug bust…and Sergeant Pepper…" he tried to explain.

"A drug bust?" she questioned dubiously. "Now listen here, Mr. Gee. You're not the only guest in our motel, and there are people here who need to get some sleep tonight. And it might surprise you to know there are people who don't necessarily care to see you running around in your underwear."

"But you don't—" he tried to inject.

"Don't you interrupt me," Amy hammered him. She was really enjoying this, but it was time to get off the line. I drew my index finger across my throat and she quickly nodded her understanding. Jeff leaned back in his chair and gave her a thumbs-up.

"Now as I said," she told him with finality, "just stay in your room and don't come out again."

Before Johnny could respond, she hung up the receiver, beaming.

"I bet he's going crazy," Amy proudly announced. "He didn't have a clue."

"Didn't sound like it," Jeff agreed.

I didn't say anything but reached for the phone.

"You're not…" Amy asked, a smile breaking across her face.

"Just need to bring this thing to closure," I said, dialing Johnny's number one last time.

"Hello," he answered. He must have been wondering what was coming next.

"Mr. Gee, this is Sergeant Pepper again."

I waited, but there was no response.

"Mr. Gee, I've talked with the front desk."

I waited again, letting this sink in.

"Listen, Sergeant, I—"

"It's okay, Mr. Gee. I understand your concern. But you've got to stay in your room. And just so you know, we found three kilos of cocaine in the back of your car."

"You what!" he exclaimed. "Cocaine!"

"Calm down, Mr. Gee," I told him. "We know you didn't have anything to do with this, but since it was in your car—well, you know. There will have to be an investigation."

"An investigation?" he asked helplessly. "But I didn't—"

"Where will you be tomorrow?" I interrupted. "We need to handle this quickly."

"I'll…I'll be in the ER, at Rock Hill General. I go in at seven o'clock in the morning. You could find me there."

"That'll be fine, Mr. Gee. We'll come over some time in the morning and get this straightened out," I told him. "Now you get some sleep."

That would be doubtful.

I hung up the phone and looked at Amy and Jeff.

"You're a devil," Amy said, shaking her finger at me.

"Me?" I asked innocently. "And what about you…*Nancy*?"

"That was a good one," Jeff pronounced. "A *real* good one."

But we weren't done, not just yet.

◈

7:02 a.m. The ambulance doors opened and Johnny Gee walked into the department. He carried his briefcase in one hand and a cup of coffee in the other. As he approached the nurses' station, he looked at Amy and said, "You won't believe what happened to me last night."

She was sitting at her station, and I was standing in front of her at the counter. Jeff, on cue, walked nonchalantly into the cardiac room.

"That so?" Amy responded, not looking up from her work. It was a good thing he couldn't see her face.

"Yeah," Johnny continued. "There was some kind of a drug bust, or something strange going on in the parking lot at the motel, and I…"

He paused, looking down at the chart I was writing on.

I had barely looked up when he came into the department, immediately resuming my writing on the record in front of me.

"Hmm," I muttered, shaking my head, obviously disturbed by the chart I was dealing with.

The top sheet was a form that we use for our cardiac arrest patients, and I had made some notes on it. At the bottom, in big, bold print, I had written:

"DOA"

As Johnny had walked up beside me, I lifted this sheet, revealing another ER record beneath it. This one was a routine encounter form, documented in Johnny's handwriting. It was the actual record of a thirty-eight-year-old man he had seen the past evening. He had complained of a simple sore throat, and his diagnosis at the bottom of the sheet read "pharyngitis."

I made sure he saw that note and his signature, then I let the "DOA" form fall back over it.

He had seen it. That's when he had stopped in mid-sentence.

"What...?" he said haltingly. "What's that, Robert? Let me take a look."

He stepped closer, putting his briefcase on the floor and his coffee cup on the counter. I slid the chart in front of him.

"This guy...did he...?" he stuttered.

"Came in just a little while ago," I explained to him. "Full arrest. Don't know exactly what happened."

Amy tucked her head down even farther and put her hand on her forehead.

"I saw him last night..." Johnny said, studying first his note and then mine. "He seemed fine, and I..."

I slid the chart away from him and said, "I read your note, and it looks fine. Vital signs were all normal, his complaint was just a sore throat. Nothing suspicious there, Johnny. Don't know what happened. Could have been his heart, a stroke—who knows?"

I picked up the clipboard, turned, and then walked toward the cardiac room.

Without prompting, Johnny followed right behind me.

"Robert, he looked fine when he left last night, and he's only thirty-eight..."

I didn't say anything.

We stepped into the room and Johnny closed the door behind us.

Jeff was standing in the corner, writing on a notepad and arranging some equipment on one of the shelves.

In the middle of the room was the cardiac stretcher. And on that stretcher was the form of a large patient, completely draped with a hospital sheet—all except for the right great toe. It was bare and was sticking out from beneath the cover. And attached to that appendage was a cotton string with a toe-tag, identifying this unfortunate individual.

Johnny stepped over to the stretcher and picked up the tag, hoping there was some mistake. The name on the tag matched that of his patient's name from last evening.

He dropped the tag and stood there, shaking his head.

"I don't know what could have happened," he said. "He seemed fine and everything. Maybe…"

He stepped to the head of the stretcher and reached down, grabbing the top of the sheet.

"Maybe there's been a mistake," he said hopefully. "Maybe this isn't the same guy, just some kinda confusion in the registration office."

Out of the corner of my eye, I saw Jeff stop what he was doing and turn to look at the stretcher.

Johnny had a firm grip on the sheet, and he pulled it back, exposing the head and shoulders of the recently deceased patient.

When the sheet came away, the man on the stretcher came back to life, bolting straight up and letting forth a blood-curdling scream that startled all of us. It was Terry Baker, one of our surgical orderlies. He was a big man, six-foot-four and weighed more than two-hundred-fifty pounds. He had been all too happy to help us with our devious plot.

As he sat up and screamed, he reached out for Johnny Gee, zombie-like. It frightened even me a little.

But it must have terrified Johnny. He jumped straight up in the air and somehow propelled himself backward, landing on top of the defibrillator. It was an amazing feat.

Then he let out a "Yow!" and tried to climb up the wall. And he may very well have wet his pants.

Jeff burst into laughter, as did Terry and I. And then Johnny figured it out. He climbed down off the defibrillator, shaking his head, his face flushed a bright red.

"You guys…" he said, straightening out his clothes.

Terry got off the stretcher and we headed out of the room. Jeff clapped Johnny on his back and said, "You're a good sport, Johnny Gee."

Johnny just shook his head, still trying to recover his composure.

Amy was looking up at us as we approached the counter. "Couldn't see anything," she said. "But I heard it all!"

"You knew about that?" Johnny asked her.

"Why of course," she answered, grinning widely.

"Well, you guys got me pretty good," he said, looking around at each of us.

Then he turned back to Amy. "This just tops off a crazy night. Like I was saying earlier, I had no more gotten to sleep last night when I get this phone call. It was a Sergeant Pepper, Rock Hill PD, and he tells me…"

Amy had startled giggling, and then she looked up in my direction.

"He…he…says…" Johnny faltered. Then he stopped. He studied Amy's face, and he then turned to me. I was trying to maintain some sort of composure, but it was too difficult. I couldn't suppress the beginning of a grin.

Johnny looked back at Amy now. She had covered her face and was shaking with laughter.

"Wha—it was you! You guys called the motel and—!"

Terry, Jeff, and I had all turned away from the nurses' station and were headed off in different directions.

"Hey, wait just a minute!" Johnny Gee called out.

"You guys come back here!"

10

Just Make It Go Away

Going a little farther,
He fell with his face to the ground and prayed,
"My Father, if it is possible,
may this cup be taken from me."

MATTHEW 26:39

S ometimes we can see the road ahead, and it frightens us. We want to find another path, another journey, another ending. Sometimes, no matter what we do, no matter how hard we struggle, we can't change our destination.

❧

Monday, 11:15 a.m. You wouldn't think a little stumble would be cause for much concern. And for Phyllis Jenkins, third-grade teacher at Piedmont Elementary, it wasn't. But she had noticed it. Just an awkward sort of stagger on level and newly mown grass. But later, back in the classroom, when the other children were busily going about their math work, something else was going on. It must have been a headache, and it must have been bad.

T.J. Blackwood had his head on his desk with his eyes closed. And he was rubbing his temples.

Phyllis walked back to his seat and asked him if he was all right.

T.J. looked up and said, "I'm okay, Ms. Blackwood. I just have a headache, and…and I don't feel so good."

He promptly gagged once and then vomited on the tiled floor.

T.J.'s mother was at the school within twenty minutes, and she brought him straight to the ER. A few minutes after their arrival, his father, Cooper Blackwood, joined us in room 2.

Lori Davidson had seen the Blackwoods out in triage, and she immediately brought them back into the department. Lori's son, Garrett, was in the same Cub Scout pack with T.J., and she and Ruth Blackwood had become friends.

"Ruth, what's the matter with T.J. this morning?" she had asked his anxious mother, leading them across the hallway to room 2.

"I got a call from the school just a little while ago," she began to explain. "T.J. had a headache and then some vomiting, and his teacher was worried. I called Cooper and told him I was on the way to the ER. T.J. was so pale, and his head was hurting, and something just seemed wrong. That's why I brought him here, Lori."

She had said this right before I walked into the room, and in less than a minute Cooper arrived.

"What's the matter with T.J.?" he asked, not addressing any specific person in the room. He stepped across to the side of the stretcher and put his hand on his son's shoulder.

Lori was in the process of checking T.J.'s temperature, and when the electronic thermometer beeped three times, she looked up at me and said, "98.5."

Then she introduced me to Cooper Blackwood. "I just got here myself," I said, "and haven't had a chance to talk with your wife. So why don't we start from the beginning?"

Ruth Blackwood told me what she knew and why the nurse had called her.

"He seemed fine this morning before he went to school. He wasn't complaining of anything at all, no headache." She paused for a moment and then added, "But he did have a headache yesterday morning. Remember, Cooper? Right before we went to church, but then it was gone. I gave him some Tylenol, and it went away."

She looked at Cooper and he nodded.

It seemed like a pretty benign story. I was going to ask a few more questions, when Ruth said, "But Phyllis Jenkins told me something unusual. I don't think it means anything, but it struck her as odd. She said that during recess, she was watching T.J. for some reason and noticed him trip or stumble. He didn't fall, but it seemed like his feet just got jumbled together and he lost his balance. The playground was as smooth as glass, and she didn't see anything he might have tripped over. She just thought it was odd."

"I'm sure that doesn't mean anything," Cooper stated. "Do you think he just has a virus or something, Dr. Lesslie?"

It *did* mean something, and it bothered me.

I asked them about any previous medical problems and any medications. Had he ever been in the hospital? Any surgeries? All of the usual questions. And then I stepped over and sat down beside T.J. on the stretcher.

"T.J., tell me how you feel," I said to him.

"My head hurts, Doctor, right here." And he pointed to both of his temples.

Then I examined him. I listened to his heart and lungs and felt his belly. When I shined the flashlight in his eyes, his pupils seemed sluggish. That's a hard call, since everyone's reflexes are a little different. But there did seem to be a delay there.

I turned the room's light out, sat down on the edge of the stretcher, and examined his eyes with the ophthalmoscope. This instrument allowed me to see the back of his eye, the retina, and to examine the blood vessels there as well as the optic nerve. Instead of clean, well-defined structures, everything seemed a little blurred. And both retinas were pale. These findings indicated papillary edema, swelling in the eyes that is usually caused by an increase in the pressure within the brain.

T.J. was sick, and would soon be in trouble.

I turned the lights back on, got off the stretcher, and stood in the middle of the room.

"We're going to need to do some testing," I told the Blackwoods. "We'll need to—"

"What's wrong?" Ruth interrupted. "What's wrong with T.J.?"

"I don't know yet," I said honestly. "The history we have, and his exam indicate that…Well, we need to find out if something is going on in his brain."

Ruth Blackwood quietly gasped and sat down beside her son, taking him in her arms.

"In his brain?" Cooper repeated, looking over at the stretcher. "That's impossible, Doctor. He's a healthy kid, and this is just some simple… some routine problem. That's all. Just a headache and, heck, he only vomited once."

Lori had stepped over beside Ruth and put an arm around her shoulder. I explained my findings. Then, trying my best not to alarm them, I told them what needed to be done.

"The first thing will be to get an MRI of his head," I said. "And we'll do that right away." I glanced over at Lori, and she immediately got up and headed toward the nurses' station.

"We'll also check some routine blood work and things like that," I continued. "But I want to see what his MRI looks like. That will tell us what we need to do next."

"What do you think this could be?" Ruth asked, beginning to suspect but not yet willing to mention the possibility.

"An MRI?" Cooper questioned. "You must think he has a…" He stopped and looked at his wife.

She sat up a little straighter. "Like Dr. Lesslie said, Cooper, we need to get the MRI and see what that shows. And then we'll go from there."

He just stood there, and quietly nodded his head.

"Let me get some things going and I'll be back in a few minutes," I told them. And then I stepped out of the room and over to where Lori was standing beside Amy Connors.

"Twenty minutes?" Amy spoke into the phone. "Okay, we'll bring him right over."

She hung up the receiver and looked up at me. "MRI will be ready for him. Anything else you need?"

I told her what labs I wanted and then turned back to room 2. Lori grabbed my arm, stopping me.

"What do you think is going on?" she asked. "He looks so pale, and his head is hurting so badly." She looked down at the countertop and stared blankly at it. "You know, Garrett is the same age. They could almost be brothers."

This was the hard part. Most of us had children, and a lot of us had kids T.J.'s age. You don't want anything bad to happen to any child. And when it does, it affects everyone in the department. And you realize all over again that it can happen to any of us.

"Let's see what the MRI tells us, Lori. Just one step at a time. If there's anything to worry about, that's when we'll worry."

She nodded and walked away. And I was worried.

Forty-five minutes later, I got a call from the radiologist who was reading MRIs that day.

"Robert, can you come around to the department and look at these films with me?" Tony Sloan asked.

I stood behind Tony and leaned over his shoulder, peering at the images on the control-room screen. He was using the tip of his pen to point out T.J.'s problem.

"This is the tumor," he stated matter-of-factly. "Pretty good size, and very aggressive, by the looks of it. Probably an astrocytoma."

This was what I had feared. So many times we get scans to rule out potential problems, thinking that the likelihood of finding a significant problem will be small. Usually, we're correct. But something about T.J. didn't feel right, and I had worried we might find something this time. What we found was worse than I had imagined.

"Is he having trouble with his vision?" Tony asked me.

"He's pretty young," I told him. "And he is not really specific about his complaints. Why?"

He shifted the tip of his pen to another area and said, "He's developing some edema here. The tumor seems to be growing pretty fast, and his ventricles are starting to dilate. He's got some increased pressure that's going to have to be dealt with."

I told him of my physical findings, confirming what we were seeing on the scan.

"Have you talked with Freddie Kleitches yet?" he asked me. Freddie was one of the neurosurgeons on staff, and he specialized in pediatric problems.

"No, not yet," I answered. "But I'm going to give him a call when I get back to the ER."

"Well, good luck with this one," he said, pushing a button and bringing up someone else's scan. "That's a tough break."

It *was* tough. It was going to be difficult telling this news to T.J. and his parents.

When I turned the corner at the nurses' station, I saw the Blackwoods standing outside of room 2, talking with Lori. They looked over at me and stopped talking. Lori searched my face and then turned and walked over to the medication room.

"What did the MRI show?" Cooper asked as I approached them. "Is T.J. okay?"

His wife shushed him, glancing back into the room at her son, and then pulling Cooper closer to the nurses' station.

"Well, what did it show?" he repeated, a little more quietly.

I stood there with my hands in my pockets and took a deep breath. Then I told them the results of the MRI. I didn't mince words, but laid out the facts as I saw them.

"The next step," I told them, "will be to get one of our neurosurgeons to take a look at T.J. And we need to do that right away."

They just stood there and stared at me. Then Ruth turned to her husband and almost collapsed against him.

Cooper held her tightly. He looked at me. "Are you sure about this?"

I simply nodded my head, not knowing what else to say.

He glanced down at the floor, silent. When he looked back up, there were tears in his eyes and he was trembling. Ruth took his hand and took a deep breath. Then together they turned toward room 2.

I followed a few steps behind them and stopped at the entrance to the room. I watched as they walked over to the stretcher and sat down, one on each side of their son.

T.J. looked up at Ruth and asked, "Momma, what's wrong with me?"

She hesitated for just a moment, and he said, "Can we still go to Carowinds this Saturday?"

❧

Saturday, 2:30 p.m. I looked up as Jeff Ryan led Curtis Mayes through the triage entrance. Curtis was one of the general surgeons on our staff. He smiled sheepishly at me, and then held up a bandaged and bloody left hand.

"What have you done to yourself?" I asked him, putting a chart down on the counter and stepping over to him.

"Just a little table-saw accident," he told me. He was sweating and appeared a little pale. Jeff was standing behind him and he shook his head.

"Let's get you back to minor trauma," I told him, stepping out of their way. "I'll be back there in just a minute."

"Okay, Robert," he said. "But it's nothing major."

They turned and headed down the hallway.

A few minutes later, I entered the room and found Jeff carefully removing the kitchen towel from Curtis's hand. One quick glance told me that this indeed *was* something major. His thumb was gone. There was a ragged and clotted stump where it should have been. It was amputated all the way back to the first joint.

He was staring at his hand and then he sighed. He looked up as I walked over to his stretcher.

"What in the world happened?" I asked him, pulling up a rolling stool and sitting down beside him.

"I was working in the shop," he began to explain. "Building a table out of knotty alder. "And as I was making a cut, I guess I didn't read the grain of the wood. Something grabbed the blade and pulled my thumb into it, and before I could do anything…Well, here it is." He held the stump up for me to see.

Curtis was an experienced and talented woodworker. I had seen some of the beautiful furniture he had made, and I frequently reminded him that this was a dangerous hobby. Saws and lathes were no friends of flesh and bone.

I looked down at his hand. There was exposed bone, and from what I could see, this was really a mess.

"How much pain are you having?" I asked him, glancing over at Jeff. He turned and reached behind him for an IV setup and fluids.

"You know, it really doesn't hurt too much," Curtis said. "But it looks like it should, doesn't it?"

It looked like it should be killing him.

"We're going to start a line and give you something for pain," I told him. "Then we'll numb up that thumb…that area, and see what we've got."

"There's not going to be much to work with," he volunteered. "It's pretty chewed up. I brought the rest of it in, just in case. But I'm not too hopeful." He reached into his pants pocket and pulled out a zip-lock baggie filled with ice. On top of the ice was a mangled piece of flesh. I took the bag and inspected what was left of his thumb.

"We'll hold on to this, just in case," I told him, knowing there was no chance of re-implanting this lost digit.

"Robert, I know better." He gave a wry grin.

We got his IV going and gave him something for pain. An X-ray demonstrated the splintered end of his first metacarpal. I held the film up in front of the overhead light, allowing him to see.

"What a mess," he sighed. "Who's on for ortho?"

I told him and explained I had already given him a call. The OR crew had been called in and would be ready in about an hour.

"Hmm…" he muttered. "Forty percent, isn't that right?"

I nodded in understanding, and then he added, "The thumb provides forty percent of the function of the hand. Good thing I'm right-handed."

Then he was silent. And I knew what he was thinking. He made his living with his brain, but also with his hands. I did too. And I wondered how I would deal with a devastating injury like this if it happened to me. I caught myself putting my hands in my pockets.

Curtis was one of the best surgeons on our staff, known for his technical skills and abilities. He was also known for his relaxed and friendly bedside manner and for his genuine compassion. When patients in the ER were informed they would need to see a surgeon, most of them wanted to know if Curtis Mayes was available.

That was going to change. This was a career-changing and life-changing event.

"It happened so fast, Robert," he said, interrupting my thoughts. "You and I both know about accidents, and how quickly they happen. We see it every day. It's just that—well, it's true. If only…" He paused, and there was obvious regret in his voice, and a quiet sadness. But his silence was brief, and he said, almost cheerfully, "Anyway, it's done, and we just need to get it taken care of."

I had sat back down on the stool when Maude Weston walked into the room. She was the OR supervisor and had come in to help with Curtis's surgery. Maude was a big woman—gruff and not known for being subtle.

She stepped over and looked down at his thumb. Jeff was getting ready to wrap it loosely in some gauze, but it was still exposed.

Maude adjusted her glasses, leaning over. "Hmm-hmm," she murmured. "You really did a number here, Dr. Mayes."

Then she stood up and patted him on his shoulder. "You know, we all have our crosses to bear. I guess this will be yours." I grimaced, wondering what she could be thinking.

She turned and walked out of the room. Jeff began wrapping the hand.

Curtis was smiling when he looked over at me. Then he said, "You know, Robert, I was about to say something to Maude, but I changed my mind. Maybe one day I will, when the time is right."

I wondered what he might have said. I had never seen him angry or heard him speak harshly to anyone. What would he have told her?

"She's wrong about that, you know," he said quietly.

"I'm sorry about that, Curtis," I said, apologizing for Maude. "Some people just don't think before they—"

"No, I mean about this being my cross to bear," he interrupted. "Now don't get me wrong, Robert. I'm not happy about this." He gestured with his head toward his wounded hand. "This is going to drastically change my life, or at least how I make a living. But Maude is referring to what Jesus said about taking up your cross daily and following him. The key word there is 'daily.' And the cross is all about dying, and about death. Jesus isn't telling me I'll have to deal with my thumb every day for the rest of my life and feel sorry for myself. He's telling me I have to *die* each day. I have to put my selfish ways to death each and every morning if I'm going to follow him. Hard stuff, isn't it? It makes this thumb seem pretty insignificant."

I just listened. Jeff was listening as well, and had stopped wrapping the gauze around Dr. Mayes's hand. When Curtis fell silent, Jeff quickly finished his bandaging and asked him if he needed anything else.

"No, I'm fine, Jeff. Thanks for all of your help."

Then he leaned back against the head of the stretcher and crossed his legs.

"You know, Robert," he said, his voice and face suddenly very serious. "There's only one real problem here."

"What's that?" I asked him, listening carefully.

"I guess now I'll need to take off one shoe when I have to count to ten."

Amazing.

❧

Saturday 11:45 p.m. "Hold steady, Mr. Jones. We're almost finished."

I was putting the last stitch in Mr. Jones's lacerated eyebrow. He was starting to move his head around, and it was difficult to find the end of the piece of suture. He had met the business end of a pool stick an hour or so ago and had a pretty big gash over his left eye.

He mumbled something, and I was once again buffeted by his alcohol-saturated breath. But at last he became still, and I was able to tie his last suture in place.

"Bad accident out on Highway 5," Jeff Ryan spoke over my shoulder. He had just walked into minor trauma and was preparing to help Mr. Jones get his wound bandaged and on his way. "Two units are working it now."

"What's coming this way?" I asked him.

"I don't think anything," he answered, his voice becoming quieter. "Three teenagers are being flown out to the trauma center, and one is dead at the scene."

I stood up from my stool and stretched. My low back was beginning to ache, and I needed to move around.

"Any idea what happened?" I asked him.

"Head-on, is what one of the paramedics reported. From the looks of the cars, he didn't know how anybody survived."

I walked up the hallway, leaving Jeff to take care of Mr. Jones.

At the nurses' station, Amy Connor repeated this information, adding that the coroner had called and would be meeting the parents of the deceased teenager in the morgue. They would have to identify their dead child.

"I wonder if it's anybody we know," she mused, not looking up from her logbook.

I didn't want to think about that. A lot of my friends had teenage children.

Forty-five minutes later, the coroner walked through the ambulance entrance.

"Evenin', Robert," he called out to me.

"Hello, Ed," I answered, looking up and then extending my hand.

Ed Ballard had been elected the county coroner thirty years running. He knew his business, and he knew just about everybody in the county.

"This is a real tough one," he told me. "Terrible accident. Those three kids who were sent to Charlotte probably won't make it. And if they do…well, they're in bad shape." He shook his head and stared at the floor. Then he looked up at me and said, "It never gets any easier. Thirty-odd years, and it never gets any easier."

I just stood there and nodded in agreement. He was a sensitive man, but the way he was acting was a little unusual for him. He had been dealing with this kind of thing for a long time. Something else must be going on.

"You might know the parents of this girl, Bob and Sandra Caldwell," he said, breaking the silence. "Her folks are friends of ours, and we all go to the same church. Her name's Trish. Beautiful girl too. And a really good basketball player. In fact, I think she was offered a scholarship to play ball at Erskine. Isn't that where you went to school?"

I told him I had, and that I couldn't place the Caldwells.

"You'd know them if you saw them. But don't worry about that tonight. Much as I don't want to, I'll meet them at the front of the hospital and take them back to the morgue by myself."

He took a deep breath and stood up straight. "Guess I'd better head over there now. They're on their way, and I don't want them waiting by themselves. See you later."

I didn't envy him his task. Having to deal with the parents of a dead child is heartbreaking. You don't know what to say or how to say it. And to walk them back to the morgue in order for them to identify their child…

The morgue was located in the back of the hospital, away from the public's eyes and ears. And it was a cold, sterile, depressing place, even in the middle of the day. At night, like this was, it was even more depressing, if that's possible.

I tried once more to place the Caldwells in my mind, but couldn't. Then I picked up the chart of the next patient to be seen and headed for the ortho room.

Ten minutes later, after examining the patient in ortho, I stepped out into the hallway and almost ran into Ed Ballard.

"Been waiting on you, Robert," he said, looking down at my chest. Then he looked to his right. I followed his glance.

Standing behind him, with their arms around each other and their eyes reddened with fresh tears, were a man and woman. With a sinking feeling, I knew it must be the Caldwells. And I did recognize them. Our children had played in the same church basketball league over the years, and I had met them on those and other occasions.

"Robert," Ed spoke, "the Caldwells here asked if you were on duty tonight, and if you would…if you'd be willing to walk around with us to the…morgue."

Only now did Ed look up into my eyes. He knew this was a difficult thing to ask, but he knew it must be important to the Caldwells or he wouldn't be standing in front of me.

"Of course," I answered, stepping around Ed and shaking Bob's hand.

"Hi, Bob, Sandra," I quietly said to them.

It was an awkward moment, but Ed quickly put his hand on Sandra's shoulder and said, "Let's go this way. Just follow me."

Then he headed to the back corridor and turned right.

They followed him, Bob's arm around his wife's shoulder. And as I walked a few steps behind, I wondered what the proper order should be. Should I be walking beside them? Or between them? And then I wondered why I was asking myself that question. It made no sense. But then none of this made any sense. This shouldn't be happening.

As if reading my thoughts, Bob Caldwell stopped in the hallway, removed his arm from his wife's shoulder, turned to me, and said, "Robert, here—walk with us."

I stepped between them, and once again we started down the hall.

"Thanks for being willing to come with us to…to…" he stammered and then fell silent.

"That's okay," I answered, searching for the right words to say here. "I'm just sorry—"

Bob interrupted without seeming to hear me. "I'm not sure what we're supposed to do. The coroner said we need to identify the…body…"

"Our daughter," Sandra injected. "We need to identify our daughter."

She spoke as if in another place, with no emotion in her voice. These were just words to her.

"Do you think there could be a mistake?" Bob whispered to me, a desperate hope in his voice and eyes.

Ed Ballard had heard the question. He turned to me and shook his head. Then he once again silently led our group past the back elevators and into a dimly lit corridor.

This was a part of the hospital I seldom frequented. Only members of the maintenance department and those who stored supplies and equipment spent much time here. And the pathologists. The hospital lab was in the front of the building, but the morgue was back here. When they needed to perform an autopsy, this was where it was done. They didn't like this walk any better than the rest of us.

The hallway became more crowded with boxes of medical supplies and storage carts. At one point we had to walk single-file to make our way past a sad and run-down portable X-ray machine. I glanced ahead, looking for the sign on the wall that read "Morgue." It seemed a long way still, and I was happy for that. But then, too quickly, we were there.

Ed stopped in front of the morgue door and turned to the Caldwells. "I know this is not going to be easy," he said to them, his voice low and calm. "But it's something I'm afraid I have to ask you to do. And we'll only be here a minute. I don't want you to stay down here. There'll be time later to…to spend with your daughter."

I knew what Ed was trying to say, but somehow that struck me as odd. That time had passed. It was gone.

The Caldwells were standing in front of me, and they slumped a little as Ed said this. Then he reached to the right of the door and flipped some switches. A bright and greenish light appeared behind the door, filtering through the cracks on the sides and at the bottom.

He reached to the left and pushed three digits on a small numerical pad on the wall. There was a loud mechanical click as the door's locking mechanism was released.

Bob and Sandra flinched as they heard this sound. They moved closer to each other.

Ed grasped the door handle. He paused and just stared at it. Then he turned to the Caldwells. "We'll only be a minute."

The door opened, and we all stepped into the room. It was much brighter than the hallway, and Sandra reflexively reached up to shield her eyes. It was cold, and I could detect the faint smell of formaldehyde. And there was a peculiar mixture of other odors, some of which I could identify, and others which I didn't want to.

The room itself was small, maybe only twelve by twelve. Two of the walls were entirely composed of stainless-steel doors. These were refrigerator units, built into the walls and stacked one on top of another length-wise, from floor to ceiling. There were eight of them, and each was numbered.

Ed Ballard reached into his pocket and took out a small piece of paper. He glanced at it and then at one of the refrigerator units. Then he put the paper back in his pocket and stepped over to the wall in front of him. He reached out, and with both hands, grasped the long handle of unit 6.

He turned and looked at the couple standing in the middle of the room.

"Mr. Caldwell, Mrs. Caldwell," he said.

They put their arms around each other and just stood there, silent, not moving. Maybe if they waited long enough, this would all go away.

Ed was patient, and he just looked at them. Then he glanced at me. I had been watching all of this, trying to somehow remove myself from this scene, trying to shield myself from this pain. But Ed's glance brought me back to the moment. I reached out and lightly tapped Bob Caldwell on his shoulder.

He began to slowly nod his head. Together the couple stepped toward the wall. Ed's hands tightened on the handle and he pulled hard, sliding the door open and pulling the unit out of the wall. It contained a metal tray mounted on rollers, and the whole thing glided smoothly out into the room. There was a faint sound of metal moving on metal. Then it stopped. And the room was deafeningly silent.

On the tray was the body of a woman, completely covered with a hospital sheet. Ed stepped around to the head of the tray and reached out, taking hold of the end of the sheet. He looked over at the Caldwells, who had now stepped beside the tray, looking down into it.

"I just need to know if this is…if this is Trish," he said softly.

Then he gently raised the sheet, revealing the face of this young woman.

Sandra gasped and then pressed her face against her husband's chest. Her knees began to buckle, and Bob grabbed her tightly, pulling her close to him. Then he closed his eyes. After what seemed an eternity, he slowly began to nod his head.

"Okay," Ed said, with a sadness and weariness that echoed coldly in this terrible place.

He once more grabbed the handles of the refrigerator and pushed the tray back into the wall. There was a faint clicking as the door sealed tightly.

And then there was nothing—only the cold of the room, the bright and greenish lights, and the quiet sobbing.

Do not fear, for I am with you;
do not be dismayed, for I am your God.
I will strengthen you and help you;
I will uphold you with my righteous right hand.

Isaiah 41:10

11

Stand by Me

If one falls down,
his friend can help him up.
But pity the man who falls
and has no one to help him up!

<small>ECCLESIASTES 4:10</small>

Friday, 6:45 a.m. I got in the car, turned on the ignition, and the radio immediately came on. I must have forgotten to turn it off last night when I got home.

As I pulled out of the driveway and headed for the hospital, a familiar and comfortable bass riff filled the car and surrounded me.

Bum, ch-bum, bum bum bum, ch-bum, bum bum bum, ch-bum…

It was the beginning lines of "Stand by Me." Like most of us, I knew the lyrics, but for some reason this morning, I listened intently and thought about the meaning of the song.

And I began to think about the people I've leaned on for help, those who have "stood by me." Of course the list would include my family, especially my wife. And most recently, my grown children. Through the years, there have been a handful of really close friends—one in particular—and my business partner. Some have stood by me when they probably shouldn't have. But they did.

The list doesn't seem very long. And maybe it's not supposed to be. But I have always been grateful for these people, and for just knowing they were there.

The song ended as I was stopped under a red light. I turned the radio off and began to think about the people who had stood by me during my medical training and my years of practice. I thought of those who had helped me in difficult situations, and especially those who stood out as teachers of medicine. I struggled for a moment because that's a much shorter list. But as the light turned green, I thought of Bob Scoffield.

⚜

Sunday 10:45 p.m. Polly Manchester had tripped on a carpet in her living room and fallen. Her eighty-year-old bones couldn't withstand the force of the fall and she had broken her right wrist. After I gave her this news, I walked back up to the nurses' station and asked Amy Connors to get in touch with the orthopedist on call.

"It's Bob Scoffield," she told me. "I'll page him."

Good. Polly's fracture was badly angulated and needed to be reduced tonight. Bob never seemed to mind coming in, and I was glad he was on call. And then I remembered. So I walked back over to the X-ray view box and put her films back in their folder.

Less than five minutes later, Bob Scoffield walked down the hallway and over to the nurses' station, where I was standing.

"How did you get here so fast?" I asked him.

"I was just around the corner in the surgical lounge. When I'm on call on the weekends, I sometimes just hang around the hospital. It's easier than driving back and forth. You guys keep me pretty busy," he added, smiling.

I slid Polly Manchester's chart over to him.

"She's back in ortho," I told him. "Nice lady. She thinks you might have fixed her hip seven or eight years ago."

He glanced down at the name on the chart. "I know Polly. And she's right about her hip. She's been doing great. But you said she fell and fractured her wrist tonight?"

"Yeah," I responded. I was about to say something else but I stopped. I knew the routine.

"Well, let's go take a look at her," Bob said, picking up the chart and heading down the hall.

I followed him, remembering the first time I had asked him to see a patient in the ER. When I had handed him the X-rays of that patient, he had put them down on the countertop. "Let's go look at the patient first, Robert. The X-ray should be used to confirm our diagnosis, not necessarily make it."

That night he had carefully questioned the patient about the mechanism of injury, and then even more carefully examined him. As we had walked up the hallway, he told me what the X-rays would show. He was right. And he was right every time we went through this exercise. I had started doing this myself, trying to anticipate what the X-rays were going to show me, trying to make a correct diagnosis without seeing the films on the view box. I was getting better at it, but was still far removed from Bob's uncanny accuracy.

He had taught me most of the orthopedics I knew, especially most of the practical orthopedics. And he had done it in a subtle, nonthreatening fashion. He had a real passion for the care of his patients, and for some reason, he had an interest in my development as a physician. Looking back now, years later, I am grateful for that interest and for his teaching.

We walked into ortho and Bob stepped over to Polly Manchester, gently taking hold of her good hand.

"Polly, what in the world have you done tonight?" he teased her.

"Now Dr. Scoffield, don't you go giving me a hard time," she fired back.

He then asked her what had happened and how. And then he examined her swollen and tender wrist.

"Polly, we're going to take a look at those X-rays and then we'll get you taken care of. It will only be a minute."

As we walked back to the nurses' station he told me what kind of injury she had and what the X-rays would show.

He was right, of course. I had already seen her X-rays, and they confirmed his diagnosis.

As we were looking at the films, he said, "I saw Jack the other day in the dining room. He said he's spending some time with you in the ER this summer."

"Yes, he's been here a good bit," I answered. "And it's been a lot of fun. I think he's seeing some things he didn't expect to see."

"I bet," Bob mused. "Hasn't had any more pugilistic mishaps, has he?"

He was referring to something that had occurred almost ten years earlier. I just shook my head, still not believing it had happened.

"Robert, I'm on my way to the ER. With Jack."

It was my wife, Barbara, and she didn't sound very happy.

"What's the matter?" I asked her.

"It's not an emergency. I'll tell you when we get there."

She hung up the phone without saying anything else. I knew that tone of voice, and I knew she was mad about something.

Twenty minutes later, she was walking through the ambulance entrance, our twelve-year-old son in tow. I was right. She wasn't very happy.

Jack was holding his right hand and kept his eyes glued to the floor.

"Let's go over to room 1," I told them. "Nobody's in there."

The three of us walked over to the treatment room and I instructed Jack to jump up on the stretcher. He was still holding his right hand, which seemed to be pretty uncomfortable.

I was about to ask him what had happened, when Barbara gave me the whole story.

Jack was spending the week at Camp Cherokee, a campground located about forty-five minutes away. All of our children had been going there each summer for a lot of years. It seems that at some point during the previous evening, Jack had gotten into an argument with one of his fellow campers. One thing led to another, and punches were exchanged. Jack thought he had gotten the better end of it, or so it had seemed at the time.

When he had awakened this morning, however, his right hand was swollen and bruised, and very painful. When I began to examine it, I knew he had broken at least one bone, maybe more. I was worried about the other boy's face, and I asked Jack how he had hurt his hand.

"That guy really ticked me off, and I just kept punching the back of his head," he explained.

Surprised by this, I asked, "You were punching what?"

"The back of his—" Suddenly he stopped and looked down at his hand. "I guess it wasn't very smart."

"The whole thing wasn't very smart," Barbara interjected, obviously disappointed in Jack's behavior.

"I know it was stupid," he said. "I told him this morning I was sorry. And I told the camp director it wouldn't happen again. He says I can go back to camp if it's alright with you and Momma."

He looked over at his mother but didn't find any sympathy there.

I looked at Barbara, trying to get a read on her thoughts. She wasn't buying it. "The camp director had a long talk with both boys," she said. "And he says Jack can come back if it's okay with us."

"I really want to go back," Jack pleaded.

"Well, son, I think you've broken a bone in this hand, and you're going to be in a cast. That's going to make things a little difficult, don't you think?"

"There's only two more days left till we come home anyway," he begged. "Please, Dad, I can do it!"

Having a cast on his right hand would be awkward, but he was determined.

"We'll get an X-ray and see how bad it is. Then we'll talk," I told him.

The X-rays of Jack's hand revealed a mid-shaft fracture of his fifth metacarpal. It was called a "boxer's fracture," but that was a misnomer. Boxers strike with the knuckles of the long and ring fingers, not the little finger. This was more of a "slugger's fracture." And that certainly fit Jack's punching capabilities.

The three of us stood looking at the X-rays. I called out to Amy Connors, "Amy, could you get whoever's on for ortho on the phone? I need to talk with them."

It was Bob Scoffield. When he called, I explained the problem. He just chuckled and said he would be over in a few minutes.

We moved Jack to the ortho room, and one of the nurses prepared the casting material Bob was going to need. When he arrived, he walked across the room, gave Barbara a hug, and patted Jack on his shoulder.

"Well, Jack, I understand you've had a little misadventure here," he said, smiling. Jack repeated the story and then held up his injured right hand. Bob gently palpated the wounded extremity. Then he looked Jack in the eye.

"You've broken your hand, right here near the knuckle of the little finger." He pressed lightly on the area and Jack squirmed on the stretcher, but didn't make a sound.

"We may need to reduce the angle of the fracture and then put you in a hard cast."

Then Jack asked him about going back to Camp Cherokee. Bob looked first at Barbara and then at me. I shrugged, leaving the medical decision up to him.

Then he looked back at Jack and very seriously said, "We want to be sure your hand heals correctly, and it will if you take care of it. But having your right hand in a cast isn't going to be easy, even if you were at home and your mom was taking care of you. Now being at camp—"

"I can do it," Jack interrupted. "I can take care of it."

While Bob put the cast on Jack's hand, they continued to negotiate. When the cast was in place and hardening, Bob asked him once more, "Do you think you can handle it now?"

Jack circled his right hand in the air and said, "Sure, no sweat."

It was agreed. Jack was going to behave himself, take care of his new cast, and go back to camp. Bob was washing the plaster off his hands and was standing by the sink, when Jack said, "Dr. Scoffield?"

His voice was hesitant, almost timid. I glanced over at him, thinking this a little unusual when instead he should be happy with the way things had turned out. But something was troubling him. He was staring at the floor and shaking his head.

Later, I learned he had been wrestling with feelings of shame and embarrassment and fear. Mainly fear. And when he could bear it no longer, he had mustered the courage to call out to Dr. Scoffield.

Bob was drying his hands, and he turned around.

"Yes, Jack, what is it?"

Jack took a deep breath, jumped down from the stretcher, and walked over to where Bob stood.

He didn't say anything for a moment, just stood there. Then quietly he said, "What about *this* one? It really hurts too."

He raised his other hand and extended it toward Bob. It was swollen and bruised as well, right over the knuckle of the little finger. And while not as bad as his right hand, it too was obviously broken.

I looked over at his mother. Steam was coming out of her ears, and her eyes were big as saucers.

Sheepishly Jack said, "I guess I was punching his head with both hands."

I stood in front of the view box, shaking my head and glad to be on the other side of those teenage years. Bob turned to me, smiling as well, and said, "Yep, he was one tough kid. And I bet he was the first camper to go to Cherokee with both hands in casts."

"And the only one," I added.

❧

3:15 a.m.—Special Care Nursery. I studied the X-ray on the view box. It was a small film, and it revealed the entire body of a three-pound two-week-old. It was what I had thought—and feared. This little girl had been born prematurely and with underdeveloped lungs. She had been on a ventilator since a few hours after she was born and had seemed to be getting stronger. Suddenly, about thirty minutes ago, that had changed. She was failing. Her color had turned dusky, and her blood gases were awful. Something bad had happened, and I needed to find out what that was and fix it.

The special-care nursery had sixteen beds, or more exactly, incubators. Most were occupied. Most of the children were stable and improving. It had been a quiet night, up until this little girl went south.

I was finishing up the first year of a pediatric residency and was alone in the unit. The third-year resident was upstairs in the call room, asleep. I was probably going to have to give her a call. But the thought didn't give me much reassurance. She was great in the pediatric clinic, but when it came to dealing with emergencies like this, she would rather be somewhere else.

I glanced over at Carolyn, the tiny girl in the incubator, making sure that nothing had changed in the past minute or so. Taped to her nose was the endotracheal tube that connected her to the ventilator beside her. It was this ventilator, with its rhythmical wheezing and sucking, that was keeping her alive.

As if she were directing some unseen and unheard orchestra, her minute and almost transparent hands were purposelessly floating in space above her.

I looked back at the X-ray. Once again I saw her collapsed lung. The entire left side of her chest was black, indicating that her lung had somehow punctured and contracted into a useless mass of tissue, much as a burst balloon would do.

It had to be re-inflated or she was going to die. In an adult or older child, this was not a difficult procedure. It was a matter of inserting a large tube between two ribs and connecting the tube to a suction device. With Carolyn, it would be much more difficult. Her entire chest was the size of a golf ball, and her ribs were no bigger around than a pencil lead.

I took a deep breath and was about to ask one of the nurses to get a chest-tube tray ready. But before I could say anything, a voice at my shoulder said, "Whatcha got, Robert?"

It was Bill Bowman. I knew it without turning around, and as I recognized his voice, I felt immediate relief.

Bill was the only pediatric surgeon on our staff. He was in his midforties and a favorite of the pediatric resident staff. In fact, he was a favorite of the entire resident staff in the hospital. Unlike a few of our surgical types, he was not in the least bit pretentious. He treated us almost as peers or even friends. Maybe that's why we always sought him out when we needed help.

He had an amazing knack, that of seeming to always know when you were getting into trouble. Or at least when you and your patient were headed to some difficult moment. And then somehow he would be there, standing behind you, ready to help. I know that was true for me. It had happened over and over again. It was uncanny, but here he was once more.

I turned to face him. "Bill, I've got this two-week old, and—well—you see her X-ray."

He stepped a little closer to the view box and adjusted his bifocals. "Yep, I see what's going on," he said, nodding his head. "She's going to need a chest tube, isn't she?"

He didn't wait for a response but called out to one of the nurses standing nearby. "We'll need a chest-tube tray and portable X-ray on the way."

Then he turned to me and said, "How many of these have you done, Robert? How many in a child this small?"

"Two, maybe three," I told him. Fortunately, we didn't have to do many of these.

"Good," he told me. "This will be your fourth."

For some reason, I had thought he might want to do this procedure. While I was still a little nervous, I was glad to hear him say this.

"Get scrubbed up and we'll get going," he added.

Bill Bowman stood at my right shoulder the entire time, not saying a word until I had made a small incision in Carolyn's chest wall and was about to insert a tiny clear tube through the opening.

"Use your blunt hemostats," he told me. "Don't use the blade anymore. You might damage the nerve or blood vessels. The hemostat is safer."

He was right, of course. I always used a hemostat at this part of the procedure with an adult. I hadn't been thinking.

"Thanks, Bill," I said over my shoulder.

"I knew you were going to use it. I was just reminding you." I could hear the smile in his voice.

Carolyn did well with the chest tube in place. Her color improved and the amount of oxygen in her blood became normal. That was the last crisis for her. Four months later she would be going home.

After we had finished and the tube was taped in place, I reached for a nearby phone and called my sleeping third-year resident. She needed to know what was going on.

I gave her my report, waited for a confirmatory grunt, and hung up the receiver. Then I turned around. Bill Bowman was gone.

Saturday afternoon, two years later. It was a busy shift in the ER. A steady rain had been falling for more than a day, and we were taking care of a bunch of auto accidents. People in the South can't drive on slick roads. And you'd better gird your loins if there was any snow on the ground. Sometimes just the forecast of snow was enough to do it.

Some of these were just routine fender benders, but some were serious. We had already sent four badly injured patients to the operating room.

We were working our way through the most recent accident victims, when the EMS radio demanded our attention.

"General, this is Medic 2," one of the paramedics on board informed us.

The charge nurse was standing near the radio and she picked up the receiver. "Go ahead, Medic 2, this is the General."

I was finishing up a chart and heard this transmission. *Here we go again—another auto accident. Will it ever stop raining?*

It wasn't the rain.

"General, we've got an eight-year-old girl—respiratory arrest."

Everyone nearby stopped what they were doing and stared at the EMS radio, waiting.

"We're still at the scene," the paramedic continued, speaking excitedly and a little out of breath. "About five minutes away. It's a birthday party at a private residence, and this girl…she was eatin' some candy and aspirated it. When we got here, her parents were doing CPR and they had tried the Heimlich, but nothing was working."

There was the sound of several people talking excitedly in the background. The paramedic said something unintelligible to them. Then he was back on the radio.

"We repeated the Heimlich…but nothing. Tried to fish out the candy but…I…I think I just pushed it further down her windpipe. She's still got a pulse of about 100 and we're trying to bag her. But we're not moving much air. Anything further?"

The charge nurse glanced up at me. I shook my head and said, "Tell him to get here as fast as they can."

She repeated this to the paramedic.

"Loading right now. Be there in four to five." And the radio went silent.

I turned again to the nurse and said, "We need to get trauma set up for an emergency trach. And find out who's on call for surgery and get them down here."

This was a long time to be without oxygen, but maybe they had been able to get some air past the piece of candy. The fact that she still had a good pulse was encouraging. But we wouldn't have much time. She needed her airway opened, and it sounded like the only way to do this was an emergency tracheotomy. I would need to make an incision just below her Adam's apple and insert a tube into her trachea, hopefully below the lodged piece of candy. If the candy was below that, if it had been sucked or pushed even further down…

I wasn't going to think about that just yet. My pulse had already quickened as I hastily walked toward trauma. The charge nurse was ahead of me. She would be opening the tracheotomy tray and getting it ready. This would be a straightforward procedure and I knew what

I needed to do—but I had only helped in three of these. And those had been different. Each of those cases had been adults, and each had involved major blunt trauma to the face and chest. One I had done myself, with a surgeon standing at my elbow. It was another one of those things we just didn't do very often.

"Any word from the surgery resident?" I spoke into the intercom on the wall by the door.

"He's scrubbed in on an appendectomy," the secretary responded. "Says he'll be down in twenty minutes."

That would be too late.

I heard the ambulance doors open and a stretcher being rapidly wheeled down the hallway. I took a deep breath, and there she was.

The paramedic and his partner quickly transferred her to our trauma stretcher.

"Didn't have time for an IV," he said, his face covered with sweat. "Still not moving much air, but she's got a good pulse."

I was quickly examining the young girl as he said this. Her color was bad, but as I listened to her chest while the paramedic bagged her, I could hear the faintest of breath sounds. Or maybe I was imagining it. Her chest wasn't moving with his attempts.

Then I took a look at her airway with a laryngoscope—and there it was. I could see a shiny, red, wet piece of candy just at her vocal cords. It was too far down to be able to grab with any instrument. Her color had gotten even worse in the past minute. She would need a trach, and right now.

After I positioned her head and neck, the nurse handed me a pair of sterile gloves and I hurriedly put them on. Then I reached for some sterile gauze, soaked it in Betadine, and prepped the front of her neck. With the long finger of my left hand locating the notch just above her sternum, I held out my right hand for the scalpel.

As the nurse placed the blade in my hand, I heard a voice behind me.

"Whatcha got, Robert?"

It was Bill Bowman. How had he gotten here? How had he known what was going on?

Before I could answer, he said, "Just a little higher, toward her head. About a centimeter."

I followed his instructions, adjusting the position of the scalpel.

"Good, that's fine," he calmly said. "Go ahead."

I made a quick and steady incision and then reached for a blunt instrument to separate the tissues covering her trachea.

"There, that's where you want to go," he said, indicating the membrane between two cartilage rings.

And we were done. The trach tube slipped easily into her windpipe and we began to bag her. Bill and I watched as her chest wall moved easily up and down. Her color quickly began to improve. Within a few minutes, she was starting to take a few breaths of her own. And then she was purposely reaching up to her neck. Everyone in the room was relieved.

This time when I turned around, Bill Bowman was still standing behind me.

"Thanks, Bill," I told him. "I'm glad you happened by."

I knew that wasn't true. It was no coincidence he was here. I didn't know how, but when I needed him, when I *really* needed him, he would somehow be there, standing beside me.

"Hey, you didn't need me, Robert. You did fine."

Then he turned and walked out of the room.

God is our refuge and strength,
an ever-present help in trouble.
Therefore we will not fear, though the earth give way
and the mountains fall into the heart of the sea,
though its waters roar and foam
and the mountains quake with their surging.

PSALM 46:1-3

12

I'm Only Doing My Job

Honor and shame from no condition rise;
Act well your part: there all the honor lies.

Alexander Pope (1688–1744)

It was the middle of the afternoon. Jack had come to the ER with me today, and we had just returned to the department from lunch. Things were caught up, and we sat down behind the nurses' station with Amy Connors.

"Dad, I've been noticing something," Jack said to me. "It seems that not too many people appreciate what all of you do around here. I mean…I don't hear too many people thanking you, or anything."

That was an interesting observation. He was right, of course. I guess it was the nature of the beast. People don't come to the ER because it's something they want to do. They're usually in pain, or worried about something, or with a loved one and worried about them, or they're unconscious. Or maybe they're inebriated. It doesn't really matter, though. Our job is to take care of them. And yet…

"Well," I answered. "You're right, I suppose. But, maybe every once in a while someone thanks us."

"Yeah," Amy injected cynically. "It was *once*, and it was a while ago."

Jack chuckled, and was about to say something when Pat Jackson walked up and said, "Well, what about Sadie Abernathy?"

Jack turned around in his chair to face Pat. She was thirty and had been working in the emergency department for the past six years. Pat worked mainly during the day, and was a solid ER nurse. She was quiet, unassuming, and steady. And she was always there. If you needed some help, or some equipment, Pat was standing right behind you. It was an invaluable skill and much appreciated.

"You're right, Pat," Amy said. "I guess I forgot about Sadie."

"You remember Pat, don't you?" I asked Jack.

"Sure, Ms. Jackson," he answered, standing. "It's good to see you. What's this about a Sadie Abernathy?"

"Well, that's an interesting story," Amy started. "You'd better have a seat for this one."

"Oh Amy, don't go telling *that* part again," Pat pleaded, blushing.

"You're doggone right I'm gonna tell it," Amy continued. "It's how Pat got her name—'Action Jackson,'" she said to Jack.

He looked at Pat Jackson, surprised by this revelation. He knew her to be anything but loud and intrusive. Certainly nothing that nickname would imply.

"Yes sir, Jack, this is the *real* Action Jackson," Amy said, leaning back in her chair. "And it all happened about a year and a half ago, around Thanksgiving."

Pat Jackson was doing her weekly shopping at her local grocery, picking up some odds and ends for the family's Thanksgiving meal. She was pushing her cart down the canned goods aisle when she noticed an elderly woman coming toward her. It turned out to be Sadie Abernathy, a seventy-year-old lady who Pat saw on occasion in the store. They were about thirty feet from each other when Sadie looked up and saw Pat. Sadie waved and then started pushing her grocery cart again, studying the confusing array of cans on the shelves beside her.

Suddenly she stood up straight, and with wide-opened eyes, stared at Pat. Then she clutched her chest and collapsed on the tiled floor. Pat says she will always remember the sound Sadie made as she fell. There was a gasp, and then an awful thump. And then there was a terrible grunt as the air was knocked out of her. The grocery cart careened down the aisle, veering to one side and knocking a bunch of cans to the floor, making a clattering racket.

Pat jumped around her cart and ran the short distance down the aisle. Sadie wasn't breathing, and when Pat checked for a pulse, she couldn't find one.

She looked around for some help and saw a teenage stock-boy standing at the end of the aisle, staring. He was carrying a case of soda, and when Pat yelled at him to call 9-1-1, he dropped it and ran.

"Sadie!" Pat shouted at the woman. There was no response.

She positioned Sadie flat on her back and struck her on the middle of her chest. Then she began chest compressions and mouth-to-mouth ventilations. She knew what to do.

The store manager appeared seconds later, and said, "We've called EMS, and they're on the way. Do you need any help?"

"I could use some help with these compressions," she told him, flushed and beginning to sweat from the effort.

"I...I..." he stammered, shuffling his feet.

"Never mind," Pat said. "Just try to keep these people back. Give us some room."

By this time, a dozen shoppers had gathered around, curious as to what was going on.

This was something the manager could do, and he quickly took charge.

"Everybody step back here," he directed them with his arms waving. "Give us some space."

Pat continued CPR for another five or six minutes, until the paramedics of Medic One arrived. They recognized her immediately and quickly relieved her, continuing the CPR. Pat leaned back on her heels and said, "We need to see what kind of rhythm she's in," she instructed them. "Let's take a quick look with those defibrillator paddles."

One of the paramedics quickly pressed the paddles against Sadie's chest and Pat studied the monitor. There was only chaotic electrical activity—nothing purposeful.

"Charge it up to 200," Pat directed. "And hand me those paddles."

The paramedic complied with her orders, pressing a button on the defibrillator and then handing the paddles to Pat. There was a faint buzzing sound as the machine responded, followed by a beeping, indicating it was ready to fire. Pat made sure the paddles were adequately lubricated and then said, "All clear!"

Everybody around Sadie moved back just a little, making sure they weren't in contact with her body. Then Pat pressed the paddles against Sadie's chest, glanced once more at the monitor, and fired the defibrillator.

There was a mechanical "thumb" as the electrical current passed through Sadie's chest and heart, and her body jerked uncontrollably.

"Just like on TV," someone whispered from behind Pat.

She continued to watch the monitor. The shock had caused all electrical activity in the heart to stop, and then, there it was. First a single complex, and then another, and another. Her heartbeat was speeding up, and looked reasonably normal.

"We've got a pulse!" one of the paramedics announced, his hand now on Sadie's neck.

Pat reached down and checked Sadie's femoral artery to confirm that her heart was pumping adequately. The pulse was faint, but it was there.

"We need to get her intubated," she told the paramedics. "And give me an angiocath. I'll get a line started."

She started the IV effortlessly, and continued to direct the code, ordering emergency medications and making sure Sadie was being properly ventilated.

"She's trying to breathe," one of the paramedics said.

And there it was. This elderly woman was dead a few moments ago, and now she was breathing and her heart was beating. A couple of people standing behind the store manager actually clapped.

I was in the ER when Sadie was brought in by the paramedics. She was still confused, but was relatively stable, considering what had happened to her. She was admitted to the CCU, where she stayed for five days. She continued to improve, and miraculously had a complete neurologic recovery. It was a real success story.

When she was discharged from the hospital, she insisted on being brought through the emergency department.

She was rolled up to the nurses' station in her wheelchair, and asked, "Is Pat Jackson working today?"

Pat was in triage, and Amy called her on the intercom. She came out and walked over to Sadie and they hugged. And Sadie thanked her for saving her life. Pat had blushed and patted her on the arm.

"I'm just glad I was there and that I could help," she told Sadie.

"And I'm glad you were too, honey," Sadie said. Then she left the hospital and went home.

"That's when we started calling her 'Action Jackson,'" Amy told Jack. "Just like in the movies."

Pat just shook her head, and smiled. She was still blushing.

"And tell him the rest of it," Amy told her. "Tell him the best part."

"Oh Amy, that's enough," Pat said.

"What else happened?" Jack asked her.

"Go on, Pat," Amy chided. "Tell him what happened."

"Well, Jack," Pat explained. "I was kneeling on the floor of that grocery store, doing chest compressions and trying to keep track of ventilations and everything. It wasn't easy, with no help and all."

She paused, and Jack leaned closer.

"And while I was doing that, I felt a tap on my shoulder. Just a light tap, nothing hard. I thought someone had come up to help me. Well, I turned around and there was this woman standing behind me. She was leaning over, and when I looked up at her, she cupped her hand to my ear and said, 'Would you mind handing me a jar of mayonnaise?' And then she pointed to the shelf beside me."

Jack's mouth dropped open. That was crazy, but then this was Pat Jackson, and he knew she must be telling the truth.

"What did you do?" he asked her.

"Well, I just reached down and grabbed a jar of Duke's, handed it to her, and just kept on doing CPR. Barely missed a beat."

"Like I said," Amy declared. "Action Jackson."

Later on that afternoon, Jack picked up the same conversation. We were alone, and he asked, "Does it ever bother you that not many people act thankful for what you guys do? I mean, there's Sadie Abernathy and all, but that must not be very common. Seems like most people just take it all for granted."

I thought about this for a moment.

"You know, Jack, it probably did bother me some at first. There might have been a couple of times, maybe when I just finished my residency and had started working here in Rock Hill," I answered him.

And then I thought about Andy Pettigrew, and that hot summer day fifteen years earlier.

❦

Thursday, 3:15 p.m. "Dr. Lesslie, it's for you," the unit secretary said, handing me the receiver. "Dr. Blevins in Fort Mill. He sounds sort of upset."

I wondered what this was going to be. Dr. Blevins was an older family practitioner in a town six or seven miles away. He usually had a few people in the Rock Hill hospital, and I had gotten to know him when he came through the ER on his way to make his rounds. He was a nice guy, and his patients seemed to really like him.

Reaching over the counter, I took the phone.

"Dr. Blevins, this is Robert Lesslie," I told him.

"Robert, listen…I need your help here." He did sound upset, and out of breath.

"Sure, what—" I began to respond.

"I've got a man here in the office," he interrupted, "Andy Pettigrew, and it looks like he's having a heart attack."

I didn't say anything, and waited for him to go on.

"He's forty-two I think, maybe forty-three, and he walked into the office just a few minutes ago, complaining of weakness."

He paused, and I heard him make some unintelligible comments to someone in the background.

"Excuse me," he continued. "I just told the staff to call 9-1-1 again and to start some oxygen. Anyway, Andy came in with this weakness, and he looked terrible. He was pale, and confused, and…Well, my nurse got him in an exam room and took his blood pressure. The first one was 60 over 40, but it's gotten lower since then. And his heart rate is pretty slow, only about 55 beats a minute."

That was a dangerous blood pressure, and a dangerous heart rate. I wondered what he had done for this man. And then I wondered what he would be able to do in his office. It was a good thing he had called 9-1-1. Andy Pettigrew was going to need some help, and quickly.

"What's his pressure now?" I asked him.

"We've…we've still got a pulse, but no…blood pressure. At least I can't hear one. But he's still responding a little, and he's breathing."

"How far away is EMS?" I asked.

"They're just down the street," Dr. Blevins told me. "And…wait, I think that's them coming in the front door."

There were some muffled sounds in the background, and I heard him direct someone to the "front exam room." Then he was back on the phone.

"Good, the ambulance is here," he said with relief. "They'll be bringing him to the hospital and I was hoping you could look at him in the ER until someone from internal associates can get over there. I'll give them a call right now."

"Sure, I'll be happy to see him," I answered, my pulse quickening a little. This would be a challenge. We had some good internal-medicine specialists in town, but at that time no cardiologists. And in the four or five months I had been in the ER, I didn't know of anyone putting in a pacemaker on an emergency basis, which is what it sounded like Andy Pettigrew was going to need. "We'll be looking for him."

Dr. Blevins hung up, and I handed the phone to the secretary. We had about ten minutes to get ready.

"Sarah," I said to the charge nurse. "Do we keep a pacemaker tray in the ER?"

She stopped in the hallway and gave me a puzzled look. Then she put her finger to her lips, thought a moment, and nodded her head.

"Yes, we keep one locked up in the medicine room. Do you think you're going to need it?" she asked me.

"It sounds like it," I answered. "How about getting it out and meeting me in the cardiac room."

As she turned in the direction of the medicine room, the EMS radio squawked loudly, demanding our attention.

"Rock Hill ER, this is medic 3."

The paramedic responding to Dr. Blevins's office gave me the current condition of Andy Pettigrew. He had a pulse but no blood pressure. He was breathing on his own, but confused and barely responsive. And the EKG that Dr. Blevins's nurse had been able to get in the office showed what looked like an acute heart attack.

"It looks like a big one, Dr. Lesslie," the paramedic told me. "His S-T segments are sky-high, but his rhythm is still nice and regular. Slow, though. About 50. O_2 going and a line of normal saline. He hasn't responded to two doses of atropine. Anything else you want us to do? We'll be there in three minutes."

They were doing all the right things, and were almost to the ER.

"No, just bring him on in," I instructed him. "Let me know if something changes."

"10-4," and the radio went silent.

I walked across the hallway to the cardiac room, where Sarah was preparing the pacemaker tray.

"Have you ever done one of these?" she asked me. The question was sincere, almost helpful, and I wasn't bothered by it. Looking back now, I should have been bothered by the fact that I had only put in a half-dozen or so of these.

But that didn't matter. It sounded like Andy Pettigrew was having a major heart attack and wasn't responding to IV medications. If he was going to survive this, he would need an emergency pacemaker. And that would be me, along with Sarah's help.

"Sure," I answered her, mustering as much confidence as I could. "How about you? Have you helped with these?"

"I've helped the surgeons put these in upstairs," she answered. "But that's always been on an elective basis. Never something like this… when it's an emergency."

She studied my face for a response and drew the correct conclusion. "But we'll get this done, Dr. Lesslie. I'll be right here."

I glanced down at the tray, relieved to see familiar equipment and supplies. The pacemaker itself was one of the ones we used in Charlotte during my training.

My relief didn't last very long. I heard the ambulance doors open and the clatter of a stretcher being quickly wheeled down the hallway.

"Cardiac room!" the secretary called out.

Seconds later, Andy Pettigrew was being transferred to our cardiac bed. The paramedics gave me his latest status.

"No BP, but he's still got a regular rhythm. Slower now, though. About 40."

Andy Pettigrew looked awful. His color was dusky, almost blue. And he didn't respond when I loudly called out his name.

Sarah quickly had him on our monitor and was hooking him up for an EKG. I watched it come off the printer, and immediately turned to the pacemaker tray, pulling it near the head of the stretcher.

He was having a bad heart attack, and his EKG indicated a potentially large amount of muscle loss. His slow pulse and low blood pressure indicated a lot of damage. Andy Pettigrew was lucky to be alive.

Sarah handed me a pair of sterile gloves, and started to put some on herself.

I felt Andy's neck for the needed landmarks. He was a big man, with a short, thick neck, and it was difficult finding anything I was comfortable with. I decided to insert my needle below his right clavicle, and then thread the pacemaker through that catheter.

Sarah stood at my side, and uttered, "Good," as blood flashed back into the syringe. I was in the major vessel, and now all I needed to do was pass the pacemaker wire through that vessel and into the right side of Andy's heart. At the tip of the wire was an electrode, and if we were successful in placing it against his heart muscle, we would be able to send a current down it, stimulating his heart, and speeding up his heart rate. If everything went well, that would improve his blood pressure and the amount of blood flowing into his coronary vessels. And it would give him a chance, the only one he had.

Sarah handed me the wire, and I threaded it through the catheter, which was now protruding from below his collarbone. I noted the markings on the side of the wire, and estimated the distance it would need to be advanced before coming in contact with his ventricle. Several things could go wrong. It could coil around on itself and go nowhere. Or it could turn and go up one of the large veins in his neck. Or it could perforate a weak area of his heart and kill him. None of those things were going to happen—I hoped.

Sarah picked up the control box and made some adjustments. She set the amount of current to a medium range, knowing that we would back down to the least amount needed. And she would be prepared to set the rate of stimulation when I gave her the go-ahead.

She stood there, and waited.

I didn't feel any resistance or unusual sensations as I advanced the pacemaker wire. When it was at the depth I wanted, I stopped, looked at Sarah, and took a deep breath. It was then I noticed that the two paramedics had not left the room, but were intently watching all of this.

"Start with 70?" Sarah asked me.

I glanced over at the cardiac monitor. His rate was now 35, and he still didn't have a pulse.

"70 is good," I told her. My eyes remained fastened on the monitor.

Sarah turned the dial of the pacemaker control to a rate of 70, and we waited.

Immediately, we could see the tall, slender pacemaker spike on the monitor. The pacer was working, and its electrical current was being picked up on our monitor. But there was no capture. His heart muscle was not responding. We should be seeing a complex on the monitor, one with every blip of the pacemaker. That would indicate the pacer was working, and his heart muscle was responding with a purposeful contraction.

I waited for a few more seconds. Still nothing. Then I advanced the wire two more centimeters. And there it was! There was the spike of the pacemaker, and immediately after that was a bizarre-appearing electrical complex at a rate of 70 beats a minute, indicating that we had capture and that the tip of the pacemaker was against his heart muscle.

Now, if only…

"We've got a pulse!" one of the paramedics excitedly reported, having placed his fingers over one of Andy's femoral arteries.

And in less than a minute, we had a blood pressure. It wasn't great, only 90 over 60, but it was getting blood to his brain, and he was starting to come around.

After another fifteen minutes, one of the doctors from internal associates came into the cardiac room. His eyes widened when he realized what was going on.

I told him about Andy, and what we had done. And I was glad to turn the case over to him.

"Thanks, Sarah," I whispered as I passed by her on the way out of cardiac.

Two days later, I decided to go up to the CCU and check on Andy. We had heard he was doing much better, and was stable, at least as stable as he could be, considering everything.

I walked into the unit and searched the patient board for his name. He was in bed 2, and I headed over, pulling the curtain aside and stepping into the cubicle.

Andy Pettigrew was sitting up in bed, watching a small television suspended from the wall in front of him. There were IVs in both arms and oxygen tubing attached to his nose. Various monitors were beeping regularly, and reassuringly.

He looked up as I entered.

"Andy," I said to him. "I'm Dr. Lesslie."

A puzzled look clouded his face, and he said, "Doctor who?"

Then I realized he had no idea who I was, or why I was in his room. He had been unconscious the entire time he was in the ER.

"I…I just came by to check on you," I stammered. "Glad you're doing well."

I turned around and grabbed the curtain, closing it behind me as I left.

"Thanks for coming by," he called to my back. Then I heard him change the channel of his television.

⌘

Saturday morning, Walmart. "Dr. Lesslie?"

The voice was coming from behind me. I was in the sporting goods department, looking for some golf tees and a soccer ball, and I was a little surprised that someone was calling my name. I turned around to see who it might be.

A few feet away stood a smiling, middle-aged woman. At her side was a teenage boy. He was tall and muscular, and he was intently studying my face. I assumed he was her son.

"Dr. Lesslie," she repeated. "I'm sure you don't remember me, but I'm Mabel Strong. And this is my boy, Samuel."

He nodded his head at me, and continued his staring. It was a little unnerving.

"Good morning, Mrs. Strong," I replied. "I—"

"Like I said," she interrupted. "I'm sure you don't remember—it's been a lot of years—maybe fourteen or fifteen. But I saw you standing over here and I just wanted to come over and thank you. And I wanted Samuel to meet you."

She nudged him gently with her elbow, and he said, "Nice to meet you, Dr. Lesslie."

I'm terrible at remembering names, but pretty good with faces.

Yet, I couldn't place either of them. Mabel Strong apparently read my thoughts, and tried to put me at ease.

"I know you see a lot of people in the ER," she explained. "And I know it's impossible to remember everyone you take care of, but I just wanted to thank you for what you did for Samuel here. He was about three years old, and we came to the ER early on a Sunday morning, around six o'clock, I think. He had bad asthma back then, and was wheezing up a storm. We had no sooner walked back into the ER when he collapsed on the floor."

Suddenly I remembered. How could I forget?

"Dr. Lesslie! Come quick! We need you right now!"

I had been dozing in the ENT chair, catching a few winks before the end of the shift. Debbie Latcher was the nurse on duty, and she had burst into the ENT room, startling me to sudden alertness.

She didn't say anything else, but turned and ran down the hall toward the nurses' station. I followed her as quickly as I could.

Standing in front of the counter was a young woman. She was obviously distraught, holding her head in her hands and staring at the lifeless body of a young boy lying crumpled at her feet.

"Please do something…" she cried.

Debbie knelt beside the child, checking for a pulse and any sign of life. There was none.

When I reached the boy, I snatched him up and headed into the cardiac room. Debbie was right behind me, and as we entered the room, she immediately reached for our airway tray.

I laid the child on his back and positioned his head to allow for the best air exchange. Debbie handed me an ambu bag and with one hand I pressed the mask to his face, covering his mouth and nose. With the other hand, I began squeezing the bag, forcing air into his lungs. His chest was rising and falling with my bagging, and I was satisfied that we were getting oxygen into him.

"We'll need to tube him as soon as we can," I told Debbie.

She reached for an endotracheal tube and a special light. It had a straight blade on it that would allow me to visualize his vocal cords. I would then be able to pass the tube through the cords and into his trachea, giving us a secure way to ventilate him.

Debbie checked the light and held it out to me. This was the moment of truth. I would have to stop bagging him while I attempted my intubation. I couldn't take much time, since he wouldn't be getting any air while I did this. I only had a few seconds.

I put the bag down by his side and took the light in my left hand. Placing it into his mouth, I moved his tongue out of the way and searched for his vocal cords.

There they were!

"Tube," I said to her, holding out my hand while not taking my eyes from these important landmarks.

Debbie placed the endotracheal tube in my hand and I easily passed it into his trachea. I immediately attached the end of the tube to the ambu bag and began inflating his chest. Debbie listened to each side of his chest with her stethoscope and said, "Breath sounds are equal. He's still tight, though."

The underlying problem of his asthma hadn't gone away, but now we would be able to make sure he was getting oxygen. And we would be able to deliver medication directly into his lungs, dilating his constricted airways. He must have worn himself out trying to breathe, and that's what had caused him to collapse. I was thankful this hadn't happened at home or in their car.

Debbie attached him to the cardiac monitor and I continued to bag him. His heart was young and healthy, and once we were able to breathe for him, it quickly sprang back into action.

"Heart rate is 120," she told me. That was good, and a good sign that he hadn't been without oxygen for very long. Now we only had to worry about his brain. But it would take a while before we would know about that. Maybe days.

"I'll get an IV started," Debbie told me. "And I'll call respiratory care."

It was then that I noticed the woman standing behind Debbie. It was the boy's mother, and she had pressed herself against the wall, the knuckles of both hands held tightly to her mouth.

I got Debbie's attention with my eyes, and motioned with my head toward the young woman. Debbie turned and immediately walked over to her, placing her arm around the woman's shoulders.

"Your boy's going to be alright," she assured her. "You can stay here if you want, or we can take you to the family room, if you'd be more comfortable."

"I'll stay," she sobbed, not moving.

"That'll be fine," I told her. "Debbie, why don't you pull that stool over here beside the stretcher, so she can sit down."

The boy was beginning to move his legs now, and was trying to reach up to his face and the tube now taped to his cheek.

"It looks like he's doing better," I said. "But he's still very sick, and will need to be admitted to the hospital. I'll need to know if he has a pediatrician or a family doctor?"

We made the necessary arrangements for him to be admitted to the ICU, and an hour after his collapse, he was stable and on his way upstairs. It had all happened so fast.

I didn't see him after that, but Debbie told me two days later that he was up and talking, and doing well.

How could I forget that?

"I remember that morning," I told Mrs. Strong. Then she told me that Samuel was a straight-A student and captain of the basketball team. And he was planning on going to Wofford in the fall.

"We're real proud of him," she said.

I had been looking at Samuel and thinking of what might not have been. Yet here he stood, strong and healthy, and very much alive. At that moment, I was humbled, and truly thankful to have had a part in what happened fifteen years ago. Then I glanced at his mother and there were tears in her eyes. She was looking up at me and thinking the same thing.

A moment ago, she and her boy had been complete strangers to me. And now, there was a bond, a special connection—something that words were not meant to describe.

"Mrs. Strong…" I said, my voice breaking.

"You don't have to say anything, Dr. Lesslie," she told me, smiling. "Anyway, I didn't think I'd ever get the chance to thank you for that morning," she said again. "And when I saw you, I just had to come over."

Without prompting, Samuel held out his hand.

"And I want to thank you too, Dr. Lesslie," he said.

I took his hand in mine and looked into his eyes. There was a genuine warmth there, and a deep and peaceful self-assuredness, unusual for someone his age. And his handshake was solid and firm.

"Take care of yourself, Samuel," I said to him. Then to his mother, "Thank you."

They turned and walked away.

I watched them as they reached the end of the aisle, turned, and disappeared from my sight.

And I tried to remember what I was looking for.

Blessed is he who has found his work;
let him ask no other blessedness.

THOMAS CARLYLE: *PAST AND PRESENT,* BOOK III

13

My Will Be Done

*There's none so blind
as they that won't see.*

JONATHAN SWIFT (1667-1745), "POLITE CONVERSATION"

Thursday, 2:15 p.m. The CBC report I had in my hand was the only thing that had come back on Andy Meadows. The rest of his labs would take another hour or so, but this would probably be enough. It confirmed my suspicions about what was going on here, and what I needed to do.

Andy was a fifty-three-year-old stockbroker. I had known him for more than fifteen years, and Barbara and I had occasionally run into him and his wife Joy on social occasions. He was a funny, friendly guy, and had the well-earned reputation of being a shrewd and capable broker and financial advisor. And he had always taken care of himself physically. He swam every day at the Y, and frequently played golf and tennis.

But something was changing with Andy. And that *something* was what brought him to the ER. Or maybe it was the insistence of his wife, Joy. She was sitting in the corner of room 5 when I pulled the curtain aside and stepped in.

Andy was sitting on the stretcher, watching his crossed ankles as they dangled below him. They both looked up as I entered.

"Okay, Doc, can I go home now?" he asked me impatiently.

"Soon, Andy," I answered. "Pretty soon."

I sat down on the other stool in the room and put his chart on my lap.

"Let's start at the beginning again," I said to both of them. "I want to be sure I understand what's going on."

I waited for one of them to say something, and it was Joy who spoke first.

"Robert, I've noticed lately that Andy has been stumbling some. He seems to be having trouble—"

"I told you I'm not doing any stumbling," he quickly interrupted her. "And I told you I don't know why I'm here. This is all your idea!"

His exasperation was apparent, and he sat there silently shaking his head. Then he said, "I bumped my shin on the coffee table the other night, and I've got some bruises on my arms from playing tennis the other day. That's all."

"Andy, you haven't played tennis in months," Joy said, almost pleading with him. "And you haven't been doing your swimming either. You've just been—"

"Don't tell me what I've been doing!" he snapped at her. "Stop putting words in my mouth and making stuff up!" This surprised Joy, and she shrank back into the corner of the room. And it surprised me.

"Andy, listen," I said, trying to calm him. "We're just trying to help you here, that's all. I'm just trying to figure out if anything serious is going on."

Something serious *was* going on. I had known it when they walked into the department. He hadn't seen me behind the nurses' station, and I had been able to watch him closely as the triage nurse led them over to room 5.

The first thing I noticed was that he looked much older than the last time I had seen him. It must have been only a few months, but he seemed stooped over and tired. And there was the way he walked. It was more of a shuffle than a walk, with his feet wide apart. "Broadbased" was the medical term. And then there were the bruises on his forearms. They were large and ugly, and multicolored, indicating this had been going on for several weeks. This was hardly the healthy and robust Andy Meadows that I knew.

When the triage nurse handed me his chart, the area for the chief complaint simply read "unsteady." That didn't narrow things down very much.

My initial exam and questioning had thrown up some red flags. But I needed to see some lab work, and we had gotten some things started. Now I was sitting in the room with them again, trying to figure out how best to handle what I was about to say.

I glanced down again at the CBC report lying on the top of his chart. It gave me a lot of information about the status of his white cells, red cells, and platelets. It was the detailed analysis of his red blood cells that caught my attention. His white cells were normal, and his platelets were borderline, but he had a mild anemia. And most significantly, his red cells were abnormally large, and they were pale. This was the kind of anemia we see with a chronic alcoholic. And it fit the picture I was seeing of Andy Meadows. As an alcoholic turns more and more to a "liquid" diet, his nutrition suffers, and he develops significant dietary deficiencies, especially of some critical vitamins. The lack of these, in combination with the toxic effects of the alcohol itself, would be causing his anemia. This combination will affect his brain, especially the cerebellum, which controls his coordination. The fact that he had these advanced findings was very troubling and needed to be addressed. Sometimes the damage to the brain could be reversed, but the longer it went on, the greater the chance the changes would be permanent.

I wasn't sure how Andy was going to handle this, but it needed to be done. This was one of the times I wished I was dealing with a complete stranger. It would be easier.

"Andy," I began, looking up at him. "How much are you drinking?"

The question must have surprised him, because he sat bolt upright. "How much am I...What are you trying to say, Robert?"

"Andy, I'm concerned about what I'm seeing here. You *are* having some trouble walking, and your initial lab work indicates that it could be from too much alcohol. I need to know how much you're drinking, and whether it's on a daily basis."

He glared at me, and I noticed for the first time the ruddiness of his cheeks. It was all coming together. Sometimes the obvious *does* escape us.

"I don't know what that has to do with anything…but…if you're going to ask me, well…I might have a glass of wine with my evening meal sometimes. But nothing excessive. Not every day, if that's what you're getting at."

"But Andy," Joy interrupted. "That's just not—"

"Just not what?" he snapped at her. "Listen, Joy, I'll answer Robert's questions. Don't you say another word!"

I glanced at her, embarrassed by this outburst. Something made me look down at her left arm, and I could clearly see the bruised imprint of a hand. It had been the grip of a strong individual, and nothing that would have happened by accident. She followed my eyes and looked down at her arm. Then she quickly folded her arms across her chest, hiding these bruises. She looked away and became silent.

This was an explosive situation, and it needed to be handled carefully.

"Andy, I know you're drinking more than that," I told him honestly. "And you know that too. The first thing here is to get an idea of where we are, and then get you some help. This is starting to take a toll on your health, and on…other things." I glanced over at Joy.

"Robert, I appreciate your trying to help," he said, suddenly becoming calm and uncomfortably solicitous. "And I know you have the best of intentions, but really, there's not a problem here. Maybe a glass of wine in the evenings, but nothing heavy. Believe me, I know about that. My father was an alcoholic, and I know what to watch out for."

Another red flag. "Andy, listen," I said, but he wasn't paying any attention.

"I think it's time that Joy and I head home, unless you're going to give me some medicine or something. And maybe you can just call us when the rest of the labs are back. Otherwise, I think that's about it."

He was firm in his resolve, and I realized he had closed this door and locked it.

"Andy, do you mind if I talk with Joy for a minute, just the two of us?" I asked him.

His eyes narrowed briefly, and he glanced over at his wife. Then he said, "Sure, I don't have anything to hide. But don't take too long. I know you're busy, and I really need to get home and check on a few things."

I stood up and motioned to Joy. "Why don't we step out in the hall and talk for a minute." She got up and followed me out into the hallway and then into an empty room 3. I pulled the curtain closed behind us, and pointed to the chair in the corner.

"Have a seat for a minute, Joy, and let's talk about this."

She sat down, and her hands dropped into her lap, once again revealing the bruises on her arms. And then she began telling me an all-too-familiar story.

Andy had always been a casual drinker, maybe a couple of beers on the weekend, or a glass of wine when they were out at a restaurant. But alcohol had never been a problem for him. Joy knew that his father had been an alcoholic, and that Andy seemed to always be afraid that he might follow that terrible path. But he hadn't, not until about a year ago.

Something had begun to change, and Joy couldn't remember what might have caused it. His work was going well and the kids were doing great. Their marriage was solid, and their passage into mid-life seemed to be going along smoothly. He was active in their church, and even taught Sunday school on a regular basis.

"Then one day, Robert, it was as if I didn't know him. At first, I would catch him drinking out on the porch, I guess trying to hide it from me. But when I found out and asked him about it, he just started drinking right in front of me. And when he told you he was having one glass of wine in the evening…"

"I know, Joy," I said. "It's obviously much more than that. This has been going on for a while, and his body is really taking a beating. This shuffling gait of his is something we see with people way down the road with this disease. I'm really worried about him. If he doesn't stop, this will kill him," I spoke as bluntly and as honestly as I could.

"I've tried, Robert, really I have," Joy sighed. "We all have. Even the boys have tried to talk with him, but he just denies that he has a problem. And then he gets mad."

She unconsciously began rubbing the bruises on her arm as she said this.

"I even asked our minister to speak with him," she continued, shaking her head. "You can imagine how that went. Andy almost physically threw him out of the house, and he hasn't been back in church since. Says they're a bunch of hypocrites and they need to get their houses in order before they go preaching to someone else."

She paused and slumped forward on the stool. "I just don't know what to do."

I didn't either. It was one thing to advise people to stop drinking, or stop doing anything that was self-destructive, and an entirely different thing to help them find some effective way to do it. Especially when they denied the problem in the first place.

But now I was worried about Joy, and I reached over and touched the bruises on her arm. "Tell me about this," I asked her.

She looked down at her arm and blushed. "He didn't mean to do this, Robert. It was just that…"

"Joy, I've seen a lot of this kind of thing," I said to her. "Too much. And I know this wasn't the first time. And I'm concerned it won't be the last. You don't have to live like this. Do you want me to confront Andy about it, or have the police get involved? This is serious business."

She thought for a moment, obviously concerned and a little afraid. Then she shook her head and said, "No, I don't want you to confront Andy. He likes and respects you, and he might be willing to talk with you at some point, so I don't want to jeopardize that. I've learned what not to say to him and when to just get out of the way. I think I'll be okay…And maybe…maybe he'll understand he has a problem, and we can get him some help. I'm just praying for that…"

There was no good answer at this point, and I said, "If you ever feel threatened, or if something else happens, call the police. Or call me. Do you hear me?" I stressed.

She sat up a little straighter. "Yes, I'll call…someone, if he…if something happens."

Andy Meadows walked out into the hallway, impatient to get going. I wrote a couple of prescriptions for him and advised that he follow up with his family doctor in a few days. "In the meantime," I told him, "you shouldn't do any drinking at all, in light of your lab work. None, okay?"

"Sure, Robert, sure," he said, not very convincingly. Then, "Come on, Joy, let's get on home."

Joy didn't call me the next time something happened. And I found out about it in an unusual way. Barbara and I were driving back home from a restaurant in Charlotte, when out of the clear blue she said, "I ran into Joy Meadows the other day." I had been thinking about Joy earlier in the day, and Barbara's statement startled me. We didn't talk much about what went on in the ER, and never about specific individuals. I hadn't mentioned anything about my encounter several weeks earlier with the Meadowses.

"We were in the grocery store, and it was kind of strange," she continued. "Almost as if she didn't want to speak to me. She had on a pair of big sunglasses, and there was some bruising around her left cheek and eye. She said she had tripped and fallen going into her back door. And then she just sort of took off. Not really like her to do that."

"Hmm…" I muttered, and then quickly changed the subject.

Two months after that, Andy was back in the ER. This time he had pneumonia, and he was pretty sick. He was beginning to develop some ascites, free fluid floating around in his abdominal cavity. It can be caused by a lot of things, but in Andy's case, it was due to his drinking and his liver damage.

We checked some lab studies, and everything was getting worse.

I told him his chest X-ray revealed a significant pneumonia, and that he should be admitted to the hospital.

"Nope, can't do that, Robert," he emphatically answered. "Just get me tuned up here in the ER and send me back home. Don't have time to be in the hospital. I'll be alright with some antibiotics and maybe something for the cough."

Joy was standing in the corner of the room, head down and silent. I glanced in her direction, looking for support. She remained motionless and didn't say a word.

"Just get me tuned up a little," he repeated.

"Andy," I said, knowing I had to go here once again, but not looking forward to his reaction. "Tell me about your drinking. That's all a big part of this, you know."

His blotched and bloated face turned beet-red and he glowered at me.

"Robert, I've had just about enough!" he almost screamed. "That doesn't have anything to do with this, and you know it! You're just meddling here, and I don't need to hear any of it. Do you hear me? I don't want you to say anything more about any drinking. I don't have a problem! Never had, never will! I just don't know where you people—" he sputtered.

"Andy, I know better than that. And I'm not talking to you as a friend now, but as your doctor. Your drinking has put you in a dangerous place. It's what has led to your pneumonia. Your liver is failing, and your kidneys aren't functioning properly. Your belly is—"

"That's it!" he shouted, swinging his legs over the side of the stretcher. "Come on Joy, we're getting out of here. I don't have to listen to this bull, and I'm not going to. Do you understand me?" He made this last statement with his finger waving in my face.

I understood, and it took my best cajoling and begging to get him back on the stretcher. We treated him for his pneumonia, and though he should have been admitted to the hospital, we couldn't make him stay, and he went home.

It was the Friday after Thanksgiving, a month and a half after this encounter, when Andy Meadows came to the ER for the last time. EMS brought him to the department and to the cardiac room. Joy was walking right behind his stretcher.

There would be no asking him about his alcohol intake, or listening to his denials, or enduring his berating responses. Andy was in a deep coma, induced by the chemicals floating around in his bloodstream from his failing liver.

He was dying. Even a liver transplant wasn't going to save him at this point. We had several specialists look at him, and they all came to the same conclusion: Too many of his organ systems were failing all at once. Actually, they had been failing over a period of time. Now they were just shutting down.

It was a matter of time, and waiting. Joy seemed to accept this, and to understand where we were. Her children, most of them grown and married, were with her in the cardiac room. It only lasted a little more than two hours. And in that room, there was a deep and somber grief. But there was also a palpable but unspoken sense of anger and resentment. And hovering over all of these emotions was a dark and smothering sadness.

There are two kinds of people:
Those who say to God, "Thy will be done."
And those to whom God says,
"All right, then, have it your way."

C.S. LEWIS (1898–1963)

14

Gone

Things said or done long years ago,
Or things I did not do or say
But thought that I might say or do.
Weigh me down, and not a day
But something is recalled,
My conscience or my vanity appalled.

WILLIAM BUTLER YEATS (1865–1939), "VACILLATION"

3:05 a.m. I had heard the question, and I was just thinking about my answer. There was a lot to consider.

"Doc," Lori spoke again, making sure I had heard her. And then she repeated herself. "What's the one thing that's really bothered you in the ER, the one thing you have trouble forgetting?"

We were sitting at the nurses' station, enjoying the quiet of this middle of the night. We hadn't been talking about anything in particular, just relaxing and discussing whatever came to mind. Then this question.

She put her coffee cup down and I felt her eyes on me.

It seemed a simple enough question, and several things immediately came to my mind. I thought of different people and experiences, and searched for those that had bothered or provoked me the most. I was sifting through layers, and through years. There were those times when I had been shocked by the way we treated each other, the violent acts that forever changed or ended lives. Then I thought about the sudden and catastrophic things that had seemed to destroy good people and good families. And then there were the children. No ER doctor or nurse can remain unaffected after taking care of tiny victims of abuse, or dealing with the unanswerable pain of SIDS, or facing the unexpected death of these little ones who aren't supposed to die.

But at the bottom of all those layers and all these years, there stood Willis Brown.

It was mid-January, and bitter cold. The clock on the wall seemed to have stalled at a little after four in the morning, a lonely but strangely peaceful time in the ER. Or at least tonight it was. The cold weather must have been keeping people at home and in bed. There were no patients in the department, and Jeff Ryan, Amy Connors, and I sat at the nursing station, talking and drinking coffee.

The conversation had turned to the topic of the desirability of growing pear trees, and Jeff was telling us why he had finally given up on peaches.

"Too many borers and diseases," he said with resolution. "Way too much trouble. Pears. That's the way to go. Asian pears."

Amy was obviously very interested in this, turning one page after another in her *People* magazine.

If this kept up, it would take more than strong coffee to keep me awake the rest of the shift.

"Rock Hill ER, this is Medic 2."

The EMS radio quickly shattered our peace and quiet. Jeff reached over to the receiver and pushed the hands-free button, allowing us all to hear.

"This is Rock Hill ER, Medic 2. Go ahead," he said, leaning close to the unit.

There was a slight pause, and then Gary James, the lead paramedic tonight on Medic 2, spoke again. "We're on the way in with a twenty-eight-year-old man, house fire. Burned pretty bad…" There was stress in his voice, something unusual for Gary. I leaned forward in my chair, listening carefully.

"Looks like mostly third-degree burns, total body…or nearly so," he continued.

In the background we could hear someone moaning, obviously in pain. He was saying something, but I couldn't make it out. We all looked at each other, and Amy shook her head.

"Is Dr. Lesslie nearby?" Gary asked.

"He's right here," Jeff answered. "Go ahead."

The radio crackled briefly with some kind of interference, then Gary said, "This guy's in a lot of pain, but…there's no place to start an IV. We've got morphine ready, but do you want me to give it IM? I might be able to find someplace to—"

"What's your ETA?" I asked, leaning closer to the radio receiver. Morphine given in the muscle would be slowly absorbed and difficult to titrate. I would much rather relieve his pain with something IV.

"We're four to five out," Gary answered. "What should I do?"

Jeff had gotten up from his chair and was heading to the trauma room.

"Hold off on the morphine," I told Gary. "We'll get a line going when you get here. What about his vital signs?"

"Heart rate's about a hundred," he told me. "His blood pressure… I…I can't find a place to put on the cuff. His burns…"

"That's okay, Gary," I told him. "Just bring him in as fast as you can."

"10-4, ER," he said, and in the background we heard the anguished cry of "Momma!"

I pushed the receiver's button to the off position and turned and looked at Amy.

"I bet it's a space heater," she said, shaking her head. "First really cold weather we've had, and I bet that's what happened. Caught fire while he was asleep."

She would turn out to be right about that. We later learned he had filled a space heater with kerosene and left it going too near his bed. The blankets caught fire first, and then he was trapped in an envelope of flame. A neighbor had happened to be awake, had seen the flames through a window, and called 9-1-1.

I stepped across the hallway to the trauma room, where Jeff was opening several emergency kits. We would need to get an IV going, probably a central line in his neck, from what Gary described. And we would need to be ready to manage his airway. It just depended on how bad these burns turned out to be.

Jeff opened one of the sterile trays, revealing its few simple contents. There were two stainless-steel cups, one for holding Betadine and one for holding sterile saline. There was a big stack of 4x4 cotton gauze, and on one end of the tray was an assortment of various scalpels. These blades were of different sizes and shapes and would be used only if absolutely necessary, and only in severe cases. This was our escarotomy tray, and the blades would be used to cut through burned tissue that surrounded an arm or a leg, or worse still, a chest. If a burn was third degree and completely encircled a body part, the burned tissue would quickly harden and tighten, blocking blood flow to that extremity. Or in the case of a chest wall, block the ability of a person to inflate and deflate his lungs. He would suffocate. The procedure was simple and gruesome. You just made a linear incision through the burned tissue, down to something that would bleed, and you made sure you had good pulses below the area. Or that your patient was able to breathe. Jeff was making sure we were ready for this, but it was nothing I wanted to have to do.

We both heard the ambulance doors open, and then the voice of Gary James.

"Trauma, right?" he asked Amy as he passed the nurses' station.

"That's right," Amy answered. "Jeff and Dr. Lesslie are in there now."

We both stepped to the head of the trauma room stretcher as Gary and his partner came through the door with their patient.

In twenty-five years I've seen a lot of burn victims, but this man before me was the worst. As gently as possible, we quickly transferred him from the EMS stretcher. Gary gave us what little information he had, confirming Amy's thoughts about a space heater and the suddenness of the blaze.

"Doc, I'm sorry about not being able to get a line started," he apologized.

As we moved this man to our stretcher, the extent of his burns became obvious. There were pieces of charred clothing stuck to his body, probably what remained of his pajamas. My search for any un-burned area of skin on his arms and legs was futile. Miraculously, most of his face and the right side of his neck were spared. He must have reflexively covered his face with his hands when he awoke and found he was on fire.

"Doc, I need something for the pain," he said in a voice just above a whisper.

It surprised me, and I stared down into his eyes. He was completely awake and clear, and was making a calm request. Somehow I couldn't put these eyes and this voice together with his destroyed body.

"Just something for the pain," he repeated, patiently pleading.

"Mr…." I looked in the direction of Gary James for a chart or note or anything that might have this man's name on it.

"Willis Brown," Gary told me. "His name is Willis Brown."

I looked down again and said, "Mr. Brown, we're going to get you something as fast as we can. We'll need to start an IV first, and it looks like the only place we'll be able to do that is here in your neck."

I was feeling the right side of his neck and the area just above his collarbone, locating the landmarks that I would use to place a catheter in his jugular vein.

"Jeff, we'll need the central line kit, and a couple liters of saline ready."

He was already preparing this, and handed me some sterile gloves. As I put them on, it crossed my mind that I would probably only get one chance at this. There weren't many, if any other options.

"And get us some morphine," I added. "A couple of vials."

I soaked some of the gauze in the Betadine and began swabbing the side of his neck.

"Willis, this is some soap, and I'm just disinfecting the skin here," I told him. "It's going to be a little cold."

He nodded his head slightly but didn't say anything.

Then I wiped the area with saline, patting it dry with some more gauze. Next I located my landmarks and then picked up a syringe. It was armed with a 14-gauge needle, a really big one, and I was glad he couldn't see it.

"Willis, you're going to feel a stick here in your neck, and then some pressure. But it should only last a second."

I looked into his face. His eyes were closed, and he whispered, "Okay, Doc. I just need something for the pain."

"I know, Willis," I told him. "We're going as fast as we can."

He flinched a little as the needle pierced his skin, and then he was quiet. There was an immediate flow of blood into the syringe and an immediate sense of relief for me. I threaded seven or eight inches of a clear plastic catheter through the needle before sliding it out and tossing it on the nearby tray. Jeff handed me the end of the IV tubing and I quickly connected it to the hub of the catheter.

"Wide open on the fluids," I instructed him. "And let's start with ten of morphine. Another five every few minutes until we get his pain under control."

It wasn't long before Willis Brown was visibly more comfortable. He opened his eyes and looked up at me. "Thanks, Doc," he said to me. "It doesn't hurt so bad now."

The morphine was relieving his pain but was not going to knock him out. He was alert and speaking clearly.

Jeff had stepped out of the room and over to the nurses' station. Amy needed him on the phone. She had called the burn center in Augusta and they had asked for more information. I was alone in the room with Willis.

"How bad is it?" he asked me, looking up into my eyes.

What was I going to say? His question took me to a place I didn't want to be. Up to this point, I had been busy doing the necessary things to get him stabilized and as comfortable as I could. And now in a moment of calm, he asked this question.

I knew the answer, and I knew what was in store for him. But that was nothing I wanted to tell him. He was going to die. He couldn't survive these burns, and he was lucky to be awake and alive at this point. *Lucky.* Somehow that wasn't the right word.

"Willis," I said quietly, leaning close to his face. "You've been badly burned, over most of your body. We're going to be sending you to a burn center, the one in Augusta. They're experts in handling this kind of thing."

"How bad is it, Doc? Am I going to die?" He was calm, yet his eyes were pleading for a response, for the truth.

I took a deep breath. This man deserved an honest answer. I would be doing him no service by telling him otherwise. He needed to know.

"These are bad burns," I said quietly. "And…I don't think you can survive this."

He closed his eyes then, and his jaw clenched. And then I thought he nodded his head.

"Willis, do you have any family nearby? Anybody in town we can call?" I asked him.

He shook his head. "No, most of my people are in Charleston," he answered.

That would be at least three hours, and by then he would be in Augusta.

"No friends here? Nobody?" I asked again.

"No. There's no one." For the first time, I noticed some hoarseness in his voice.

And then, as if on cue, he started having trouble breathing. I knew it was coming, I just didn't know when. The burns on his chest were beginning to constrict his breathing, and he was having trouble moving air. It would only get worse.

Jeff had come back into the room and now stood beside me at the head of the stretcher.

"The helicopter is on the way," he told me. "Should be here in thirty to thirty-five minutes." Then he looked over at the monitor. "Pulse ox is 88 percent."

The oxygen in his blood was beginning to fall, and I needed to do something.

I heard the scraping of a metal stand being pulled up behind me and turned to see Jeff opening another sterile kit. It was our emergency intubation tray, the one we used for rapid sequence intubation. Willis Brown needed his airway controlled, and would need a tube placed in his windpipe. The process was simple. First he would be given some IV medication that would sedate him, and then more medication that would completely paralyze him. Then we would place the tube. If everything went well, it would only take a moment. He would be on a ventilator and would have to remain paralyzed, and completely sedated. And I knew Willis Brown would never again wake up.

"Pulse ox is 84," Jeff said, nodding in the direction of the monitor.

Willis was having more trouble breathing, and his pain was coming back.

"Doc, I think I need something more…for the pain." He was struggling now, and his voice was more raspy.

"Sure, Willis," I tried to reassure him. "Jeff, how about giving him another five of morphine. And we need to go ahead with rapid sequence," telling him what he had already anticipated.

Jeff had been organizing the escarotomy tray, and had opened three of the scalpels. He knew where we were headed.

"Okay," he answered, moving easily to the counter and drawing up the morphine. Once he had given it through the IV tubing, he turned to the intubation tray and began drawing up the necessary medications.

I glanced at the monitor. His oxygen saturation was still at 84 percent, but his color was getting worse. We didn't have much time.

"The chopper's twenty minutes out," Amy Connors said, standing in the doorway of trauma. "You need anything?"

Jeff looked up at me and then at Amy. "I think we're okay. Just tell us when they get here."

"Sure thing," she said, closing the door of trauma as she walked back to the nurses' station.

Willis seemed to be more comfortable now, and we were ready for the intubation. I caught Jeff's eyes and he looked away. Why was this so hard? I had performed dozens of these intubations and wasn't worried about that part of it. It was just…Maybe the people in Augusta would be able to do something miraculous. Maybe they would be able to save Willis Brown, and somehow keep him alive. Maybe…

But I knew better.

Once I gave him the sedative he would be gone. He would never again wake up. The people in Augusta would have to keep him on a ventilator, asleep and paralyzed, until he died. And that would probably be a matter of days, if not hours.

I stood there by his head, wondering what to say. Wondering if I should say anything.

Jeff silently picked up the first syringe and inserted the needle into the IV tubing. He looked up at me, waiting for my order to give the medication.

"Willis, this medicine is going to make you drowsy," I explained to him. "And then you're going to be asleep."

He opened his eyes and looked up at me. "Thanks, Doc," he whispered peacefully. And he seemed to understand what all of this meant.

Suddenly the magnitude of this moment was overpowering. Should I say something more?

I nodded at Jeff, and then it was done.

The trauma door opened and Amy stuck her head in. "They're almost here."

I shivered in the cold night air, watching the helicopter lights as they disappeared into the black sky. For a few moments I just stood there in the dark, cold and troubled. I was thinking about Willis and wondering if I had failed him. I should have said something more to him, I should have made sure that he understood what was happening, that his life was ending. I should have given him the chance to say something, or maybe…I'm not sure what.

Then I said a prayer for Willis as the beating of the chopper faded into silence.

15

Speechless

God, give me sympathy and common sense,
And help me home with courage high.
God, give me calm and confidence,
And please—a twinkle in my eye.

DOROTHY DAY

In the ER, we take what we do very seriously.

But in order to *survive* in the ER, you have to learn to never take yourself very seriously.

❦

Wednesday, 3:45 p.m. Virginia Granger stepped out of her office and stopped, hands on her hips, and surveyed her department. She looked over in the direction of the nurses' station. I thought I detected a faint smile when she saw that Jack was again spending the day with us in the ER. He was sitting there with Jeff Ryan and me. Amy Connors had just rolled her chair over. A big thunderstorm was rolling through Rock Hill, and for the past half hour the ER had been really quiet. That would all change, once people got out on the roads and started skidding into each other.

But for the moment, we had a break and were just sitting and talking.

Jeff had just asked Amy to share some of her most interesting and peculiar experiences in the ER.

"You've seen some pretty crazy stuff over the years," he said. "Tell us some of your favorites."

Amy thought for a moment and was about to say something, when Virginia walked over.

She had heard this question, and after gathering what we were discussing, she pulled over one of the rolling chairs and sat down. In other places or other circumstances, this might have been the end of any lighthearted discussion. After all, Virginia Granger was the head nurse of the ER—and she was, well, she was Virginia Granger. But the nature of the ER, and of especially this ER, was one of family. We went through a lot together and we shared the same experiences—good, bad, or peculiar. And so it was only natural that Virginia should join in our conversation.

When she was comfortably settled, she looked over at Amy and said, "Yes, Amy. Tell us one of your favorite stories."

Amy grinned sheepishly and said, "Actually, Ms. Granger, it involves you and something you did a few years ago."

"Hmm…" Virginia mused. "Well, that makes it even better. Go ahead."

Relieved and encouraged, Amy began her story.

A Saturday in July, 6:32 p.m. Sheila Rice walked through the triage door and over to the nurses' station. She just stood there for a moment, shaking her head.

"What's the problem?" Amy Connors asked her.

"There's a woman out in the waiting room that's driving me crazy," Sheila answered her, obviously exasperated. "I don't know how to handle her."

Sheila was one of our more experienced nurses, and it was unusual for her to lose her patience or composure. It must have taken a lot to get under her skin.

But then again, everyone was a little on edge this evening. The ER had been busy all day. Every bed in the department was occupied. It was "standing room only" in the waiting room, and EMS was on the way in with three people from a wreck out on the interstate. There was no relief in sight.

"What's she doin' out there?" Amy questioned, her curiosity growing.

Virginia Granger walked up behind Amy as Sheila began to answer.

"Well, you can imagine what it's like in the waiting room." She glanced up at Virginia. "There are people everywhere. Most of them understand how busy we are and that we're trying to get to them as fast as we can. But this one woman, Bertha Wiggins, is really making a nuisance of herself. Every time I step out there, she gets right up in my face and demands to be brought back into the ER. She gets really loud and upsets the people around her. I keep telling her that we'll get to her as fast as we can, but—"

"What's her complaint?" Virginia asked matter-of-factly.

Sheila shook her head again. "That's just the thing. When she first came in, she complained about her wrist hurting. Then it was her back. And then it was her neck. I can't remember what it was last time, but her vital signs are completely normal and she looks fine. There are a lot sicker folks out there than Bertha Wiggins."

"Hmm…" Virginia murmured, pursing her lips. "I think I'll go out and have a chat with this Ms. Wiggins," she said, her voice low and ominous.

Amy glanced up at Sheila and their eyes met. Both of them knew the fate of those who landed in Virginia's crosshairs.

A few minutes later, Virginia walked back in from the waiting room. She didn't say anything, but nodded at Amy and then walked over to her office in the back of the department.

Half an hour went by, and Sheila brought several people back through triage. After she had led an elderly man into room 5, she stopped at the nurses' station and said to Amy, "Apparently Bertha Wiggins doesn't know who she's dealing with. She didn't pay any attention to Ms. Granger and just got in my face again. This time she told me she had a rash, and that it was probably contagious. That cleared out a few chairs around her. But as I turned to come back here, a woman sitting close to her got up and followed me to the door. She stopped me and said that Bertha had told her that the real reason she was in the ER was to get a note to be off from work tonight. She's supposed to work third shift at one of the nursing homes in town and doesn't want to go in because some of her friends are having a big party. I guess some people will do just about anything to—"

"She said what?" Virginia Granger interrupted. She had just stepped out of the cardiac room and heard most of what Sheila had just said.

Surprised, Sheila turned around and repeated Bertha's shenanigans.

"Well, we'll soon put a stop to this," Virginia huffed. Then she strode off toward the triage entrance.

A few minutes later she walked back up to the nurses' station with a look of satisfaction on her face.

"I guess that takes care of that," she announced.

"What happened?" Amy asked her. "What did you say to her?" This was going to be good.

"I didn't say anything," Virginia stated. "Ms. Wiggins was nowhere to be found. Some of the other people in the waiting room said she just got up and walked out. Didn't say a word. I expect she finally got the message."

Amy looked over at Sheila and shook her head, feeling just a little disappointed.

"We need some help in cardiac!" one of the doctors called out. Virginia immediately headed in that direction, Sheila walked back out to triage, and Amy resumed her work at the desk. Bertha Wiggins's unruly and inappropriate behavior was quickly forgotten.

Twenty minutes later the ambulance doors burst open, and the two paramedics of EMS 3 came rushing into the department, transporting a young woman on their stretcher. She was screaming and moaning, rolling from side to side. It was all that Bill, one of the paramedics, could do to keep her from falling off onto the floor.

Lori Davidson hurried over to the stretcher. "What's going on? What's the problem?"

Within a minute there was a crowd of ER staff surrounding the patient.

Bill, flushed from exertion, began to explain. "We got a call from dispatch that there was a woman down in the parking lot of the hospital. No other information, but we were just down the street so we responded. Found her out on the pavement by the ER," he continued, nodding at the writhing and wailing woman before him. "Didn't take the time to call in or anything. We just loaded her on the stretcher and came in." He paused, catching his breath. "Hope that's okay," he added.

"Sure, that's fine," Lori quietly assured him. "But what's she complaining of?" she asked him, stepping closer to the stretcher and picking up the woman's wrist. Her pulse was 80 and regular. Normal.

"Well, I don't know the answer to that one," Bill responded, scratching his head. "She won't say anything. Just keeps rolling around and carryin' on like this."

Sheila Rice walked through the triage entrance, bringing in a young mother with two children. Her attention was drawn to the commotion at the ambulance entrance and she glanced over in that direction. A puzzled look crept over her face. The woman on the stretcher somehow looked familiar...

Just then, Virginia Granger walked over from around the nurses' station. It was as if Moses were parting the Red Sea. Only Virginia didn't need a wooden staff or a booming voice. Without saying a word she simply approached the EMS stretcher, and the surrounding crowd of people parted, making way for this imposing figure.

The area quickly fell quiet, except for the persistent moans of the young woman. She still squirmed from side to side, her eyes tightly closed.

Virginia reached the side of the stretcher and just stood there, feet apart, fists clenched and on her hips. She stared down at the woman and didn't say a word.

Bill looked at the head nurse, then down at his patient, and then back up. Something was going on here, but he didn't have a clue what it might be.

Then Virginia spoke. It was but a single word and was uttered quietly, but with an unmistakable firmness.

"Bertha."

The name pierced the air at the ambulance entrance, and now even the young woman on the stretcher fell silent.

Her thrashing stopped and she lay quietly on her back, her head facing up. Then ever so slowly, her right eyelid began to open. Without moving her head, Bertha began looking around, searching for the source of this word that still seemed to hang in the air above her.

Her eye came to rest on the resolute face of Virginia Granger. Then there was a drawn-out, pitiful sigh, and she seemed to be trying to disappear into the thin mattress of the EMS stretcher.

Virginia just stood there, looking down at Bertha Wiggins.

Finally, Bertha opened both eyes and slowly sat up. Without saying a word, she slid to the end of the stretcher, jumped down, and stood dejectedly in the hallway, a child caught in the middle of some forbidden act.

Bill looked on in amazement, wondering at the sudden healing of his previously distressed patient. Sheila Rice quietly shook her head and then led her new patients down the hallway. And Amy Connors stood at her vantage point behind the nurses' station and chuckled.

Bertha was silent, speechless, as she followed Virginia out through the triage entrance, back to the waiting room, and to the end of the line.

⋘⋙

Amy leaned back in her chair and glanced over at Virginia, who just shook her head and muttered, "Humph...the nerve of some people."

We were quiet for a moment, and then Amy said, "Now, Ms. Granger, it's your turn. Why don't *you* tell us about some of the things you've seen that really stick out in your memory? Some of the crazy stuff."

We all turned to her, anticipating something good. She was silent for a moment, and then she pursed her lips and began to stroke her chin.

"There've been a lot," she began. "But the ones that really stick out are the times when I've been taken completely by surprise. Didn't know how to respond or what to do. In fact, I didn't even know what to say."

At this, Jeff cleared his throat and looked off into the distance. The thought of Virginia Granger being speechless was an unimaginable event in itself.

This didn't go unnoticed, and Virginia stopped, adjusted her bifocals with her right hand, and peered over them at the now squirming Jeff Ryan.

"As I was saying," she continued with exaggerated gravity, "those are the times I remember."

Then we waited. Amy rolled her chair a little closer, and out of the corner of my eye, I saw Jack edge forward in his seat.

"Before I came to Rock Hill," she began, "I worked in a big hospital upstate. I was the head nurse in the ER there as well, and we were really busy. There were several residency programs in the hospital. The orthopedic program was especially good. We always had some of their residents in the ER, and they were always busy.

"Now we were set up a little differently there than we are here. We had two 'ortho rooms' in the back of the ER, connected by a sort of closet. That's where we kept our casting supplies and crutches and whatnot. And that's how we were able to go from room to room without going out into the hallway.

"Because of our volume, we had several ER techs. That's a luxury we don't have here. Their job was to sort of float around the department and help where needed. Usually, that was back in the ortho rooms. The residents would need help putting on a cast or splinting someone, and they would need an extra pair of hands. Two of our techs, James and Willis, were really good at this. The ortho residents had come to depend on them. They were both in their fifties and had a lot of experience. And it was my job to ride herd on them. You see, they were both… well…they always got their work done, yet they always seemed to have a good time. I guess that's why everyone liked them. Sometimes they weren't always as serious as I would have liked."

Virginia paused here, and for some reason, glanced in my direction.

"Anyway," she continued, "we couldn't have managed without them. Then one afternoon…hmm-hmm." She stopped and shook her head. "We had called the ortho resident down to see a middle-aged woman with a badly fractured ankle. She was a vice president in one of the local banks and had tripped on the curb as she was getting into her car. As she fell, she twisted the ankle. It looked awful. She was going to need surgery, and the resident was putting a plaster splint on it to get it stabilized until that could be arranged.

"She was back in one of the ortho rooms, sitting in a chair and facing away from the door. I just happened to walk by, and I stopped in the doorway to check on what was happening. The resident was sitting in a chair beside her, wrapping the plaster around her foot, ankle, and lower leg. Willis was standing in front of her, carefully holding her foot in the air. It isn't easy, holding a foot and leg in the air by just the toes. But Willis could do it, and without so much as a tiny twitch. And that was important for the resident. He wanted a good splint, and he didn't want that leg to move one little bit.

"Willis looked up as I stepped into the doorway and gave me just the tiniest of smiles. And maybe a slight nod of his head. He was intent on what he was doing. Nothing was going to interfere with his holding that leg still.

"I was about to move on down the hallway when I caught sight of James coming out of the closet in the back of the room. Something made me stop at the edge of the door. Apparently he hadn't seen me standing there. If he had, I can assure you things would have turned out differently.

"He nonchalantly walked into the room and politely nodded to our patient. Now, we had all of our techs wear surgical scrubs, since it could be messy work and they frequently got plaster on themselves, and other stuff. Willis and James had on their scrubs that afternoon, just like always.

"James seemed to glide across the room. Then he stopped right behind Willis. I saw him reach into his pocket for something, but I couldn't make out what it was. Not at first. Then I caught a glimpse of something bright and shiny, and all of a sudden, I knew what he was going to do. But it was too late.

"His hands were out of sight of that patient, and of course Willis had no idea that James had taken out his cast knife and snapped it open. James was quick as a flash with that blade. Before anybody knew it, he had grabbed the drawstring of Willis's scrubs and cut it clean in two. Then he just turned and walked back toward the closet just as calm as could be, and he was gone. Then it was like…all slow motion. Willis knew what had happened and his eyes got real big. But he couldn't move. He had to hold on to that woman's foot, and he didn't dare budge. The resident didn't have any idea what was going on—at least not until Willis's scrubs started heading toward the floor.

"And then there it was. Willis was standing in the middle of the room, holding this woman's foot in the air, his pants bunched on the floor at his feet. That's when I noticed his underwear, or 'drawers,' as we used to call them. He was wearing these extra-long boxers made of black silk, and they were covered with little red hearts. The resident glanced over at him and then at the patient, and then he just kept putting on that plaster. Never said a word. And the patient never said anything either. Not then, not even later.

"I was speechless, and just turned away and started looking for James. But I knew he was going to have much more than me to be worrying about."

We were all laughing, and Virginia added, "And you know, from that afternoon on, anytime someone mentioned those black drawers with little red hearts, Willis would just get real quiet and leave the room."

She shook her head, smiling.

"But," she went on, "that really doesn't compare to what your father did one night in the orthopedics room. A Halloween night, I believe it was." She looked over in my direction and waited. I knew what she was talking about, but I just sat quietly and shrugged innocently.

"Why don't you share that one with us, Dr. Lesslie?" she goaded. "I'm sure your son would find it quite interesting."

They were all looking at me. There was no obvious avenue of escape. But in reality, I didn't mind telling this story. I considered it one of my finer moments.

Halloween night, 10:15. J.D. Howell was sitting back comfortably on one of the beds in the ortho room. The curtain between the two beds was drawn, and the other bed was occupied by a patient with a fractured wrist. We had contacted the orthopedist on call, and he would be coming in to take care of that patient.

J.D. was all mine, and he was proving to be somewhat of a challenge. He was forty years old, looked twice that, and his blood alcohol was probably four times the legal limit. He had swayed into the ER listing from side to side, complaining of right knee pain. He couldn't recall any specific injury. But he knew it hurt and he wanted something for the pain.

He had no limp, at least when he thought no one was watching, and his examination was completely benign. Just to be sure, I had ordered some X-rays of that knee. They were normal, as expected. I had given him all of this good news and advised that he get home, put some ice on it, and try some Tylenol or ibuprofen. I had been writing up his chart at the nurses' station when Lori walked up and said, "Your friend back in ortho wants to talk with you again. He's determined to get something for pain before he leaves, and if he doesn't, he's planning on spending the night." She smiled as she said this, but then walked off, clearly leaving me to deal with this problem.

That bugged me a little, and as I walked down the hallway toward the ortho room, I planned to make quick work of this.

I was halfway there when someone behind me called my name.

"Robert. Hey, Robert!"

I turned around and glanced back at the nurses' station. And I couldn't help but laugh out loud. Standing across the counter from Amy Connors was one of my partners, Andy Rogers, and his wife, Joanna. It turned out they had just left a Halloween party, having won the "best costume" award for a couple. This was a number of years ago, and they were dressed as "Ghostbusters," replete with silvery outfits, boots, backpacks, and "ray guns." Now these were no little toy pistols, but big multicolored complex-looking contraptions. As I walked toward them, they both raised their ghost-fighting weapons and blasted away. The noise was hilarious, and several people peeked out from behind their curtains to see what was going on. It was a combination of a siren, some kind of whistle, and maybe a hoot owl. And all the time the ray guns were making these noises, they were flashing all kinds of different colored lights. It was great.

And that's when it came to me.

"Andy, I need to borrow that ray gun for just a minute. Would you mind?"

He glanced at me dubiously. "Okay, but what do you have in mind?"

"Just an idea," I answered. "An inspiration."

I took the gun in my hand and test-fired it a couple of times.

"This is perfect," I told him, then turned and walked quickly down the hall. As I passed one of the supply carts, I grabbed a towel and wrapped it around the gun, completely hiding it.

When I walked into ortho, J.D. was still lying back on the stretcher, singing some strange and unrecognizable tune. He looked over at me and said, "Listen, Doc. I really need something for the pain. This knee is killin' me. How about helpin' me out?"

Then I heard the voice of Doc Wiggins from behind the curtain. He was on for ortho tonight and was talking to his patient.

"We'll just inject this wrist with something to help with the discomfort, and then we'll put it back in place. It's gonna smart a little, but then we'll be done."

I'm sure Doc had a first name, but I never heard anybody call him by it. I never did. He was always "Doc Wiggins" from the first moment I met him until the day he died. He was probably the first orthopedist in the area, and even though he was in his early 70s, he was still active and took calls on a regular basis. I think he had treated everyone in York County at some time or another. Everyone liked and respected him. He was always straightforward and a man of few words. Just like tonight.

I walked over to J.D., holding the covered ray gun carefully in one hand, and gently patting his "injured" knee with the other.

"J.D.," I said to him, mustering as much seriousness and professionalism as I could. "We're going to get you something for the pain, and I think you're going to feel a lot better in just a few minutes. In fact, we're going to try a brand-new, experimental treatment."

"A what? Now, just a minute—" he protested, waving his hands in front of me.

"No, no, don't worry," I reassured him. "This is all very safe and approved by the ABC people."

"ABC? Ain't those the people who run the red-dot stores?" he asked, obviously not totally inebriated.

"No, the ABC is the, uh, the…Anyway, it's approved and everything," I stammered, caught off guard.

It was then that Doc Wiggins stuck his head around the curtain, curious as to what was happening. J.D. couldn't see him, and Doc just stood there, staring. I nodded slightly at Doc, and then refocused my attention on J.D.'s knee.

"Now, as I was saying," I resumed. "This is really going to help you. And all I need for you to do is just lie real still and straighten out your leg."

Through the fog of cheap bourbon, J.D. was still skeptical.

"Are you sure about this, Doc? I mean, wouldn't it be easier just to—"

At this point, I dramatically removed the towel from the ray gun, and with a flourish, tossed the towel onto a nearby counter. J.D. stared at the gun in amazement and, for a moment, was silent. Then his eyes began to grow bigger, almost popping out of his head. I glanced over at Doc Wiggins. He was just shaking his head.

"What in the world is that thing?" J. D. asked, reflexively grabbing both knees with his hands.

"Don't worry, J.D.," I reassured him. "This is not going to hurt at all."

I stepped closer to the stretcher and gently patted his knee again. Reluctantly, he straightened it out. Then he tightly gripped the rails of the stretcher.

Very professionally, I examined the ray gun, making sure all of the settings were correct. "Don't want it on full blast," I told him. "Maybe about half strength."

I heard Doc Wiggins clear his throat at that, and I struggled to keep a straight face.

"Okay, J.D., here goes." I placed the tip of the gun on his knee and waited for just a few seconds, just for effect. Then I squeezed the trigger.

J.D. jumped a little at the noise and the flashing lights. Then, when he realized it wasn't going to hurt, he seemed to relax and watch curiously.

I moved the tip of the gun all over his knee for at least a minute, making sure to not miss a spot. Finally I stopped, and pointed it at the ceiling.

"How is that?" I asked him. "Better?"

J.D. felt his knee with both hands and then moved it around, flexing and extending it.

"Nope, feels the same," he said, shaking his head. "Still hurts."

I stroked my chin and then said, "Well, according to the directions, this might take two treatments. Especially with a bad injury."

He nodded his head. I again made some adjustments to the ray gun, twisting anything that looked technical.

"This time, I'm going to turn on all the juice," I told him. "Full power."

His eyes got even bigger as I again approached him with the gun. But he didn't say anything, and he didn't move.

I fired the weapon and began moving it all over his knee, just like before. This time I did it a little longer, maybe a minute and a half. When I finished, I touched the side of the gun, then quickly snatched away my fingers as if it had overheated.

"Be careful there, Doc," J.D. advised.

"How does that knee feel now?" I asked.

He did the same thing again, palpating his knee with both hands, and then stretching it out fully.

"You know, it *does* feel better! Yes sir, Doc, it doesn't hurt nearly like it did! I think that thing really helped. What did you say it was?"

Without hesitating I said, "It's a joint techno-atomizer." Where that came from, I don't know. But it sure sounded good.

"Well, whatever it is, it really works. Just wait till I tell the boys."

I grabbed the towel from the counter and wrapped up the "techno-atomizer" once again. Then I stepped over to the doorway.

"J.D., the nurse will be back with your papers in just a minute, and you can be on your way."

He was still rubbing his knee and didn't look up as he said, "Okay, Doc—and thanks."

As I turned to leave, I happened to glance in the direction of Doc Wiggins. He was still standing at the edge of the curtain, looking at me. He was smiling and shaking his head. And he didn't say a word.

...And a time to laugh.

ECCLESIASTES 3:4

16

Another Word for **Love**

It is in pardoning
that we are pardoned.

St. Francis of Assisi (c. 1181–1226)

We try to define love in a lot of different ways—ways that are most often superficial, "feel-good," and transient.

Real love requires work, sacrifice, and understanding. Mainly it involves being willing to live beyond ourselves. Once we are able to do that, we can learn how to truly forgive—and accept forgiveness.

❧

4:45 p.m. Edna Strait was rolled into the ER on the stretcher of EMS 2.

"Go ahead and take her back to the family room," Lori Davidson told the two paramedics with her. "I'll be back there in just a minute." Then she added, "And be sure to stay with her."

The family room doubled as our "psychiatric room," providing privacy and security for those patients who needed to be watched closely but didn't have a significant medical problem.

Edna fit in that category. She was 62 years old, and we had been witnessing a gradual decline in her mental status over the past few years. That decline had accelerated over the past three or four months, after she finally received the official diagnosis of Alzheimer's disease.

Her husband Charlie had been faithfully taking care of her all this time, in spite of her growing dependency. They had no children and no relatives in town. Some of their church friends had tried to help out when they could, but the disease is grinding, and after a year or so, Charlie was mainly on his own.

We saw Edna on a regular basis, with minor bruises from falls, an occasional urinary tract infection, and once with a bad case of pneumonia. It was during the pneumonia episode that we approached Charlie with the idea of some kind of care facility for Edna. He was a slender man, probably ten years older than Edna, and was becoming feeble himself. None of us thought he could continue with this for very long. But he would have nothing to do with a nursing home, telling us without hesitation that he was going to care for his wife as long as he was alive. He was determined, and we understood that. But we couldn't have known that those words would soon come back to haunt him.

Lori grabbed the clipboard for the family room and headed down the hallway. Then she stopped and turned to me. "When is Charlie getting here?" she asked.

I looked up at the clock on the wall. EMS 1 had called in with their ETA about five minutes ago. "Should be in just a few minutes," I told her. "No more than five."

"I guess we need to keep them apart," she thought aloud. "Edna won't know where she is, but Charlie will be looking for her. I'll make sure they're separated."

"Good idea," I agreed.

Lori walked down the hall and I waited for our next ambulance.

It wasn't long before EMS 1 brought their stretcher through the ambulance room doors.

"Take Charlie back to the trauma room," I directed Denton Roberts. "Everything still stable?"

They brought their stretcher up beside me and I looked down at Charlie Strait. He had an IV going in his right forearm, and a sheet was drawn up to his chin. A bloody bandage covered his face. There was only a small hole for his mouth and nose, and I could see nothing else.

"Dr. Lesslie, is that you?" a small voice asked from beneath the pile of gauze.

"Yes, it's me, Charlie," I answered him. "You're in the ER now, and we're going to take care of you."

"Where is Edna?" he asked, anxiety in his voice. "Is she here yet? How is she? I need to see her."

"Just relax, Charlie," I told him. "Edna's going to be fine. Right now though, we need to take care of you."

His hand came up from the stretcher, the IV tubing preventing free movement. He was searching for me, and I grasped his hand in mine.

"Dr. Lesslie, she needs me," he pleaded. "You know how she gets…"

I did know. And Lori would be taking the necessary precautions to be sure Edna remained calm and didn't do anything to hurt herself. Over the past few weeks, she had shown us an unpredictable and violent side of what remained of her personality, especially when Charlie was not with her.

"We're going to take care of Edna. Try not to worry about that," I assured him.

Then I nodded to Denton in the direction of the trauma room and he began pushing the stretcher down the hallway. It was with some difficulty that I was able to release myself from Charlie's grasp.

When we had received the call forty-five minutes earlier, it had been unusual. There were two EMS units on the scene and a couple of police officers. Some neighbors had called 9-1-1, reporting they had heard some gunshots coming from the Strait house. When the first policemen had arrived, they knocked on the front door and were greeted by Charlie Strait. He was standing in the doorway, blindly groping for the screen-door latch, trying to let the officers in. Blood was streaming down his face and onto his shirt. His eyelids were swollen shut and his face had a strange peppered appearance. In the background, walking from side to side in the living room, was Edna Strait. She was carrying a rifle in her hands and mumbling incoherently.

She didn't resist as they slowly approached and unarmed her. She had no idea where she was nor what was happening.

Charlie grabbed the shoulders of the first person he came in contact with, still groping blindly. "Don't hurt her!" he begged them. "She doesn't know what she's doing!"

Denton arrived on the scene shortly after that, and then he had called us.

I walked across the hall and into the trauma room. Jeff Ryan was carefully removing the blood-soaked bandages from Charlie's face.

"His blood pressure and pulse are fine," he told me. "No evidence of any other bullet wounds, just his face. Chest and belly are clear. Nothing on his back."

Hearing this, Charlie spoke up. "Dr. Lesslie, she only shot me one time, just in the face. No place else. And I'm going to be fine. Just…"

I stepped over to the stretcher and patted his shoulder, waiting for Jeff to finish his work.

"Just relax, Charlie, and let me take a look," I said.

Jeff peeled off the last piece of gauze, and I couldn't help exclaiming, "What in the…"

"Rat shot, doctor," Charlie said matter-of-factly. "Edna shot me with rat shot."

That explained what I was seeing. Charlie's face was a peppered, swollen mess. She must have shot him at close range, because the pattern of the tiny pellets was very tight.

"How far away was she when she did this?" I asked him.

"Well, she was in the living room," he began. "And I was getting her something to drink from the kitchen. We keep a .22 rifle in the closet, 'cause we've got bats in the attic, and when she hears them, she kind of goes crazy. Anyway, when I turned the corner into the living room, there she was, maybe eight or nine feet away, and she had the rifle in her hands. Then she drew down on me and fired. I really didn't think she would. She's pointed that gun at me before, and I thought I had it pretty well hidden. But…I guess not."

He was reaching up to touch his face, but Jeff grabbed his hand.

"Better not do that," he told Charlie. "We need to get it cleaned up."

"Oh, sorry," Charlie muttered, putting his hand back on the stretcher and tucking it under the small of his back for good measure. "I understand."

I picked up some sterile gauze and soaked it with saline. Gently, I began to clear away the clotted blood from around his eyes.

"How is Edna?" he asked me again.

"She'll be fine," I told him. "Now, tell me what you can see."

I had cleared the blood from around his right eye. The lids were swollen, and there were a few pellet holes just above his upper eyelashes. I gently pried the lids open, trying to get a look at his eyeball. I didn't see any obvious wounds of the eye itself, and his pupil was round and it reacted to the light of the overhead lamp.

"I can see your face, Doctor," he told me.

"Good," I said, relieved. "Now, how many fingers do you see?"

I held up two, then four, then one, and he identified them all correctly.

"That's good Charlie. I think this eye is going to be okay. We'll need to get some X-rays, since there are a bunch of pellets here."

I had been relieved to learn that rat shot had caused his wounds. These were tiny pellets, a bunch of them, and they were designed to be fired in an attic without blowing a hole in the roof. There wouldn't be any deep bony penetration, but we had to worry about an injury to his eyes.

I began to clean the blood from around his left eye. This one looked different. There were about ten pellet wounds of the upper lid, and when I pulled the eyelid up, it was obvious they had penetrated the globe. His pupil was dilated and irregular in shape, and I could easily see blood within his eye.

"Doctor, I don't see anything yet. Am I supposed to?" Charlie asked me.

Jeff just shook his head, and I heard a faint grunt as he turned away.

"Charlie, this eye looks pretty bad. I think there are some pellets lodged within the eyeball itself, and…well, we're going to need to get the eye specialist involved here. You're probably going to need surgery."

"Am I going to lose that eye?" he asked, more calmly than I would have.

"I'm afraid there's a good chance of that," I told him honestly. "We'll just have to wait and see what the specialist finds, and what he thinks."

"Wouldn't surprise me," Charlie said. "She was standing right in front of me, and Lord knows I ought to be dead."

Jeff placed clean dressings on his face and then started an IV. We would be giving him antibiotics and something for pain.

"How long do you think this will take?" Charlie asked me. "I mean, how long do you think I'll be in the hospital? There's nobody to take care of Edna, except me."

Jeff looked at me and shook his head, amazed, as I was, by this man's dedication to his wife.

"Charlie, Edna might be in some trouble with the law here. After all, she shot you in the face, and you might lose—"

"No, no, no!" he stated emphatically. "If it's up to me, of course I won't press charges. She didn't mean to do this. I know that for sure. She's not in her right mind, you know that. And my Edna would never try to hurt me. I can't let the police do anything to her. She'll just…just…I need to get her back home, and we'll…everything will be alright."

He tried to get up from the stretcher, but Jeff gently yet firmly made sure this didn't happen.

"Charlie, you need to sit still and relax, okay?" I told him. "I'll go and check on Edna. And I'll talk with the police and tell them your concerns."

"Thanks, Dr. Lesslie. She's not in her right mind, you know. And she'd never want to hurt me."

He was right about the first part. And yet she *had* hurt him. He was going to lose an eye and his face would be disfigured for the rest of his life. And yet his main concern was for her.

I glanced back at him as I opened the door. Charlie Strait was a pitiful sight, sitting alone on that stretcher, his face completely bandaged, and his bloodstained shirt clinging to his slender chest and arms.

"She didn't mean to…"

Saturday, 9:45 p.m., in August. "10-4, Medic 1," Jeff spoke into the ambulance radio. "Major trauma on arrival."

He hung up the phone and turned to Amy Connors. "Better get X-ray on the way, and lab. Sounds like a bad one."

I had heard the tail end of this and asked him, "What's coming in?"

"Head-on accident on highway 21, near where the four-lane becomes two. The driver of a pickup truck crossed the median doin' about 90 and ran into a Toyota sedan. They're bringin' in the driver of the pickup. Head injury, it sounds like. Vitals are okay, and no other evidence of any injury. But he's unconscious, and smells of alcohol."

I slid the chart of the patient I had just seen in ortho over to Amy. "How about getting some films of this guy's hand? Got in a fight with his girlfriend and punched his car door. Pretty smart—but then, it *is* Saturday night."

Turning back to Jeff, I asked, "What about the people in the Toyota?"

"Just one," he answered. "Twenty-one-year-old girl. She's dead at the scene."

He shook his head and added, "Medic 2 is bringing her in, and taking her straight back to the morgue. The coroner is on his way now."

"Drunk drivers…" Amy muttered angrily. "Why can't we keep them off the road? How many people will they kill before something is finally done about it?"

It was a valid question. Most of us read about fatal auto accidents in the newspaper, and the subtle mention that "alcohol may have been a factor." And then we forget about it and turn the page. But in the ER, we see the devastation intoxicated drivers wreak on our highways.

We see the aftermath, and we're the ones trying to put the pieces back together. All too often, that can't be done. And then we deal with the family and friends whose lives have been forever changed.

"You know, Dr. Lesslie," Amy said, looking up at me. "This is a little unusual. The drunk is usually the one who walks away with barely a scratch."

She was right about that, or at least so it seems. I knew she would never wish anyone harm, but I also knew these accidents were hard on all of us.

"I'll get X-ray on the way," she said with businesslike resolution. She would do her job.

Ten minutes later, Medic 1 came through the ambulance doors with their patient and headed for major trauma.

"Vital signs stable," Denton Roberts told me as they passed the nurses' station. "But he's still unresponsive."

Jeff and I followed them down the hallway and into trauma.

"What's this guy's name?" Jeff asked.

"Clayton Andrews," Denton answered. He was sweating profusely, as was his partner. "Took us a while to get him out of the truck. He's just nineteen years old. And his parents are coming in right behind us. They don't live far from where this happened, and they were on the scene. In fact, they got there just after we did."

Jeff helped them move Clayton onto the trauma stretcher. I began to examine him, trying to elicit some response, some sign that his brain was working. There was nothing, not even a reaction to forceful rubbing over his sternum.

The paramedics had placed him in full spinal immobilization as a cautionary exercise. After we cleared his neck of any injury, we freed him from his collar and splints. He had good muscle tone, and no evidence of an abdominal or chest injury. The only physical evidence I could find was some bruising over his left eyebrow and some blood at the edge of his nostril.

And he *did* smell of alcohol.

"The girl didn't stand a chance," Denton said, referring to the driver of the Toyota. "She probably never knew what hit her. His tire marks just suddenly veered across the median and he struck her head-on. No sign of brake marks anywhere. She was wearing her seat belt, but nothing was going to save her. Head, chest…She was pretty messed up."

"Hmm…" Jeff muttered, rechecking Clayton's oxygen saturation.

"And you know her parents, Dr. Lesslie," Denton added. "Or at least her mother."

"Who is she?" I asked him, bothered by this new information.

"The girl's name is Jill Mackenzie. And her mother is Annie," he told me. "Annie Mackenzie, who used to work in the lab."

Oh, no. I knew Annie well. We had worked together for more than ten years, when she had been in charge of the second shift in the hospital's lab. I didn't know her husband or her daughter. But I knew that Annie was a wonderful woman. She was dependable, professional, and she was always smiling when she came to the ER.

"Do they know what happened?" I asked him. "Do they know their daughter's dead?"

"Yeah, they do," Denton said quietly. "They have to meet the coroner in the morgue and identify Jill. I just can't imagine…"

He didn't have to finish his thought. None of us could imagine that long walk down the dimly lit back hallway of the hospital.

Clayton turned out to have a terrible brain injury. His CT scan demonstrated a massive and inoperable shearing and separation of his brain matter. The impact of the accident had caused his head to whip back and forth. He must have struck his forehead on the dash or steering wheel. He wouldn't survive this injury.

His blood alcohol came back at four times the legal limit.

I sat down with his parents in the family room and gave them this awful news. They had been at the accident scene and had seen their son being loaded onto the EMS stretcher. And though they were expecting the worst, you can never really be prepared.

I gave them some time to be alone. After they collected themselves, they of course wanted to see their boy. Jeff led them up the hallway to major trauma, and I met them there. They were silent as they came into the room, and then the first words came from Mr. Andrews.

"What about the girl?" he asked me. "What about the driver of the other car? Will she be alright?"

They didn't know, and I told them what had happened. They looked at each other. Then he took his wife in his arms.

I was about to leave the room when Mrs. Andrews said, "Dr. Lesslie, do you think he will hear me if I speak to him? Will he understand me? There are so many things I want to say, and…and…Is there any way he can hear me?"

Her voice trailed off as she looked down at her son. I had seen his CT scan and knew the extent of the injury to his brain. The doctor in me would tell her no, he was completely unconscious and completely unaware of what was going on around him. But how did we really know? How could we know for sure?

"Mrs. Andrews," I quietly said to her. "There's a chance. Talk to your son."

She was leaning down over her boy as I left the room.

A few minutes later, the door of major trauma opened, and the Andrewses stepped out. I was standing at the nurses' station, and they started in my direction.

But something stopped them.

Something caused Mrs. Andrews to pause and look behind her.

Walking up the hallway, walking directly toward them, were the Mackenzies, Tom and Annie.

"Oh Lord," Amy whispered from behind the desk.

Annie Mackenzie's reddened eyes caught mine, and then she looked away and focused on the couple in front of her.

They didn't know each other, but somehow they knew. The coroner had told the Mackenzies about the condition of the Andrews boy, and that he was in bad shape. And Annie had wanted to come to the department to speak to me.

I didn't know what to expect. This could be a volatile encounter. Several thoughts flashed through my mind, none of them good.

But things were beyond my control, and the two couples were now facing each other in the hallway, only inches apart. They just looked at each other, motionless, in what seemed like an eternity. One couple's boy had just killed the daughter of the other couple. I waited, ready to intervene.

Then Annie Mackenzie stepped closer to Clayton Andrews's mother and put her arms around her. She didn't say anything, neither of them did. And they began to cry. Tom Mackenzie was standing beside his wife, and he reached out his hand and laid it on Mr. Andrews's shoulder.

And they stood there.

Tuesday, 8:15 a.m. It was about eight months ago that Henry Bartlett had started coughing. It was only a little a first, every now and then. But then there had been a little blood when he coughed. He had hidden this from his wife and hoped it would just go away. But it hadn't. Finally, when he could no longer ignore it, he went to see his family doctor.

Twenty-five years of cigarette smoking had given him lung cancer, and at fifty-three years of age, it had given him less than a year to live.

It wasn't long after the initial diagnosis that we began seeing Henry in the ER. Once he had pneumonia and needed to be admitted to the hospital for IV fluids and antibiotics. As the weeks passed, he began losing weight and strength. Then he would come in with vomiting or shortness of breath. And there was the time last month when he had fallen and broken his wrist. He was having a hard time with this, at least physically.

His spirit remained amazingly positive. Even at the very end, he was never depressed or anxious. And he was always patient with the ER staff. He just rolled with whatever came his way and let us do what we needed to do.

A big source of strength for Henry was his wife, Jean. She had no misunderstanding of where all this was headed, and she was always there with him, always encouraging him.

His positive spirit was sorely tested that last morning in the ER. Henry had had a rough couple of days and had tried not to come to the ER. He knew the end was fast approaching, and he wanted to be at home when it came. But he had developed a high fever and his shortness of breath was worse. Jean insisted that he come to the hospital, even if only to be made more comfortable. Somehow she knew this would be the last time.

Lori was with them in room 2. She and Jean had gotten to know each other over the past months, and had become friends.

By now, Jean knew the routine. She helped get Henry situated on the stretcher. She rolled up his bathrobe sleeve in anticipation of Lori starting an IV, and then she covered him with a blanket. He was having bad chills along with his fever.

I had seen Henry a week earlier. I was shocked by the change in him in such a short time. He seemed to have lost even more weight and was now little more than a skeleton. His temperature was 103, and his respirations were rapid and labored.

"Pulse ox is 88," Lori told me, reaching for the oxygen tubing hanging on the wall. This was a low reading, indicating that he wasn't getting much oxygen through his lungs and into his blood. But what could we do, other than provide him with some temporary relief? Lori secured the tubing's nasal prongs and then turned the valve on. "Three liters okay?" she asked.

"That's fine," I told her, and then turned to Henry. "How are you feeling, Mr. Bartlett? Do you need anything for pain?"

"No, no. I'm fine, Dr. Lesslie," he understood. "Well, maybe something for the fever. That might help with these chills."

"Coming right up," Lori said, handing him a medicine cup containing two white tablets. In her other hand she had a glass of water. Jean took this from her, and stepped over to Henry's side to help him.

A portable chest X-ray showed that Henry's left lung was completely full of fluid. His right side, where the cancer had started, was barely functioning. It was the worst X-ray I had ever seen, at least in someone who was still alive. His cancer doctors had advised us there was nothing to be done, other than trying to keep him as comfortable as possible.

After I had looked at the X-ray, I motioned for Jean to follow me out into the hallway. I wanted to tell her where I thought we were.

In a quiet voice, I told her. "Jean, this is the worst I've ever seen Henry."

She looked down at the floor and nodded her head. "He seems to be getting weaker and weaker by the minute."

Then she looked up and asked, "How much longer do you…I know you can't be sure…but…"

"You're right, Jean," I said to her. "There's no way of knowing, but he is wearing out fast, even since he got here. I think we need to anticipate that…well, it could be this morning."

There was a painful silence. Then she nodded her head and smiled. "Okay. I need to get back there with him."

"Jean," I said, gently taking her elbow. "Is there someone we can call? Some family member? I've heard the two of you mention Eric in the past. Isn't that your son?"

She stopped, completely still now, and stared at the door in front of her.

"Yes, Eric is our son, Dr. Lesslie. But it won't do any good to call him."

I thought she was referring to where he lived, and that the distance would be too great for him to get here soon enough. "Where is he?" I asked her.

She turned and faced me. "He lives in Charlotte."

That was a surprise. Charlotte was only twenty or thirty minutes away. Surely he would come to Rock Hill if he knew his father was dying.

"But it's no use calling him," she said with a sad resoluteness. "He won't come."

She saw the confusion on my face and then explained, "Eric and Henry had a falling out several years ago. Actually, Eric had the falling out. It was about money, or something like that. Henry was only doing what he thought was best, and he tried to explain that to Eric. But he only got mad and said he'd never speak to Henry again. And he hasn't. Henry has called him and written him, and when we finally figured out the computer, he even e-mailed him. But Eric has never responded. It's broken my heart, and I know it's broken Henry's."

She paused, and I said, "What if I called him? What if I explained what's happening, and that it…it might be the last chance he has of seeing his father alive."

"It won't do any good, Dr. Lesslie, but thank you. I know my son, and he's just too headstrong."

You don't become an ER doc by being timid. I was sure that if I could only talk with this man, I would be able to convince him to make the short trip to Rock Hill.

"Jean, if you don't mind, please give me his number," I asked her. "It can't do any harm."

Reluctantly, she opened her purse, took out her organizer, and read the number to me. I wrote it on a scrap of paper and walked over to the nurses' station. Jean returned to her husband's bedside.

"This is Eric Bartlett," the voice said. I was calling him at his work number. Maybe that was why he sounded all business.

"Eric, this is Dr. Lesslie, and I'm calling from the ER in Rock Hill."

I proceeded to explain the condition of his father, and that he didn't have much longer to live. I minced no words, making it as plain as possible.

When I finished, there was only silence. And then, "So?"

It was a simple word, but utterly cold and heartless. I wasn't sure how to respond.

"Eric, your father is dying, and—"

"There's nothing I can do about that, is there?" he coldly stated.

Wow. This was going to be difficult.

"I thought you would want to be here with him," I said. "And I want to be sure you understand he's not going to live much longer."

"Listen, Dr.…whatever your name is. I'm not coming to Rock Hill. Do you understand that? And you can just call me when it's over."

I didn't say anything. I just kept searching for some word, *something* that would change his mind.

"You get that?" he added tersely.

"I got it."

There was a click on the other end. And I hung up the receiver.

I took a deep breath and walked over to room 2. As I entered the room, Jean and Henry looked up at me. There was expectation in their faces, and I had trouble meeting their eyes.

It was Henry who spoke. Jean must have told him what I had been doing.

"Did you talk with my son?" he asked, gasping between each word.

I looked at Henry and silently nodded my head. And I just stood there, not knowing what to say, and not wanting to say anything.

A sadness seemed to pass over him, and then it was gone.

Henry took his wife's hand in his, looked up at her, and smiled.

Then he turned to me, nodded his head, and with that same smile on his face, he said, "Tell him…tell him I forgive him."

Forgiveness is another word for love.

GEORGE FIELDS, JULY 8, 2009, CAMP JOY

17

Dancin' in Heaven

Earth has no sorrow
that heaven cannot heal.

Thomas Moore (1779–1852)

Monday, 10:15 a.m. Danny Miller. It had been awhile since we had last seen him in the ER. A few years ago, it had seemed we were seeing him once or twice a week, but something must have changed.

He was twenty-one or twenty-two now. Could it be that many years since we'd first seen him? He'd been four years old then and had celebrated his birthday earlier that afternoon. His parents had brought him to the ER after he had fallen out of his wheelchair.

Danny had suffered some unrecognized problem during his birth, and sustained brain damage due to a lack of oxygen. Cerebral palsy was the technical name for his condition, though that isn't a very specific term. It covers a wide range of problems and conditions. In Danny's case, it affected his motor system but not his ability to think.

During the first few months of his life, it had become apparent that something was wrong. He was alert and responsive, but he had difficulty moving his arms and legs, and his development was way behind other children his age.

When his parents received the news of his diagnosis, they didn't believe it at first. They had two older children at home who were perfectly normal, and this kind of thing just didn't happen, not to them. They weren't prepared for all that lay ahead.

The next couple of years were difficult, but they seemed to be adjusting to the challenges of taking care of a child with special needs. Danny couldn't walk or even crawl, and was placed in a special stroller at about the age of two. As he grew, his arms and legs became more contracted. His head, always too heavy for his weakened neck, began to tilt to one side. They had tried physical therapy and constant stretching exercises, but the changes in his body were inevitable. When he was a little more than three, they had a special wheelchair made for him. It allowed him to be moved from place to place, but he wasn't able to propel himself, and needed almost constant attention.

He couldn't speak, due to the lack of development of his facial muscles. But he tried. There was nothing wrong with his brain, and he didn't miss a thing. He just couldn't express himself.

I had been in the ER the afternoon of his fourth birthday. Somehow his wheelchair had slipped over the edge of their driveway, and he had tumbled onto the pavement. They were worried about possible fractures and had brought him straight to the hospital.

He had some bad bruises and abrasions of his right elbow and leg, and some on his face. But nothing was broken.

I can remember him looking up at me, and seeing the smile in his eyes. He was trying to say something, but I couldn't make it out. His parents were unable to decipher what he was mumbling and just told me not to worry. Danny continued to look at me, and I felt helpless. Finally I turned away and talked to his parents.

It was obvious then they weren't doing well. They were becoming more frustrated with his condition and the constant demands on their time and energy.

They motioned for me to step out of Danny's room. His father said, "Dr. Lesslie, we're getting to the end of our rope with Danny. We love him, of course…but you can imagine how hard this is on us. And on his brother and sister. He needs so much attention, and it somehow doesn't seem fair to them."

He was right about his first statement. I couldn't imagine how hard their daily life must be. The part about this not being fair, though—that bothered me. But I wasn't the one whose life had been totally redirected by the birth of this young boy.

Then Danny's mother said, "We're looking into a special home for him. Some place where they know how to care for him, where there are…others just like him."

They seemed a little embarrassed sharing this with me, yet they were determined. A few months later, Danny came back to the ER with a fever and bad cough. He was in his same wheelchair, but this time he was accompanied by two people I didn't recognize. It turned out they were staff members of a group home in Rock Hill, one that served the needs of children like Danny.

He was his usual bright and engaging self, still unable to speak. He had pneumonia on that visit, but didn't require hospitalization. We were able to get his treatment started and get him on his way back to the group home.

I asked Danny's attendants about his parents. Did they know he was in the ER?

"Well, I don't think they know," one of them told me. "They moved… Where did they move to, Frances? Wasn't it somewhere in Tennessee?"

Her co-worker answered, "Yes, somewhere near Memphis," Frances answered. "And we have directions not to notify them unless something is really bad. Do you think we should call them, Doctor?"

I told them that his condition was not that serious, and they needed to follow the request of his parents. Maybe their supervisor could make that decision when they got back to the home.

After that visit, we saw Danny on a regular basis. It seems he was in the ER every few weeks with an assortment of problems. Nothing ever really bad, just bumps and bruises and sometimes another fever. These were straightforward things that could be diagnosed and treated without his being able to talk with us.

And we watched him grow up. He had to get another wheelchair, something bigger and sturdier. And his useless limbs became more contorted. Still, he maintained a bright and cheerful spirit every time we saw him, speaking his happiness to see us through his eyes.

Then, when he was about sixteen years old, he sort of disappeared. He just kind of stopped coming to the ER. After a few months someone mentioned this, and we realized it was true. He hadn't been in the ER for quite a while.

One evening, when I was taking care of a young girl from Danny's group home, I decided to ask the woman with her about Danny. I glanced down at her nametag. Apparently she noticed my hesitancy in trying to pronounce her name.

"I know, Doctor," she said smiling. "Nobody can pronounce my name. I'm from the bayou country in Louisiana. Just call me 'Miss B.' That's what all the children do."

Having been rescued I said, "Thanks, Miss B. Do you have any idea where Danny Miller is? We haven't seen him here in quite a while."

"Oh, his family moved him to another facility, somewhere in the lower part of the state. He's been gone quite a while now. And you know, we really miss that boy. He was something special."

I told her we all agreed. I was turning to leave when she added, "I just don't know, though. I've been working at the home for over five years, and I've never once seen his parents. That's just never made any sense to me. To none of us. Like I said, he is such a special young man. He has 'the light,' you might say. Every Sunday afternoon, we would gather all the children together and read Bible stories to them. Not all of them understood what was going on, mind you, but Danny certainly did. He always wanted to be up front, and he listened closely to every word. And though he couldn't tell us, we knew he understood. The Lord had touched that young man, that was for sure. And it's that light of his, that spirit that touches everyone around him."

She paused and patted the arm of the little girl on the stretcher in front of us.

"Yes sir, we all miss him."

And now here Danny was in the ER again. He hadn't changed much during the years he had been gone. Maybe some more facial hair, and a little more weight. And though still in a wheelchair, imprisoned by his misshapen body, his eyes hadn't changed. His gaze was still bright and engaging, and there was still that "light" that Miss B had talked about. He had clearly become more animated as he was rolled into the department through triage and he seemed happy to be back in our ER.

I was glad to see that Miss B was once again with Danny. When I asked her where Danny had been living, she told me that he had been moved back to Rock Hill several weeks ago and had been placed in the same group home. They had brought him to the ER because he had a low-grade fever and seemed to be uncomfortable.

"You know, Doctor, it's difficult trying to figure out if anything is hurting Danny," Miss B told me. "He's been gone for a while and I haven't had a chance to work with him. I just can't understand what he's trying to say. But something's different today, and I somehow thought we should bring him in to the hospital."

I assured her we would take care of him, and directed the triage nurse to take Danny to room 4. Brandy Phillips was covering that room, and she walked over to help them get Danny settled.

Brandy was young, twenty-four at the most, and had been in the ER for only a few months. She came to us with some critical-care experience in another hospital and was still "learning the ropes" in our department.

Miss B and her co-worker walked out of Danny's room and over to where I was standing at the nurses' station.

"We'll be going back to the home now," Miss B said to me. "Just give us a call when he's ready to come back, and we'll be right here."

They turned and left the department. I resumed writing up the record in front of me.

Ten minutes later, Brandy Phillips came walking out of room 4, shaking her head. She walked up to me and said, "Dr. Lesslie, I have no idea what is going on with the patient in room 4. I can't understand anything he is trying to say, not one word."

She was obviously frustrated, and I gave her a second to collect herself.

"His temp is 100.1, but I can't be sure about his blood pressure," she continued. "The cuff is too big, and his arms are...well, they're just so small and hard to get to. What should I do? I guess I could try a pediatric cuff."

She had put Danny's chart on the countertop. I picked it up.

"Let me go and see if I can figure out what's going on," I told her. "And don't worry about not being able to understand Danny. None of us have ever been able to, and we've had a bunch of years to try."

Lori Davidson had been sitting behind the nurses' station, and she stood up when I said this.

"Let me go with you, Dr. Lesslie," she said. "I'd like to see Danny again. It's been a while, and maybe I can help."

"Sure," I told her. "Come on."

We walked into room 4, where we found Danny curled up on the stretcher. The rails had been pulled up, and he was leaning against one of them. He was unable to move and was in an obviously uncomfortable position.

Lori quickly stepped over and helped him to be more comfortable.

He looked up at her and then at me, and his expression was one of recognition and then relief.

Then he seemed to become more serious. He tried to say something. He was working hard, and when he saw our lack of comprehension, he seemed to become frustrated. That was unusual for Danny. I had never known him to lose his patience. He had always seemed to accept our shortcomings.

Lori leaned over and spoke quietly and slowly to him. "Danny, can you tell or show us what's the matter? Do you hurt anywhere?"

He tried again, mouthing his words with great effort and obvious difficulty. But we couldn't understand what he was trying to get across to us. I examined him the best I could. But couldn't find any obvious problems. It was a difficult exam, and I knew it was only of limited value.

"Lori, I'm going to the desk to get Amy to order some labs and a urine. And we'll get a chest X-ray." I looked down again at Danny and added, "We probably need to send him around in his wheelchair for that. The stretcher will be too clumsy."

Lori looked over at me and said, "I'll stay with him for a few minutes, and see if I can make any progress."

I went out to the nurses' station and ordered the labs and X-ray. Then I just stood there and wondered what I was going to do with Danny. A few minutes later, Lori walked over and shook her head.

"I'm sorry," she said. "I just can't understand him. I tried, but I just can't."

Forty-five minutes later, he was being wheeled back to the department from X-ray. The tech with him stopped in front of Amy and asked which room Danny was in. As she rolled him toward room 4, Amy slid the results of his lab work across the top of the counter.

His urine was completely clear, but his CBC was abnormal. His white count was 15,500, an elevated level that probably indicated an infection somewhere. When I put his chest X-ray up on the view box, I had to step back and get my bearings. His thorax was contorted, just like the rest of his body, and it was difficult to make out the important physical landmarks. After a few minutes, I was satisfied that there was no pneumonia present. His lungs were clear.

That was when Jack walked up and quietly stood at my shoulder.

"That's an unusual X-ray, isn't it?" he asked, startling me a little. I had almost forgotten he had come to work with me this morning. One of the radiologists had come through the ER earlier and asked Jack if he wanted to sit in on a few MRIs. There were a few heads scheduled, and at least one lumbar spine. I thought it would be a good experience for him, and he had gladly followed the radiologist down the hallway.

I turned and faced him.

"Yeah," I answered. "There's not much normal on this chest X-ray. This is a tough case. It's the young man in room 4 with a fever and elevated white count. He's probably got an infection going on somewhere, but he can't communicate with us. And it's going to be difficult to find out where it's coming from."

"What do you mean he can't communicate?" Jack asked me, glancing over in the direction of room 4. The curtain was still open, and the X-ray tech had left Danny sitting in his wheelchair, alone in the room.

I explained Danny's problem and the impossibility of getting any kind of complaint or history from him.

Jack nodded his head and said, "Mind if I try?"

That might be a good idea. I guess I had been too busy to remember Jack's years of experience at Camp Joy.

This was a summer camp that the Associate Reformed Presbyterian Church had been operating for the past thirty years. Three sessions each summer, a group of fifty or sixty individuals with special needs would spend a week at Bonclarken, the denomination's retreat located just outside of Hendersonville. Each one of them would be paired with a counselor, a "special friend" who would spend the entire time with them, 24-7. Some of these campers were pretty self-sufficient and high-functioning, while others required a lot of help with everything, including eating and bathing and using the restroom.

It was an intense week for everyone there. For the campers, their week at Camp Joy was the highlight of their year. And for the counselors, the week spent in selfless and sometimes difficult service was life-changing. Not everyone could do this, but for those who dedicated themselves to their camper, the experience taught them a lot about these "special needs" individuals, or as they soon came to understand, these "special people" with needs. It also taught them about love, and what "unconditional love" was all about. These campers placed no conditions on their affection and loved freely. There really is no place on this earth quite like it.

Jack and his two sisters and brother had all been counselors at Camp Joy, and it had impacted each of their lives. In fact, Jack would be heading up to Bonclarken in a few weeks for his sixth session as a counselor. During those summers, some of his "special friends" had been high-functioning and mainly required a lot of emotional support and encouragement. Later, as he became more experienced, he was given the assignments of more complex campers, those who required a lot of physical help, and those who had great difficulty in communicating with others.

I hadn't thought of that.

"Sure, Jack, see what you can do with him," I told him. "His name is Danny. But don't be surprised if you can't understand anything he's saying. We've all tried."

I quickly told him about Danny's level of mental functioning and that it was a matter of communication, nothing else.

He walked over to room 4, and I watched as he stepped over beside Danny's wheelchair. He knelt down and put his arm around Danny, then leaned his head close to Danny's. I watched as Danny's eyes lit up and I saw his mouth began to move excitedly. I couldn't hear what they were saying and walked back over to the nurses' station.

Ten minutes later, Jack walked up and stood beside me. He had picked Danny up from his wheelchair and placed him on the stretcher. Then he covered him with a hospital blanket before leaving his room.

Lori was standing on the other side of the counter beside Amy, helping her log in some orders for one of our patients.

"Well, what did you learn?" I asked, hoping that he had discovered something, but not really expecting him to have anything to offer.

"Wow!" Jack exclaimed. "Danny is really a special spirit. But I guess you guys know that, though."

Lori looked up as he said this, and tilted her head, waiting.

"He kept apologizing for causing so much trouble. He knows how difficult it is to understand him."

That was an understatement, but I was surprised and anxious to hear what else Jack had learned.

"Well," he said to me, "Danny thinks he has appendicitis."

"He what?" I responded. "Appendicitis? Did he tell you that?"

It suddenly made sense, with his low-grade fever and elevated white count. It was almost impossible to examine his abdomen since his rib-cage almost touched his pelvis, so that could certainly be the source of his problem.

"He's not sure," Jack explained. "But he thinks that's what it might be. He has pain in the right lower part of his belly, and he's nauseated. Doesn't that sort of fit the picture of appendicitis?"

Lori chuckled and smiled at Jack.

"It does fit the picture," I told him. "But we'll need a CT scan of his abdomen to be sure."

Then I looked down at Amy and said, "Can you get that scheduled as quickly as possible? We need it done right away."

It turned out that Danny Miller in fact did have appendicitis. He was taken to the OR later that afternoon and had his appendix successfully removed, with no complications. A few days later, he would be going home.

That evening, as we drove out of the hospital parking lot, I asked Jack how he had been able to understand Danny. "A lot of us tried, you know," I told him again. "But it just wasn't any use."

He looked over at me and matter-of-factly said, "You know, Dad, you just have to take your time and listen. That's all. If you listen closely enough, you can begin to understand. And then suddenly, it becomes clear."

He was being completely serious, and fully expected me to understand. I just shook my head. I realized this was a gift that not all of us possessed. Or maybe we do. Maybe we just don't work hard enough at having "ears that hear." One thing was for certain, though. It was because of Jack and this gift that we had been able to help Danny.

We were silent, and then Jack said, "I overheard Miss B, from the group home, say something that really makes a lot of sense. She said that though Danny is trapped in that body and in his wheelchair, some-day he will be dancing. 'Dancing with the Lord' is the way she put it. I know that's true. And it will be a great day."

He paused, reflecting. "There will be a lot of people dancing."
I looked over at my son, and marveled.

Behold, I make all things new.

REVELATION 21:5 RSV

18

New Beginnings

There is a time for everything,
and a season
for every activity under heaven:
a time to be born and a time to die.

ECCLESIASTES 3:1-2

Thursday, 7:15 a.m. Jack and I had just sat down at the nurses' station. We were talking with Amy about her husband's big dirt-track race the following night, and she had asked Jack if he wanted to come.

Before he could say anything, the ambulance doors burst open and someone began screaming.

"Help me! Somebody come quick!"

We all turned in the direction of this outburst. Standing in the entrance, holding the doors open with both hands, was an obviously distraught young man. He was barefooted, dressed in blue jeans, and his shirttail was flapping in the slight vacuum created by the automatic doors.

He was frantically searching the department and when his eyes caught mine, he repeated, "Help me! My wife's havin' a baby in the car!"

I immediately turned to Amy. "Who's out in triage?"

"Lori," she told me, reaching out and pressing the triage intercom button. "I'll give her a call."

She leaned down over the speaker and said, "Lori, we got a woman havin' a baby in the parking lot. Might need some help."

The atmosphere of the department was suddenly changed. Lori barreled out of triage and headed straight for the open ambulance doors. She paused only long enough to grab the emergency OB kit that we kept on a shelf in the hallway.

"Help me, please!" the young man said again, this time turning and starting out into the parking lot. Lori was right behind him.

Jack looked at me and said, "Shouldn't we get out there? I mean, if she's…"

I had stood up and was making my way from behind the nurses' station. Apparently I was not moving quickly enough for Jack.

"Don't you think we need to…to run or something? What if—"

We were moving through the ambulance doors and I turned to him and said, "Lori is out there, and she'll holler if there's a problem."

I understood his excitement and his anxiety. But my response was tempered by a few decades of hearing many of these same emergent cries for help. Usually there was no cause for alarm and certainly not for running. Nonetheless we took each one seriously, and I could see that Lori had reached the back door of a late model maroon station wagon, parked at an awkward angle near the ambulance entrance. The young man had opened the door and Lori was bending over, peering inside the interior.

We were ten yards from the car when Lori straightened up, turned around toward me, and beckoned with a wave of her hand. She was calm as always, yet I sensed an urgency in her unspoken request. This was confirmed when she set the OB kit on the pavement at her feet and began to open it.

Immediately my pulse quickened, as did my step. Racing through my mind were the steps I needed to perform. It had been a while since we had done this. Usually we were greeted by a young woman in active labor, but who had not progressed beyond the point of no return. We were able to get her on a stretcher and up to Labor and Delivery before any precipitous activity. It was always a little disappointing, tempered with a significant measure of relief.

Hearing the rattling wheels behind me, I turned to see Amy Connors pushing a stretcher across the parking lot. She was having a little trouble navigating the cracked and uneven pavement, but had almost reached us.

Lori looked up at her and with a slight shake of her head said, "Not yet."

It was then that I noticed Jack. He was standing just behind me, wide-eyed, and trying to get a glimpse of what was going on in the backseat of the car.

"What've we got?" I asked Lori, reaching the door and leaning in.

"She's crowning and pushing," she calmly reported. "And this is her third baby."

That was cause for more concern. This was going to happen and it was going to happen quickly.

"Ohhhh, doctor, make sure my baby is okay," the young woman moaned between pants.

I caught a quick glimpse of her face. She was frightened and obviously in pain. Her damp hair hung limply across her forward and into her eyes. She tried without success to brush it aside.

"Everything's going to be alright," I said, trying to calm her. "But it looks like we're going to have a baby here in the car. Try to relax as much as you can and just let us help you."

She looked at me with wide-opened eyes and just nodded.

She was reclining in the backseat, her left leg draped over the back of the front seat. It must have been an uncomfortable posture, but that was the least of her concerns. Looking down, I could see the black-thatched top of the baby's head pressing through the birth canal. I felt something at my left shoulder and turned as Lori handed me sterile gloves. I quickly put them on and noted that she stood ready with a suction bulb, prepared to clear the child's airway as soon as it was accessible.

Then she did something that barely registered on my consciousness, but which I was able to recall later in a calmer moment. She turned to my son and quietly said, "Jack," nodding her head and shifting slightly to make room for him. I *sensed* more than saw his presence behind me.

I delivered the baby's head and then its shoulders. In a split and slithery second, I had a baby girl in my hands. She was screaming and objecting to the syringe that Lori was inserting into her nostrils and mouth. And it sounded good. She was healthy. Her color was good, she had all of her arms and legs and fingers and toes.

"Can I see him?" her mother asked, lying flat on her back, exhausted.

"It's 'her'," I said. "And yes you can, in just a second. Let us get her cleaned up first."

"It's a girl?" the voice came from somewhere behind me. It was her father, the young man who had just burst into the ER, and he was clearly excited.

"Yes," I heard Lori tell him. "It's a girl and she's doing great."

"A girl? Are you sure?" he asked again. "We have two boys at home and we've been hopin' for a girl and…Are you sure?"

"Yes, it's a girl," Lori told him. "We're sure. And she's perfect."

She reached down to the OB kit and handed me the umbilical cord clamp. And as I snapped it into place, she gave me the scissors. I was almost ready to sever the white, rubbery cord when I thought of Jack. He was at my elbow, and I handed him the scissors, motioning for him to step a little closer. I held the cord taut, one finger directing where he should cut.

He stared at me but didn't say anything. An insistent nod of my head made my intentions clear. Lori prodded him with an elbow.

His hands were shaking as he reached out and opened the scissors, placing them where I pointed.

"Here?" he mumbled nervously.

"Right there," I answered, waiting.

His first attempt was a little timid, barely nicking the cord. Then without any further prompting on our part, he gathered himself and made a clean cut.

"Good," Lori approved. Then, wrapping the little girl in the warming blanket, she handed her carefully to her mother, laying the baby on her chest.

"Here, Mama," she said to her. "Here's your baby girl."

Jack and I backed away from the car and the young father moved to the door.

Then he turned and grabbed Lori, giving her a big hug. And then he grabbed Jack, hugging him and lifting him off the pavement. Jack looked at me over the man's shoulder, with his eyes big and a sheepish grin spreading across his face. He didn't know what to say.

Then, just as suddenly, he put Jack on the ground and turned to his wife.

"Honey, are you okay?" he asked her, gently patting her knee.

Amy pushed the stretcher next to the station wagon and within a few minutes mother, father, and newborn little girl were all on their way to Labor and Delivery.

Jack and I stood beside each other as Lori finished cleaning up the remains of the OB kit. She then walked off toward the ER, leaving the two of us in the parking lot.

"Well, what'd you think?" I asked him.

"Wow, Dad, that was...that was something else! And it all happened so fast. I mean, one minute there was nothing, and then...then there was a baby. Just like that."

"Uh-huh," I agreed.

"And thanks for letting me cut the cord. I mean, that was really...I wasn't expecting that."

"You did great, Jack. But don't tell your mama. I promised her you'd only be 'observing.'"

I knew that wasn't going to happen.

Later that morning, during a quiet moment between patients, Jack and I had walked back to the lounge for some coffee. As we stepped out into the hallway, he stopped and asked me, "Dad, how often do you do that?"

I knew he was talking about the parking lot delivery, and I said, "Not very often, maybe once or twice a year. But it's always fun. Pretty exciting, wasn't it?"

"Yeah, it was," he agreed. "But do things ever go bad? I mean does it sometimes turn out differently?"

I thought for a moment before I answered. Prior to my residency training in emergency medicine, I had spent a year and a half in pediatrics. As peds residents, we responded to all C-sections and all difficult deliveries in a large community hospital. And sometimes things did go bad. There had been too many terrible tragedies, most of which had been anticipated. But there had been some that came out of nowhere and were devastating for all of us. Looking at Jack's eager and still excited face, I knew I shouldn't go there. Not right now.

"The good thing about delivering babies in the ER—"

"Or in the parking lot," Jack interrupted.

"Or in the parking lot," I agreed, smiling at him, "is that these expectant women are usually healthy and are multips."

"What's a 'multip'?" he asked, puzzled by the term.

"It just means that they've had multiple babies. This might be their second, third, or fourth child. Labor for them is usually much shorter, sometimes less than an hour. That's why they frequently don't make it to the hospital in time, like this morning."

"Hmm," he mused, nodding his understanding. "I guess Mama was a 'multip' when she had me."

Jack was our third child, and he was right.

"Yeah, she was. And you introduced yourself to us pretty quickly," I told him, remembering that spring evening twenty-two years ago.

He looked me square in the face and said, "You know, Dad, I've always known that you delivered me then, but until today, I never really thought about what that meant. I don't remember too much about it myself," he quipped. "But what was it like for you? I mean... what were you thinking?"

I leaned against the hallway wall and looked at him. What had I been thinking?

It had all happened so fast. One minute I was standing by Barbara in the labor room, talking with Eddie Blanchard, our obstetrician. He had just completed his exam and determined her status.

"Barbara, looks like we're ready to go," he had said to her.

And the next minute we were headed down the hall toward the delivery room. Eddie was on one side of the rolling bed and I was on the other.

"Robert, you want to deliver this one?" he had asked me.

It was a bolt out of the blue. He hadn't even looked in my direction and the question had been nonchalant, as if this was some everyday occurrence and just routine.

A thousand thoughts had sped through my mind. I had delivered a reasonable number of babies and I knew what to do. And I knew Eddie wouldn't have considered this had he not been confident in my ability to handle it. Then again, I knew he would be standing right behind me.

But what would Barbara think? Would she be comfortable with this?

I looked down at her. She was white-knuckling the bedrails, experiencing another painful contraction. Her eyes were opened wide and she looked straight at me, nodding and somehow finding a smile.

"Sure, Eddie," I answered, wondering if it was really me saying that. "That would be great."

"Good," he responded, still not looking in my direction. "Then let's get going. Go get scrubbed up."

And then we were in the delivery room. Barbara had been moved to the delivery table and I was putting on a gown and gloves and mask. Eddie was standing behind me, his arms folded casually across his chest, not bothering to put on gloves or gown himself. That was when I knew this was going to be me.

"What was I thinking?" I repeated Jack's question.

He had leaned a little closer, expectantly awaiting my reply.

"Well, just like this morning, it all happened pretty quickly," I began. "And it was pretty amazing. You were easy, once things got started. Your mama pushed a couple of times and there was your head and then your shoulder. And I can remember thinking, *Don't drop this one!* I wasn't about to do that, and I grabbed you for dear life. The doctor in me took over and I made sure you were breathing and that we cleared your airway. You were perfect. Well-shaped head, everything where it was supposed to be. And then the father in me took over. We hadn't known whether you would be a boy or a girl, but now I knew. I was standing there holding my firstborn son. Your mama asked, 'Is everything okay?' But I couldn't answer her. I couldn't speak. I just stood there, holding you, and trying to get myself under control."

Suddenly I remembered those feelings, that awesome sense of something…almost holy. I felt my face flushing and tears beginning to form in my eyes. Then I looked over to see Jack staring at me intently with those same big, dark eyes that had first looked into mine twenty-two years ago.

"It was Eddie who told your mother we had a healthy son," I continued. "And he took you in his big hands and placed you in her arms. And then she was crying and I was crying and you were crying. It was a wonderful moment. And it was a rare and wonderful gift."

We were silent for a moment, and then he said, "Thanks for that, Dad."

I put my arm around his shoulders and we turned and walked up the hallway.

⌒◎⌒

It was five 'til seven, and Tom Anders, my relief, was walking into the department. He was carrying a grocery bag of supplies for the night ahead. A bag of chips was precariously perched on its top.

"Ready to go home, Robert?" he asked cheerfully. Tom didn't mind working nights, and in fact signed up for more than his share of them. "No hospital politics at 3 a.m.," he frequently said.

"Yes, we're ready to go," I answered, glancing in Jack's direction. "Nothing to turn over to you. Everything's been taken care of."

"Great. Thanks," Tom said to me. Then turning to Jack, "Do any brain surgery today?"

"Not today, Dr. Anders. Maybe tomorrow," Jack answered, smiling.

"Good. Well, I guess I'll see you in the morning." He turned and walked down the hall toward our office.

We were standing in front of the counter at the nurses' station and I turned to my son.

"Jack, if you have just a little more time, there's someone I want you to meet."

"Sure," he said. "I don't have anything planned for this evening. Actually, I'm kind of tired, and I'll probably just stay home tonight."

"This won't take long. And I'm not sure how many opportunities you'll have to meet this man."

We walked to the back of the department and then to the staff elevators. The doors closed behind us and I pushed the button for the fourth floor.

We stood in silence as we smoothly ascended, stopping at the highest level of the hospital. The doors silently glided open and we stepped out.

"This way," I instructed him, pointing to our left. "We need to go to 4-B. It's a general medical floor."

We walked into a deserted waiting area and I stopped.

"Jack, let me tell you something about the man you're going to meet," I began.

He looked up at me, his expression open and waiting.

"His name is Duncan MacKinnon, and he's quite an interesting fellow."

I then told him how I had first met Duncan. It had been a cold December morning, about a year and a half ago. He had come into the ER complaining of nausea and some difficulty swallowing. And though he was able to swallow and to drink liquids, he had gotten to the point where he couldn't get anything solid down. This had been going on for a week or so and he finally had enough and came to the ER to get it checked out.

"He was almost eighty, but looked like he might have been sixty," I told Jack. "He was lean, strong, and his mind was as sharp as a tack. And he had a great sense of humor," I remembered.

Duncan MacKinnon had no family in the area and he lived alone. His story was bothersome, and when he told me he had lost ten pounds over the past two weeks, I became more concerned.

A suspicious chest X-ray had led to other imaging procedures and within a short period of time, I had to inform him of his diagnosis. He had esophageal cancer, and from the looks of his studies, it was inoperable. A surgical consult confirmed our worst fears, offering little if any hope.

"Maybe some radiation," the surgeon had told Duncan. "That might slow things down. But I'm afraid there's nothing else we can offer."

He had stoically accepted the news, seemingly expecting this death sentence. I think he had known when he first came to the ER. And yet, there was a peace about him, something different that we didn't often see in this circumstance.

I hadn't seen Duncan for several months after that. Then, about a year after we had made this diagnosis, he had come back to the ER. He had become dehydrated, now finding it difficult to even keep fluids down. Prior to that time, he had worked hard at maintaining his weight and energy levels, drinking a lot of liquid supplements. But that was no longer working.

We began to see him on a regular basis after that. He didn't want to be admitted to the hospital, but just wanted to be given some IV fluids and then be sent home. Amazingly, he was blessed with little to no pain.

A week ago, he had come to the ER in pretty bad shape. We had started an IV and had given him a couple of liters of saline. But I knew what I needed to do.

"Duncan," I told him. "I can't send you home this time. You need to stay in the hospital."

"I know, I know," he had said softly, nodding at me. "I locked up the house and gave the key to my neighbor."

And that was it. He had been in the hospital ever since that day.

I paused and gazed down at the floor. Then I looked up at Jack.

"This is a good man," I told him. "And he has an interesting outlook on life. You'll see."

I tapped on the door of room 417 and pushed it open. There was no response, and I assumed Duncan had not heard us. We stepped quietly into the room and I closed the door behind us.

He was lying on his back in the hospital bed, his failing body barely forming any contours under the thin hospital blanket.

His eyes were closed, and he was humming a familiar and haunting melody. Then, somehow sensing our presence, he stopped his humming, opened his eyes, and turned his head in our direction.

"Dr. Lesslie," he greeted me, still with surprising strength in his voice. "Glad you could come by this evening. And who is this young man with you? This must be one of the young Lesslies."

Jack stepped toward the bed and held out his hand to Mr. Mackinnon.

"I'm Jack Lesslie," he said, but now he was hesitating. Duncan was struggling to free his right hand from the hospital sheets. It was fettered with the IV line, taped securely in place on the back of his wrist. His arm and hand were covered with bruises and his skin was paper-thin. He looked down and shook his head in frustration.

"Doggone it…" he muttered, still struggling to free himself.

Jack reached down and patted the back of his wasted hand, and then grasped it gently. It was something his mother would have done.

"Yes, I'm Dr. Lesslie's son, and I'm glad to meet you."

Duncan relaxed at this, and his arm settled back on the sheets.

If possible, he had lost even more weight since I had last seen him, just two days earlier. He was disappearing, melting away. Yet his spirit remained strong and his eyes were bright and engaging. For a moment I wondered if bringing Jack up here had been a mistake. But when he looked at Jack and smiled, my initial thoughts were confirmed. This would be a good thing.

"So," Duncan said, "I understand you're not sure what you want to do with yourself. Not sure about going into medicine, or architecture, or…Well, you're just not sure."

Jack was about to respond when Duncan continued.

"Well, that's okay. In fact, that's good. You need to be sure about how you want to spend the rest of your life. At least, as far as work is concerned. But you know, that can always change. You can change direction most times, though it becomes more difficult as we get older."

He told Jack about some of the things he had done during his life, careers he had pursued, jobs he had worked. And then abruptly he said, "Let me tell you about something your father did for me. He might not even remember this, but I do. Always will."

He looked at me knowingly, but I had no clue where this was headed.

"Last fall," he continued, "I was having some problems and needed to come to the ER for some fluids. It was a Saturday afternoon and I tried to put it off as long as I could, but…Well, I had to come in. The problem was, it was the Clemson–South Carolina football game and I was going to miss it. My nephew had gone to Clemson, and Lord forgive me, I had become a Tiger fan. Didn't want to miss that game, but I had no choice.

"When I got to the hospital, your father was on duty, and he got an IV going and all that, and I just happened to mention something about the ballgame. Well, the next thing I know, the nurses are putting me in a wheelchair and rolling me somewhere down the hall. They took me into your father's office and into the call room. Then they propped me up in the bed and turned on the TV. Never missed a minute of the game. Got to watch the whole thing."

He smiled and looked in my direction. "Yep, Dr. Lesslie came back to peek in on me a few times, said he was just checking on the score of the game, but I knew better."

I remembered that visit, and asking the nurses to take him back to our call room. It was a small thing, and certainly no sacrifice to me. I was a little embarrassed.

"Yes, I won't forget that," Duncan repeated. "Can't remember who won that game, but I'll never forget what your father did for me."

We were silent for a moment, and then he said, "You know what I really regret? I really wish we had had a chance to play some cribbage." He looked over at Jack and winked. Then he continued. "Your father was talkin' about how he could whip me and all. Sounds like he needs a little lesson in humility, and this old navy hand could probably give him one. We used to play a lot of cribbage, me and…me and the boys." These last words trailed off, and there was an awkward silence. I sensed it was time for us to leave, and I stretched and made a tentative move toward the door.

"One more thing, Dr. Lesslie, Jack," Duncan said, his voice once again strong and clear. "The hospital chaplain came by yesterday. Good fellow, well-intentioned and all. I suppose he just wanted to make me feel better, share some warm and fuzzy thoughts. Well, he got to talking about the 'circle of life,' about how we are born, then we live our lives, and then we die. About how that comes full circle somehow. I guess he thought that would make me feel better about where I am, close to the end and all."

He glanced at me briefly, but then looked directly in Jack's eyes. "But you know, son, I don't think that's the case at all. Life is not circular, with us somehow coming back to where we started. No, I think it's more linear. We're on a path, and that path starts the day we're born. And whether we understand it or know it or even believe it, we are all on that same path. And that path leads us all to one place. We are all marching to God's throne. And standing at the side of God's throne is Jesus. And you know, it's all about Him, isn't it? The problem is we don't all understand that. If we did, we would live our lives differently. We would pay more attention to the journey, and to the people who are on that journey with us. But it still remains, we're all on the same path. And when we reach the throne, well, that will be the best beginning of all."

He stopped, and I could tell he was tired. This time we needed to leave and allow him to rest.

We told him goodbye, made sure that everything he needed was within reach, and then we stepped out into the corridor.

As we walked down the hallway, Jack said, "Thanks for bringing me up here."

"He made me promise to bring you with me the next time I visited," I responded. "That was good for him. It was good for all of us."

We reached the waiting area, still deserted, and I stopped once more.

"Did you hear him humming when we first went into his room?" I asked Jack.

"I did, but…I couldn't quite make it out. It sounded like something I had heard before."

"He was humming 'It Is Well with My Soul,'" I told him. "It's a great old hymn, but one you've probably not sung in our church. Do you know the words?"

"No, I don't think I do," he answered.

"There's some interesting history behind the writer of the lyrics, and the words are very powerful. The first verse is the only one I can remember, and it goes like this,

> When peace, like a river, attendeth my way,
> When sorrows like sea billows roll;
> Whatever my lot, Thou hast taught me to say,
> It is well, it is well with my soul.

The next day, Jack and I took our lunch break and went around to the cafeteria. After we had eaten, we were walking back to the department and passed the staff elevators.

"Dad, why don't you go on back to the ER? I think I'll go upstairs and check on Mr. MacKinnon. You think that would be okay?" he asked me.

"I think he'd like that," I said. "And take your time."

I walked on to the ER and Jack got on the elevator.

At the nurses' station, I had picked up the chart of a child in room 3.

"Fever and cough." I was turning to go to that cubicle when I noticed Jack walking up the hallway toward me. He had his hands in his pockets, and there was a troubled look on his face. He stood before me, looking down at the chart in my hands, not saying anything.

Then he looked up at me and quietly said, "I went up to room 417... and it's empty."

Later that night, after I had taken a shower, I walked back into our bedroom and over to the bed. There, on top of my pillow, was a piece of paper. Jack had sat down at our computer and searched the web. He had found the lyrics to Duncan MacKinnon's hymn and printed a copy. As I glanced at the sheet of paper, I noticed he had circled the fourth verse.

And Lord, haste the day when faith shall be sight,
The clouds be rolled back as a scroll;
The trump shall resound, and the Lord shall descend,
"Even so"—it is well with my soul.

About the Author

D r. Robert Lesslie, author of the bestselling *Angels in the ER,* is a physician who lives and actively practices medicine in Rock Hill, South Carolina. Board-certified in both emergency medicine and occupational medicine, he is the co-owner of two busy urgent care/occupational clinics.

For more than 25 years, Dr. Lesslie worked in and directed several of the busiest ERs in the Charlotte, North Carolina, area. He also served as medical director of the emergency department at Rock Hill General Hospital for almost 15 years. During his tenure as medical director, he received the American Medical Association's Continuing Education Award. He also traveled around the country, giving lively, innovative lectures to the Emergency Nurses Association at their annual meetings in major cities.

For seven years, Dr. Lesslie wrote a weekly medical column for *The Charlotte Observer* presenting a wide variety of topics, both medical and editorial. He also pens a regular column on medical, philosophical, and personal topics for the YC, a monthly publication in York County, South Carolina.

Dr. Lesslie enjoys the fast-paced environment of the ER and the need to make rapid and accurate diagnoses. He views his medical career as an opportunity to go beyond simply diagnosing and treating individual patients. For him, it is a way to fulfill a higher calling by meeting the real physical and emotional needs of his patients.

An active member of his home church in Rock Hill, Dr. Lesslie serves as an elder, and he and his wife, Barbara, teach Sunday school and sing in the church choir. They are also involved with an outreach program for disabled/handicapped individuals, Camp Joy, where Dr. Lesslie serves as the camp physician for a week each summer. He also enjoys mentoring high school and college students considering a career in medicine.

Dr. Lesslie and his wife, Barbara, have been married for more than 35 years. Together they raised four children—Lori, Amy, Robbie, and Jeffrey—and are now enjoying five grandchildren. In his spare time, Dr. Lesslie enjoys gardening, golf, hunting, reading, and bagpiping.

More Great Reading
from Harvest House

Angels in the ER
Inspiring True Stories from an
Emergency Room Doctor
ROBERT LESSLIE, MD

If you don't believe in angels… you should spend some time in the ER. You'll learn that angels do exist. Some are nurses, a few are doctors, and many are everyday people.

…Sometimes you have to look hard for their wings, as with well-starched head nurse Virginia Granger, whose heart of compassion hides behind a steely gaze that can quell a belligerent patient with a glance.

…Sometimes they bring a grin, like William Purvis—a.k.a. "Max Bruiser"—a beefy pro wrestler who lands in the ER after a tussle with an unexpected opponent.

…And sometimes you have to shield your eyes from the glow that surrounds them, as with asthma sufferer Macey Love, whose determination to love the two granddaughters in her care—and everyone else she meets—is expressed in just the radiance of her smile.

In this bestselling book of true stories—some thoughtful, some delightful, some heart-pumping—you'll see close-up the joys and struggles of people like you. Along with them, you can search your own heart for answers to finding grace and peace in the darkness, and living well in the light.

The Whispers of Angels
Stories to Touch Your Heart
ANNETTE SMITH

This bestselling collection of true stories will help you find a heavenly perspective in the midst of everyday experiences...as you meet people like Hope, a ten-year-old blind girl who found her place in a brand-new school. Or Sam and Lily, childhood sweethearts whose love never stopped growing. Or Mr. Simmons, a heart-attack patient who taught his nurse about proper healing. Take a few moments to stop and listen, and perhaps you too will hear the sounds of heaven—*The Whispers of Angels*.

Horse Tales from Heaven
Reflections Along the Trail with God
REBECCA ONDOV

Gifted writer and avid horsewoman Rebecca Ondov invites you to experience life in a wilderness horse camp. Drawing on 15 years of living "in the saddle" while guiding pack trips and working as a wilderness ranger, Rebecca shows how the outdoors can open up people's hearts and minds in true stories about...

- a frisky cayuse and an early morning chase
- the special friendship between a night-blind horse and a mule
- snoring at base camp—and a startling cure for it
- a wilderness "drive-thru" cafe

Horse Tales from Heaven captures authentic Western life and reveals how God gets involved when you hit the trail with Him.

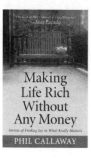

Making Life Rich Without Any Money
PHIL CALLAWAY

With wisdom and laugh-out-loud wit, Phil Callaway shares six fascinating characteristics of rich people—characteristics that have nothing to do with money and everything to do with wealth. You'll nod your head knowingly as you read about…

- Phil's new appreciation for his wife after a memorable "Mr. Mom" experience

- one family's surprising response when their house is "creamed" by a dairy truck

- a lasting friendship forged over the murder of a lawn mower

- the perils and joys of a SITCOM family (Single Income Three Children Oppressive Mortgage)

- a startling phone call that changed Phil's life

The best things in life are not really *things*, says Phil…and surprisingly, they just may be in your own backyard.

Four Paws from Heaven
Devotions for Dog Lovers
M.R. WELLS, KRIS YOUNG, AND CONNIE FLEISHAUER

Friend, family member, guardian, comforter—a dog can add so much to our lives. These furry, four-footed creatures truly are wonderful gifts from a loving Creator to bring joy, laughter, and warmth to our hearts and homes. These delightful devotions will make you smile and perhaps grow a little misty as you enjoy true stories of how God watches over and provides for us even as we care for our canine companions.

To learn more about other Harvest House books
or to read sample chapters, log on to our website:

www.harvesthousepublishers.com

HARVEST HOUSE PUBLISHERS

EUGENE, OREGON